POSITIVE HERDING 101
Dog-friendly training

Barbara Buchmayer

with **Sally Adam**

DISCLAIMER
The information in this book is meant to supplement, not replace, in-person herding training. Like any sport involving speed, equipment, balance, livestock, and environmental factors, herding poses some inherent risk. This work is sold with the understanding that neither the authors nor the publisher are held responsible for injuries or damage incurred while engaged in this training.

First published in 2021 by Positive Herding 101, LLC
14649 Hwy M, Purdin, MO 64674

Go to *www.positiveherdingdog.com* to purchase a copy of this book or to sign up for news from Positive Herding Dog.
Go to *www.positiveherdingdog.com/book2* to purchase the second book in this series, *Positive Herding 102*, or to sign up for news from Positive Herding Dog.

Photographs by Barb Buchmayer: p292 and all photos not listed below
Sally Adam: pp 11, 12
Laurie Burbank: Back cover (Barb & dogs), all other full page photos
Pam Eloff: pp 11, 22, 30, 98, 260
Tania Quarmby: Cover, back cover, pp 13, 124

Typography by User Friendly, Cape Town, South Africa
Set in Zapf Humanist 10.5 on 15pt

ISBN (print): 978-1-7368443-1-1
ISBN (epub): 978-1-7368443-8-0

Contents

Foreword

I know Barbara as a student of mine, and a good one. Far from her usual training border collies, in my class she trained chickens to do complex tasks and in a short time. Using what she learned from training her barnyard fowl on a tabletop she quickly learned to train exemplary behavior in her herding dogs. One reason for her success, I would suggest, was her willingness to accept the philosophical view of what she learned from the "white ladies" – in my opinion, she did an excellent job translating the training of chickens in a classroom to training dogs to herd sheep in the field.

Herding and guard dogs have been used for millennia. In its present form, sheepdog herding has been around for centuries. Herding dog trainers have evolved their own vocabulary over that time. Barbara describes and defines many of the words and phrases used by the herder in the field to "command" the dogs to perform various maneuvers necessary to direct the herd from one place to another. But there is another language introduced in the book, the modern language of psychology, operant conditioning to be exact. To the uninitiated, operant conditioning terminology can seem obscure. Fortunately, in everything I read, the language used is simple and with a minimum of jargon.

Barbara describes the stepwise introduction of novice dogs to the various skills the dogs will need to become proficient herders. Some of the chapters depict the best herding dogs as those that are swift and accurate "decision-makers", changing their behavior as required to accomplish the task. Barbara writes knowledgeably about teaching the dog "problem solving", such as getting sheep out of small corners. She also shows how to best make use of the instinctive behavior of dogs, especially the herding breeds, by timely reinforcement of appropriate behaviors to the efficient movement of stock. Barbara also describes those procedures most efficient to the elimination of unwanted behavior.

All in all, Barbara Buchmayer has written an introductory "How to" I believe would be useful to trainers new to herding, as well as to veteran trainers looking for new ideas, and maybe even a different training philosophy. The book accentuates the process of "splitting" behaviors into small parts rather than "lumping", or training whole or large parts of behavior. This process of splitting behavior is one step toward simplifying behavior which can then simplify training. There is an old saying: "Training is simple, but not easy!"

Robert E Bailey (Hon PhD)
October 2020

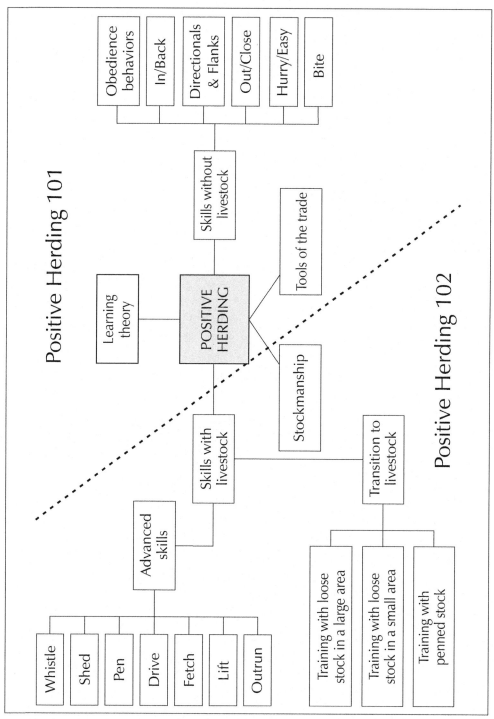

Positive herding mind map: Positive Herding 101 covers the basics of herding through building skills, strengthening behavior, and adding penned livestock. Positive Herding 102 covers the transition from basic to advanced skills, stockmanship and on-farm skills. Read diagram clockwise from 'Learning Theory' (top center).

Section 1
Getting and Building Behavior

May all of your dogs be as good as Gold.

CHAPTER 1

The experiment

As I read the short email in 2011, I had no idea that destiny was knocking at my door. The message was from a woman in South Africa asking if I would help her train a herding dog using positive methods. She had never trained a dog for herding, nor had she even worked a herding dog. In fact, she knew virtually *nothing* about herding! If she had not mentioned that Kay Laurence, a mutual friend and teacher of positive reinforcement-based training, had given her my name, I may not have considered working with her. I immediately realized it would be foolish to get involved with this project because we would be limited to using email, video, and Skype to communicate tons of precise information and complex concepts. Yet I was deeply into figuring out how to train herding using positive reinforcement and I *knew* it could be done. So the question was: Could two people with the same vision, but very different backgrounds, living on different continents thousands of miles apart, turn a rambunctious border collie pup into a useful herding dog?

This is a view of Sally's small farm in South Africa, a patch of semi-flat, cleared land amid rugged steep hills covered in natural vegetation.

This book grew out of my quest to learn the science of positive training and then apply that knowledge to herding. Besides working with my own dogs I am blessed to have had an amazing experience working with that woman from South Africa, Sally, whom I now count as one of my closest friends. In this book I will share with you both the theory I have learned and the practical exercises I have developed to train herding positively. Plus, Sally has generously agreed to share her triumphs, trials, and tribulations as we collaborated to train her red border collie Renn. You have met Sally and Renn on the cover of this book and soon you will be properly introduced.

So how did Renn turn out? Sally will tell you that her greatest achievement is that Renn is a first-class farm dog. Renn can race out of sight to gather the flock and then be cued by whistles to bring the sheep to Sally or take them wherever they need to go while Sally stays up on the hill directing her. Renn easily and happily does *everything* Sally needs her to do with the sheep on their small farm.

What is even more amazing to me is that Sally was also able to gain the skills necessary to successfully trial with Renn. In 2016 Sally and Renn became the South African Sheepdog Association's National Reserve Junior Champions.

I am honored to introduce you to my special friend Sally Adam and will let her tell you her story as she sees fit. Her thoughts will be woven into every aspect of this book and are sure to offer a fresh and unique perspective.

Sally has positively trained several dogs, horses, cats, and two donkeys (plus driving lessons on the lawn with her niece, a clicker and a bag of choccies). She was one of the first to use clicker training in South Africa in 1996.

Sally's story: Starting a sheepdog – an alternative approach

. . . .

Sally says

We got our first internet connection in 1996. I had no idea what one actually did on the internet but I found a search engine and, lacking imagination, typed in "dog training". On the first page of results was a bizarre concept called "clicker training". It sounded daft but I ordered a couple of clickers from the US and quietly began playing around with my dogs – at the time we were concentrating on agility. The results were magical and I ordered another batch of clickers and started handing them out to my agility students. I've used clicker training ever since, on all sorts of different animals including horses, cats, and so on.

When the time came to train a sheepdog I knew there was only one method I was interested in exploring. It didn't appear that there was anyone in South Africa using a clicker for herding training, but I was lucky enough to hook up with Barb Buchmayer, a trainer/triallist from Missouri. Barb has over 25 years of experience in the field but was keen to experiment with gentler methods. Renn and I would be the guinea pigs, and Barb would review our training videos and give direction and encouragement while thinking up new strategies as situations developed.

● ●

Barb: I met Sally by email through a mutually known clicker trainer. Sally did not yet have Renn but we discussed our mutual desire to train herding in a more positive, gentle way. I particularly wanted to be able to tell my dogs when they were right instead of only telling them when they were wrong.

● ●

It was a massive challenge – I had never worked a sheepdog before, let alone trained one, and I would be starting a dog from scratch using an untried method, working on my own. I was constantly terrified of losing control of the situation and having sheep injured or killed, which in hindsight probably meant I was more meticulous in my planning of each training session – not a bad thing! I was so ignorant I didn't even know what a flank was and I constantly pestered ever-patient Barb with questions.

Sally says

● ●

Barb: I was very apprehensive when Sally came to me looking for help because I know how difficult it is for experienced trainers to start a dog traditionally. Not only was she not a herding trainer but she also had *never* "run" a dog. It would not be easy, but we would communicate by email, Youtube video, and occasionally Skype. This would not be my preferred method of teaching a student, but it garnered amazing results in this instance!

Renn working sheep at a trial in South Africa with Sally handling.

Sally says

Our initial plan was to teach Renn the basic commands (flanks, stop, walk in, and so on) before she ever got near the sheep. This way she'd have some clue of what was required later on. We worked on basic clicker training, obedience skills, tricks, and self-control before we attempted to teach circling or flanking.

To teach flanking, circling, I set up a ring of traffic cones and had Renn circle outside while I stood inside. She was rewarded with food or a toy. Once she had the idea, the circle was extended (fortunately we have a large lawn) and I moved outside of the circle (see Fig. 1). This was also a great time for me to learn the flank commands without the distraction and chaos of working with sheep. Working this way means you get to train flanks several times a day without the hassle of getting sheep involved. To teach "get out" and "come in" I used a second, larger circle of cones around the original circle.

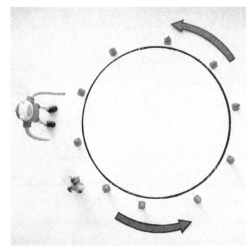

Figure 1

Barb: One of the best things about teaching a dog using marker/clicker training is that the herding skills become fluent away from stock. Without the sheep, the handler can develop their and their dog's skills without the huge distraction of the sheep.

Sally says

At the same time we wanted to get Renn listening and thinking around sheep. If a dog is completely obsessed with sheep, we reasoned, it won't be thinking or paying attention and would be in no position to actually learn anything. Self-control had always seemed to me the most essential thing one could work on with a sheepdog puppy.

Barb: I reasoned that if a dog cannot do simple obedience or tricks near sheep then there is no way they would be able to perform herding cues around sheep.

I started by putting my little training flock of four in a small pen. I would approach the pen with Renn on a lead. Renn would be rewarded for paying attention to me and responding to my requests (I had a range of tricks that we used for this purpose, such as spins and backing up). I would reward her with a toy or by letting her get closer to the sheep (her preferred reward). We worked on this for some time, until she could pay attention to me even when we were right next to the pen with sheep moving around inside. "Sheep are just another distraction!" Barb would remind me, daily ...

Sally says

Barb: This took much longer to accomplish than Sally envisioned, but it is an essential part of training in this way. Initially, Sally told me this was not possible, and she kept wanting to skip over this step, but I realized how crucial this was to her success.

So now we had a dog with good flank and stop commands, I had worked on the stop command from the moment I got Renn home at five weeks old. At first I lured her into a down, and soon asked her to down before every meal. Once she did this reliably I introduced the whistle cue. Training this way means the pup is exposed to the cues at least four times a day and is highly motivated to comply. We also had a dog who could pay attention to me in the presence of penned sheep. Next we needed to combine the two exercises. I set up a pen in the middle of a field inside a ring of traffic cones and started doing short casts or gathers (see Fig. 2). Gradually we extended the diameter of the circle and the length of the cast.

Sally says

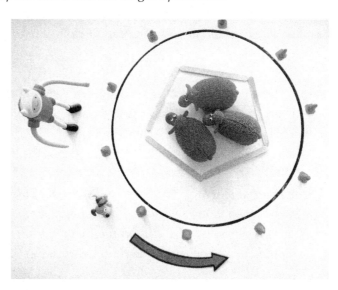

Figure 2

I also worked with the pen against a fence, sending the dog in half-circles with cones to encourage Renn to stay on the arc (see Fig. 3).

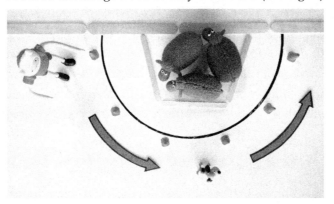

Figure 3

After a few months, I could delay the inevitable no longer: it was time to let Renn play with the sheep. But we wanted to keep things as calm as possible so Renn would be on a long line. We worked on the assumption that what a sheepdog wants most is to have the sheep in balance and what the dog wants least is to be taken off the sheep. We would use this to our advantage in moulding the dog's behaviour.

My neighbour had a suitable fenced area, of about 10 m × 5 m [33 ft × 16 ft], and we lured in the training flock with feed. I brought Renn in on a line and I walked to the inside of her while encouraging her to stay out on the fence – I used a PVC "crook" (made from plumbing components) if I needed to block her from the sheep. There was no shouting or harsh pressure from me on the dog – if she attempted to leap at the sheep or bite them, I simply dragged her away and gave her a time-out of a minute or so, away from the sheep. If things went well, Renn was allowed to continue circling for a short period and was rewarded with a toy or by being permitted to hold the sheep in a corner. We would work for short periods of a minute or two with lots of rests where we just hung out with the sheep – we didn't want her thinking that being around sheep meant constantly hurtling around like a maniac. We strove at all times to keep Renn in thinking mode.

Barb: A time-out is just matter of factly removing the dog out of the pen to a place where they cannot see or interact with the sheep and then standing there for a minute or two before re-starting work in the pen.

Sally says

We then moved to a larger training area (25 m × 28 m) [82 ft × 92 ft], and I'm afraid that Barb despaired over whether I would ever remove the training line, such was my fear of losing control. But I did finally take it off and got used to the fact that there would inevitably be the odd train wreck and that probably no-one would die.

Barb: This was definitely the most difficult step for Sally to do on her own. I knew she and her dog were more than ready for this step, but I also understood that as a novice handler she was totally out of her comfort zone.

. . . .

So, much to my surprise and relief, I've ended up with a dog who is incredibly useful on the farm and responsive enough to trial with. And all this without resorting to heavy handler pressure and punishment. In fact the dog is so unaffected by my position that I can sit on a horse or in my bakkie (truck) and Renn still retains the strong desire to go to balance and bring the sheep to me.

> **Sally says**

. . . .

Barb: It has been a pleasure and a privilege to work with Sally and Renn. I feel Sally and Renn have achieved a mastery of basic and intermediate herding with a foundation solid enough to allow them to achieve whatever level of herding they aspire to.

. . . .

It would have been quite impossible to have achieved anything without Barb's dedication to our project – no question went unanswered and Barb would patiently repeat advice until I eventually listened. I hope I can pay it forward some time!

> **Sally says**

. . . .

Barb's story: Winning a sheepdog trial sets me on a new path

My herding story is a bit different from Sally's. I also started learning herding with a border collie puppy but all of my herding training consisted of traditional methods. I had never heard of clicker training and am not sure it was talked about much back in the early '90s. I took some lessons from a trainer about five hours away from our dairy in upstate NY and tried to educate myself with herding DVDs and books. It was slow going.

In the beginning, I could only work with my trainer every couple of months and my progress seemed like it was one step forward and two steps back. I was overwhelmed with all of the movement; I moved, my dog moved, the sheep moved. One kind soul allowed me to work her sheep, once I had some control of my dog, and her only comment was, "You always move in the wrong direction". Probably an accurate assessment but not particularly helpful.

Several years later, my family moved to a farm in Missouri and I found a different herding teacher, Nyle Sealine. One of Nyle's first directives was for me to stand still.

What a relief! Now there were only two moving variables to keep track of instead of three. At weekly lessons, I slowly grew from a novice to an intermediate handler and finally to an open handler. Over those early years, I trained seven border collies using traditional methods. All of my dogs were purchased as pups or untrained dogs except for one which was given to me after she quit herding due to excessive pressure.

I took weekly herding lessons for eight years and I don't think the learning would ever have ended, there was always more to learn and there still is. I was extremely fortunate that my teacher was not only a master trainer and handler but a master stockman as well. He taught me stockmanship, the knowledgeable and skillful handling of livestock, which I later found out is knowledge that not all handlers possess. Learning herding was a long, sometimes frustrating, journey but it was also an addictive one.

Since things were going extremely well after 20 years of traditional punishment-based herding, why was I suddenly at a crossroads?

In 2008 I had just won an Open sheepdog trial and brought home an impressive trophy, a double dog box decorated with a lovely tri-color border collie in stalking mode.

Mattie was the first dog that I ever trained to the Open trial level. She was a very special dog who taught me many important lessons about herding at an advanced level. She had a huge heart and never gave up on controlling livestock, sheep or cattle.

Since I didn't have use for the dog box to transport dogs, I sat it in my large living room and found myself contemplating it often. Did I want to upgrade my handling skills in order to run with the "big dogs" at the prestigious trials, or did I want to learn a whole new way to interact with my dogs? I knew I desperately wanted to be able to say yes to my dogs after years of saying no but, did I want to start all over again when I had finally had significant success? It had taken me two decades to learn the skills of traditional herding and gain my current level of proficiency, how could I go back to being a novice again? Eventually it became clear, the right choice for me was to start over and become a positive herding trainer.

Similar to Sally, I started my investigation of positive dog training on the internet since I live on a dairy farm in rural Missouri. I was searching for a method that allowed me to reward my dogs when their behavior was correct and punish when it was incorrect. I became a "balanced trainer" for a matter of days before I learned it really was not good training to combine reinforcement and punishment in equal parts. (See Chapter 3, The un-balanced trainer.) Plus, while on the internet I had found tons of information about positive training using a clicker and had immediately ordered *Shaping Success* by Susan Garrett that relates her trials and tribulations while training agility with her red border collie Buzz. I was off and running on an odyssey to learn positive training and then apply it to herding.

I would like to say that my journey from traditional to positive herding has been fast and easy but it has not. My trek closely mirrored my first interaction with a box clicker. I held this simple plastic box in my hand, clicked it a few times, and mused, "How hard can this be?" I was about to find out I had a *lot* to learn.

Over the years I have been fortunate to learn from some of the top positive trainers, either directly or online, but probably my best teachers have been my dogs and the White Leghorn chickens I worked with at Chicken Workshops. Lessons in a classroom combined with applying those concepts to training an animal other than a dog are a recipe for extraordinary learning. Was it possible to teach a chicken to discriminate colors, go to a target on cue, change from walking a figure 8 to a circle on cue, climb a ladder, shoot a ball into a goal, or do chicken "agility"? "Yes!" (Bailey and Farhoody 2015)

In the 2015 Chaining Chicken workshop I trained my chicken to perform a chain of behaviors:
- Go up a ladder
- Pull out a squishy ball from a container on the platform
- Go through a tunnel while traversing a balance beam
- Pull the duck with the blue pipe cleaner handle from three choices in a bowl (pond); blue, green, or red (a color discrimination)
- Go down a ladder
- Peck a ping-pong ball into a mini-goal

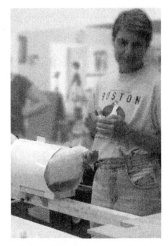

Chained behaviors including a tunnel on a balance beam, a color discrimination, and descending a ladder. Note (far right) the chicken's lowered head as it goes down the ladder.

Things were slowly coming together at home with my dogs, and I was having success getting my border collie Qwest working sheep using positive training when I got that fateful email from Sally years ago. The ultimate test would be to teach Sally to train Renn to be a capable helper on their small acreage, as well as a competent trial dog, while we were thousands of miles apart. If Sally had had experience with herding, I would have felt more confident that we would have been successful, but since she was a rank beginner I knew it would take years to accomplish our goals, if we could get there. Conversely, the advantage I had was that she *was* a rank beginner, and thus she had no preconceived ideas about herding or bad habits to overcome.

To watch Sally working Renn at a distance visit
https://www.youtube.com/watch?v=67gGkIGRx7c

Sally and I worked together for several years, since she had gotten Renn as a tiny pup. I feel fortunate that I was able to work with a positive trainer as skilled as Sally and that I had input on training Renn from the time Sally brought her home. Sally did a fantastic job with Renn and I am proud of my part in helping her and Renn become the amazing herding team that they are!

Safety first, fun always
A word of caution is in order. Eventually, you will be working with both your dog and livestock at the same time. Safety for you, your dog, and the livestock should always

be your first priority. Anytime you train with your dog there is the chance that you or your dog may be injured and herding livestock increases that risk. If you ever feel uncomfortable, trust your intuition and seek help from someone experienced whom you trust. Always, safety first!

Training herding positively should first, last and always be fun. If you and your dog are not having fun, you are doing something wrong. You should also be aware that herding is tremendously addictive. The more you learn and participate in herding, the more addictive it becomes. You have been warned.

Some encouraging words

You are setting out on a wonderful and exciting journey. You will be stepping out of your comfort zone, but that can be a very good thing. Instead of a wall that protects you, your comfort zone can be a shell that restricts your growth. Fear is what usually keeps you in your comfort zone. Fear of failure can prevent you from growing, and the only alternative to growing is dying.

Although it is our fear of failure that often holds us back, in reality, our biggest fear should be of regret. Don't allow your desire to prevent failure stop you from pursuing success. What would you attempt if you knew you would succeed? As George Tilton reminds us, "Success is never final and failure is never fatal". At least usually not fatal in positive dog training.

Mastery is a marathon, but along the way don't confuse hoping and worrying with actually doing something. Hope is a good friend but a poor dog trainer. As you gain victories and struggle through failures, be as positive and kind to yourself and other trainers as you are to your dog.

The most difficult part of any journey is getting started, so set small, easy goals that you know you can accomplish. These small accomplishments will give you confidence and propel you forward. Plan to train for 2 minutes and you will find yourself having so much fun that you will have to stop yourself after 20. Just do it.

On your herding journey I wish you much success, little failure, and kind livestock.

CHAPTER 2

A brand new world

The primary goal of this book is for you and your dog to have *fun* as you both learn about and gain proficiency herding. With this book you will learn how to teach herding to your dog, initially using toys or treats as reinforcers and later using access and the working of livestock as reinforcers. This should be a fun experience for both you and your dog. As noted previously, if you are not having fun, something is wrong!

There are three main building blocks that you will use to grow skills into basic herding competence:
1. *Build skills* – Start with basic obedience skills/tricks and then add herding skills.
2. *Strengthen self-control* – Grow basic skills into fluent behaviors by working up to using massive distractions.
3. *Add livestock* – Bring fluent behaviors to livestock in a totally controlled setting and increase access to stock as your dog demonstrates their ability to think and respond appropriately.

I was able to successfully guide Sally and Renn, whom you met in Chapter 1, to herding proficiency using positive methods. This book can be your guide to herding success. How you define that success is totally up to you. Success could mean having a capable herding companion for your farm or a competent trial dog to pursue prizes or titles. Although there have been some truly spectacular herding dogs, I believe the most amazing herding dogs are yet to be trained. If we release our dogs from the fear of physical punishment they will show us just how brilliant they can be.

We will still seek to decrease unwanted behavior which is, by definition, punishment. There is a huge difference between the type and severity of positive punishment used in traditional dog training and employing negative punishment, removing the opportunity to work livestock, as used in positive herding. Our goals include preventing rehearsal of unwanted behavior with a long line, employing no reward markers, managing the environment, and relying primarily on positive reinforcement and negative punishment. The better positive trainer you are, the less punishment, of any type, you will need to use. The foundation of this herding training is to foster, not force, behavior. I call this type of training *compassionate herding*.

Sir practicing his paw wave with deer and moving lawn tractor in background.

Compassionate herding has three legs:
1. Handler friendly
2. Dog friendly
3. Livestock friendly

Handler, dog, and livestock are all calm. Sir is attached to a long line to prevent lunging at the stock.

The goal is for you, your dog, and the stock to be safe at all times with interactions being as low stress as possible. Your dog training and livestock handling should both aim to minimize stress.

Who this book is for

This book targets two main audiences: positive trainers new to herding and experienced traditional herding trainers looking for a more positive and scientifically-based training method. Sally brings her experience as a positive trainer who was new to herding, and I bring my experience as a cross-over herding trainer with more than 25 years of herding experience.

Traditional herding trainers have produced some amazing herding dogs. For decades these trainers and handlers have astounded us with the precision, capability, and intelligence of their dogs. But there have also been dogs and handlers who have not fared well in this traditional punishment-based herding system. This book offers a way to train herding dogs using primarily positive reinforcement.

I have found that the better the positive trainer, the less positive punishment they need to use. Through experience and education, the savvy trainer learns to set their dog up for success by slicing behaviors into small pieces that are easy for their dog to learn. This type of training is called shaping. Almost all of the training in this book is based on shaping.

The exercises in this book have been developed for one handler working with their dog alone, since the majority of dog trainers spend most of their time training by themselves. The training environment will be set up so that you can help your dog to learn as quickly and safely as possible, especially around livestock.

Almost any dog of any age can learn the *Positive Herding 101* foundational herding behaviors:
- Directionals/flanks
- Stop
- In/back
- Out/close
- Easy/hurry
- Here (recall)

The amount and type of inherent herding instinct your dog possesses will determine which behaviors will be easier to train and which will be more difficult. The amount of instinct your dog possesses will also determine, to a certain extent, how aroused your dog will be by livestock. The more highly aroused your dog is by movement and livestock, the more you will need to strengthen your dog's self-control, or responsiveness to cues, the second important building block of herding competence.

The type of instinctual herding behaviors your dog possesses will also vary greatly. For example, some collies have more eye while others have more chase. If you are training a non-border-collie breed (Aussie, Belgian Tervuren, Malinois, or Sheltie), you will find that they have different herding instincts/styles (barking/silent, driving from the rear vs outrun, chest-bump vs eye).

Herding instinct is a double-edged sword. On one hand, it gives your dog the ability to naturally read and control livestock. On the other hand, the ability to read and control livestock may initially interfere with your dog's ability to perform herding cues that are contrary to what their instincts are telling them.

If your dog lacks herding instinct, they will essentially be performing obedience around livestock. This means that they will rely on you, as the handler, to tell them every move to make. Although it initially may be easier to train the basic herding skills with a dog lacking herding instinct, with these dogs you will ultimately be responsible for reading the livestock and positioning them appropriately.

How this two-book set is organized

This book, *Positive Herding 101,* covers the basics of herding through building skills, strengthening behavior, and adding penned livestock. A companion book, *Positive Herding 102,* will complete the training by transitioning the basic herding skills into more advanced skills, stockmanship and on-farm skills.

Throughout this book, various icons will alert you to important information and helpful hints. **Before you start** will outline specific pointers for the training session that follows.

The **RAM**s indicate **R**ules **A**nd **M**echanics for a particular behavior or exercise.

The **Rules** are guidelines for the exercise and may include:
1. Goal of the exercise
2. When to begin teaching
3. When to move on
4. Appropriate environment
5. Setting up the environment

6. What props are needed
7. Criteria in one sentence
8. Reinforcement to use
9. Cue(s) to use

The **Mechanics** are all of the moving parts of doing an exercise and may include:
1. Your position
2. Your dog's position
3. What is marked or clicked
4. How and where the reinforcement will be delivered
5. How to build the behavior
6. When to practice without your dog

Before starting an exercise, learn the **R**ules **A**nd **M**echanics you will be using. For each exercise, the criteria will be defined in one sentence. A **criterion** is a definition of the specific part of a behavior you want to increase. It is paramount that you understand the criterion you want because it determines when your dog is successful and thus when you will mark and reinforce your dog. Much more on setting and changing criteria is discussed in this first section of the book.

In herding we always treat rams, male sheep, with the utmost respect as they can be powerful and potentially dangerous animals. Give this same respect to the **RAM**s of training each exercise and don't start an exercise until you are confident you know and understand what and how you will be training. Always practice *without* your dog whenever you are not totally confident of your **R**ules **A**nd **M**echanics, which will probably be nearly all of the time! Even simple exercises can be tricky to get right initially with so many new things to think about and precise mechanics to perform.

TNT indicates Tips 'N Tricks which are helpful hints or important points.

These tidbits will be applicable to the topic being discussed. Included will be quotes that inspire, lessons Sally or I have learned, or important or interesting information.

Look out for video clips that illustrate the training sessions and behavior, and make it easier to follow the exercises outlined in the text.

Meet Shandler, Dawg, and the flock

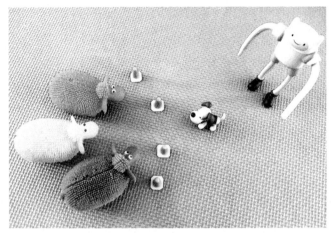 

In place of drawn diagrams, I use photo dioramas or pictures of props. Shandler the handler is pictured to the left with her crew (and cones) and a close up of Dawg is on the right.

Sally speaks

You have already met Sally and Renn. Throughout the book, Sally will occasionally chime in. Her comments in the text are placed between gray dotted lines. Sally's comments will always be in a serif font and mine will always be in a sans serif font.

Sally says

....

Sally will be adding her unique insights, relating experiences, giving encouragement, or chipping in with whatever else strikes her fancy.

....

Speaking of sheep

I train herding on sheep and use my dogs almost exclusively on the sheep on our farm, although we also have dairy and beef cattle. In this book I will use the terms *livestock, stock,* and *sheep* interchangeably, unless noted. All three terms will represent cattle, sheep, goats, or ducks throughout the book, unless one species is specifically noted. Many dogs work all types of livestock, but some prefer one type over others. I like to start training my dogs on sheep because they flock together well and usually move freely away from even tentative dogs.

Puppies

Finding a pup that will become a great herding dog is no easy task. If you want to do herding with a dog that has a lot of innate herding instinct, make sure both parents work livestock and, if at all possible, watch the parents herd. Remember that having working parents does *not* guarantee your pup will work. Working parentage increases the odds in your favor but no one can guarantee a pup will turn on to and work livestock.

Keep your pup safe when around livestock! Many pups have been ruined by being injured or scared by livestock. Safety first!

Also realize that unwanted puppy behavior does not automatically change into desirable adult behavior by the process of maturation alone. Obnoxious puppy behavior, left unaddressed, will become obnoxious dog behavior.

Welcome to a brand-new world!

In the world of positive herding, things are much different than in the traditional herding world. Dogs are primarily reinforced, handlers use markers and clickers as well as crooks, and sheep are just another distraction.

Positive Herding 101 will move you through the initial stages of positive herding training based on the laws of behavior. You will find exercises that you can do with your dog in your home and later move on to ones that require more room, so are best done outside or in a larger building. You will work through a series of step-by-step exercises that will move you from working with your dog and cones, to eventually working with penned sheep, ducks, or cattle. But before we get to the point of a dog circling a pen of livestock we have a lot of work to do.

The most difficult part of dog training is ... starting!

So, let's get started.

CHAPTER 3

The un-balanced trainer

I found positive training methods when I started searching for a way to tell my dogs they were right, rather than only telling them when they were wrong. The first method I came across, on the internet, that seemed to be just what I was looking for, was balanced training.

Balanced training relies on both positive reinforcement and punishment, in roughly equal amounts or slightly weighted toward the side of reinforcement. If the dog does something correctly, they are reinforced. If the dog does something incorrectly, they are punished. Yes! This was exactly what I was searching for. Not only would I tell my dogs when they were wrong but I also could tell them when they were *right*! I was over the moon! Why hadn't I heard of this method before? Certainly balanced training made more sense than only telling my dogs when they were wrong. On a rational basis this approach seemed just the ticket. I definitely wanted to learn more about balanced training and why it was not more widely embraced in the dog training world.

As I continued to research and learn about balanced training, I began to encounter more about clicker and marker training. This second method advocated using primarily positive reinforcement while ignoring unwanted behavior. Hmmm… I was not sure that was going to work. I knew that herding dogs found many herding behaviors, especially undesirable behaviors associated with livestock, to be *very* inherently reinforcing. Maybe I better stick with balanced training after all.

Never one to jump ahead without thorough investigation, I continued to read and ponder what the internet dog training community had to say about both methods. And they had a *lot* to say! Obviously, there was no clear-cut method that everyone

Sir was looking for direction too.

agreed upon. Positive training was permissive. Traditional training was too punishing. Balanced training was worse than using either all reinforcement or all punishment. What? Wait a minute! How could using a lot of reinforcement with only a small amount of punishment be worse than using all punishment?

Dr Jekyll and Mr Hyde

The problem with balanced training is that the dog never knows if they will be receiving a treat or a collar pop. By routinely switching between reinforcement and punishment the trainer does tell the dog when they are right and when they are wrong, thus giving the dog clear feedback. That seemed like a win-win to me.

The problem is that dogs often become apprehensive because they are unsure which response will be elicited in this unpredictable environment. This uncertainty tends to shut them down and they wait to be told what to do, which is very similar to how dogs respond to traditional punishment-based training. In the case of traditional punishment-based training the dog can learn the rules and, although the rules may not be ideal, at least they are consistent. The dog can change behavior to survive, if not thrive, in this environment.

Using both reinforcement and punishment equally means that the dog can never ascertain the rules and thus may become apprehensive. When rules change inexplicably it is difficult to grow confidence and offered behavior often disappears. Although I do not advocate using positive punishment, my advice is to use reinforcement *or* punishment, but not both equally. I choose to use reinforcement as much as possible.

Is silence golden?

Has anyone ever told you, when using punishment as the basis of teaching or training, that the absence of a correction or criticism is reinforcing? In other words a correction or criticism = punishment and no correction or silence = reinforcement. Every time the dog or handler does something incorrectly, they are either punished or criticized, while every time they do something correctly, there is silence but no correction.

I thought that this could possibly be an improvement on the balanced training method. Instead of punishment and reinforcement you would use only punishment and lack of punishment. This theory rests on the hypothesis that silence is golden, or at least reinforcing. I had the occasion to experience just this scenario. I had been training with a teacher who relied almost totally on corrections for the dog and criticism for the handler. They espoused that when the dog was not being corrected they "knew" they were correct and thus were more likely to repeat the behavior that was not punished. By definition they were saying that an absence of punishment is reinforcing.

I needed to find my way before I was able to give Sir direction.

I had finally gotten to the point of being a fairly proficient handler. I clearly remember one afternoon when I was working my dog and the usual criticism was blatantly absent. Did I feel highly reinforced? Not exactly. Instead, I felt my level of anxiety rising as I waited for the inevitable criticism. If my anecdotal experience is comparable to what dogs feel, then I can unequivocally say that a lack of punishment is definitely not reinforcing!

An un-balanced trainer

I proudly proclaim myself as a positive trainer, a definitely un-balanced trainer. The more skill I acquire using positive reinforcement training methods only convinces me that both I and my dogs are happiest, and most likely to reach our potential, when I strive to be the best positive trainer I can be. I don't always succeed. There is always more to learn and new obstacles to overcome. But I love to see the gleam in my dog's eyes and the enthusiasm they show for working with me, around and away from stock.

As doctors swear in the Hippocratic Oath, "first, do no harm". When you train positively, you may not get what you want, but you can always go back and re-train a behavior because you have done no harm.

Unfortunately, balanced training does not live up to the panacea it promises. Instead, I advocate becoming the absolutely best positive trainer you can be. The good news is that as your level of proficiency as a positive trainer increases, your need to use even mild positive punishment decreases.

CHAPTER 4

Learning theory

To efficiently get and build behavior you need to understand basic learning theory. The laws of behavior impact all of your training. Along the way we will be revisiting them to emphasize their importance and impact on specific exercises or behaviors.

Many books are far more capable of explaining learning theory in detail than this one. All mistakes regarding learning theory and its application as explained in *Positive Herding 101* and *Positive Herding 102* are my own. I have gained my knowledge of learning theory over two decades, but am far from an expert concerning it. I believe I have garnered a solid, workable foundation as it applies to training positive herding, but there is always more to learn! If you find learning theory as intriguing as I do, I encourage you to look at the references listed in Resources, which is found at the back of this book.

The value of knowing learning theory is that once you understand the principles of getting and building behavior you can adjust exercises, teach new behaviors, and deal with problems more easily because you understand how your dog learns. If you just follow a training recipe you will be lost if your dog doesn't respond as expected. Throughout the books, I will include common problems and how to solve them, but each dog and handler team is unique and you will face some issues you will have to deal with on your own. If you understand the principles underpinning your training, you will be much more prepared to overcome problems that arise.

A science and an art

Science-based positive dog trainers are technicians (Bailey and Farhoody 2013–2015). The advantage of being a technician is that anyone can learn the foundational principles and how to apply them to dog training to become a proficient trainer. There are no secret handshakes or special inborn talents necessary to become a good trainer. It is very helpful to work with an experienced mentor to learn positive training, but there are many other ways to become a proficient dog trainer.

In herding, there is also an element of art. Watching the timing and choreography of a well-trained dog/handler team, as they control and direct stock around a field or through a trial course, is like watching a beautiful dance. The training may be based on science but the expression of that training is akin to an art form.

Animals are always learning

As trainers, we may set aside time for training sessions, but our dogs are always learning, even when we are not intentionally training. Animals learn in order to survive and thrive. They are constantly doing more behaviors that are reinforced and fewer that are punished, either by humans, other animals, or the environment. We reinforce behaviors not animals (Burch and Bailey 1999).

Reinforcement is anything that strengthens a behavior, increases the probability of a behavior occurring; *punishment* is anything that weakens a behavior, decreases the probability of a behavior occurring (Chance 2006). As your dog learns, behavior changes. The laws that govern these changes of behavior are classical and operant conditioning.

Classical conditioning governs *involuntary* responses while **operant** conditioning explains how consequences determine **voluntary** behaviors (Reid 1996). Both classical and operant conditioning happen at the same time. For example, if you teach the sit behavior using treats your dog will learn to sit and will also have a positive association with the sit behavior. If you teach sit using a choke chain and collar pops your dog will also learn to sit, but will probably have a negative association with the sit behavior.

Reinforcing a calm sit near sheep builds the sit behavior and encourages relaxation near sheep. Both operant and classical conditioning are part of all training.

Classical conditioning

Classical conditioning (also known as Pavlovian or respondent conditioning) is based on the work Russian scientist Ivan Pavlov did with dogs in the 1890s. Pavlov (1849–1946) noticed that the dogs he was using to study salivation started to salivate whenever he entered the room, even when he did not have food for them. He later was able to ring a bell, present food, and the dogs would salivate. Finally, he could just ring the bell and the dogs would begin to salivate. Thus he had classically conditioned the dogs to respond to hearing the bell in the same way they would respond to the presentation of food (Burch and Bailey 1999).

This ability to change the sound of the bell from an unconditioned stimulus to a conditioned stimulus, by pairing it with food, is the basis of classical conditioning. In classical conditioning the animal has no choice, their response is involuntary or automatic. I am classically conditioned to become anxious when I encounter the smell of a dental office, even if I am just passing by on my way to another destination, and my stomach will clench. The smell of the dental office has become classically conditioned and I react to that smell automatically.

In my example of teaching sit with treats, the dog will come to associate treats with sitting and the behavior of sitting may develop a positive Conditioned Emotional Response (CER), which can be seen in the dog as tail wagging, ears up, and muscles relaxed (Reid 1996). The same sit behavior, taught with a choke chain, will also have a CER, but this time it may well be negative: muscles tense, ears down, and head lowered. How the dog learns a behavior impacts the emotion the dog associates with that behavior.

In herding we want our dogs to have a positive association with the livestock they will be working. If we use punishment to train herding we may cause our dog increased stress. This anxiety can increase our dog's arousal level such that they may lose self-control and chase or bite the stock, or alternatively, they may shut down and avoid interacting with the livestock. The higher our dog's arousal level, the more self-control they will need to control themselves around livestock, and most dogs find livestock inherently arousing.

Gold developing a positive Conditioned Emotional Response to the flirt pole.

Operant conditioning

One of the most important additions to learning theory was the development of **operant conditioning** (also known as Skinnerian or instrumental conditioning), which is based on the work of psychologist B F Skinner (1904–1990). Operant conditioning is an explanation of how animals operate on their environment and that the consequence of their behavior is the primary determinant of their future behavior. In operant conditioning, animals have a choice of how they will respond and their future response is determined by the consequence or result of their past behavior. If a consequence is desired or *reinforcing* the behavior will tend to be repeated, but if the consequence is undesired or *punishing* the behavior will tend to diminish (Burch and Bailey 1999).

Two of Skinner's graduate students, Keller Breland and Marion Kruse, assisted him with "Pigeon in a Pelican", which taught pigeons to guide missiles. After seeing the commercial potential of operant conditioning, Keller and Marion abandoned their doctorate studies to set up Animal Behavior Enterprises (ABE). They married and together at ABE trained more animals and animal species than any other trainers. Keller died at age 50 and Marion continued ABE. She also worked with autistic children and belatedly finished her doctorate. Bob Bailey came to work at ABE and after Keller's death married Marion. Together they began Bailey & Bailey Operant Conditioning Workshops, which taught animal training using chickens as the animal model (Bailey and Farhoody 2013–2015).

The majority of the training that will be discussed and implemented in these books is based on the knowledge that was acquired and passed on by Keller and Marion. They were truly pioneers in bridging the gap between the lab and the field (Farhoody 2018).

Shaping a chicken to do agility at a Bailey–Farhoody Chicken Workshop (2015). Training is training!

Most of the training we do with our dogs is based primarily on operant conditioning, although classical conditioning is always present, happening in the background. Our dogs have a choice in how they will respond in a given situation and we reinforce the response that we want repeated. Our job is to set up the environment for our dogs to make the correct response easy and the incorrect response difficult, especially during the initial phases of learning.

As our dogs progress, we ask for a bit more of the desired behavior, until they learn the behavior to our criteria. This is called shaping behavior. **Shaping** is a training procedure that uses the reinforcement of successive approximations to build a desired behavior (Chance 2006). Almost all training is shaping!

Once our dog knows the initial behavior, we can make it more difficult for them to be correct and easier for them to be incorrect, thus helping our dogs to strengthen their mastery of the behavior when faced with distractions. In herding, distractions are paramount because most dogs find the presence and movement of livestock to be extremely distracting.

*The key to operant conditioning is that **consequences drive behavior**, either increasing or decreasing the behavior. This means that what happens after the behavior, desired or undesired, determines the likelihood of it being repeated.*

In operant conditioning:
- **Add = Positive**
- Take away = Negative
- ***Increase in behavior = Reinforcement***
- *Decrease in behavior = Punishment* (In operant conditioning, *punishment* is defined solely as a decrease in behavior.)

There are four ways consequences can be applied (Reid 1996):
1. **Add** something to ***increase*** behavior. (**Positive *Reinforcement***)
2. **Add** something to *decrease* behavior. (**Positive** Punishment)
3. *Take away* something to ***increase*** behavior. (Negative **Reinforcement**)
4. *Take away* something to *decrease* behavior. (Negative Punishment)

The operant conditioning quadrant

The OC quadrant is based on consequences and the definitions above. Although the OC quadrant looks simple, it can be difficult to ascertain exactly what quadrant you are using at certain times. Rather than get hung up on pinpointing which quadrant a certain training situation is in, I find it much more helpful to simply strive to train using primarily positive reinforcement, reinforcing behavior to build wanted behavior, and some negative punishment, removing the chance to earn reinforcement, to weaken unwanted behavior.

The advantage of understanding the quadrants is that you realize that reinforcement and punishment can take many forms and things can be added or taken away to increase or decrease behavior. If a behavior is increasing or maintaining, it is being reinforced, either positively or negatively. Similarly, if a behavior is decreasing it is being punished, either positively or negatively.

Remember that in operant conditioning there is no moral judgement attached to the terms punishment or reinforcement. Punishment is neither good nor bad, it just indicates that behavior is decreasing. Reinforcement is also neither good nor bad, it just indicates that behavior is increasing.

The following table gives examples of the four ways of using operant conditioning to increase or decrease behavior, by adding or taking away something (Bertilsson and Johnson Vegh 2010). The examples provided are my own.

		Positive (add)	Negative (take away)
Reinforcement – behavior increases		**Positive *Reinforcement*** = Something is **added** that ***increases*** behavior. When my dog recalls to me off of livestock, I give a treat. I have added a treat which increases the probability that my dog will recall off of livestock again.	Negative **Reinforcement** = Something is *taken away* that ***increases*** behavior. When my young, insecure dog walks into light sheep, the sheep easily move away. The sheep have taken away pressure from my dog which increases the probability that my dog will walk in toward livestock again.
Punishment – behavior decreases		**Positive** *Punishment* = Something is **added** that *decreases* behavior. When my dog bites the tail of a cow, the cow kicks my dog. A kick has been added, which decreases the probability that my dog will grab a cow's tail again.	Negative *Punishment* = Something is *taken away* that *decreases* behavior. When my dog noses a foot target, I remove it for a moment. I have taken away the foot target so my dog has lost the opportunity to earn reinforcement by touching it, which decreases the probability that my dog will nose it again.

Extinction

Another important part of operant conditioning is **extinction**, the gradual lessening of a behavior due to lack of reinforcement (Chance 2006). In this situation, the behavior will gradually die out or extinguish. If I no longer give my dog food from the table, eventually my dog will stop begging at the table.

All shaping involves extinction! Shaping is a series of steps that move a behavior from a rough approximation to exactly the goal behavior. As you reinforce the behavior closer to your target behavior, you are also extinguishing the behavior that was a step below your current level. If I am shaping a turn to the left, I may first reinforce an eye flick to the left. Once I've reached my goal for this approximation, I will withhold reinforcement until I get a head turn to the left, then a weight shift, followed by a paw movement. At each step I am reinforcing a new behavior and not reinforcing the old behavior, thus putting the old behavior on extinction.

If a behavior continues even after you have quit reinforcing it, the problem may be that your dog finds the behavior inherently reinforcing. Many dogs find chasing livestock inherently reinforcing, so you cannot extinguish that behavior by simply allowing your dog to chase stock. Any behavior that maintains or increases is being reinforced.

As a behavior extinguishes it will often return in full force for a short period, often right before it finally extinguishes. This reoccurrence of a dying behavior is known as an **extinction burst** (Burch and Bailey 1999). Don't be disheartened when this happens because an extinction burst is just a signal that the behavior is growing weak. If you can stay the course through an extinction burst, you usually have seen about the last of the unwanted behavior.

The five basic principles of operant conditioning

These operant conditioning principles were originally determined by Keller Breland and Marion Bailey, from their graduate work with B F Skinner and their years of training animals in their business, Animal Behavior Enterprises, to be of paramount importance for changing behavior.

The five principles are:
- Stimulation and stimulus generalization
- Reinforcement
- Punishment
- Extinction

In addition to *reinforcement*, *punishment*, and *extinction* that have already been briefly discussed, we have two other ways to affect behavior: **stimulation** and stimulus **generalization** (Burch and Bailey 1999).

In operant conditioning, a **stimulus** is a thing or event that sets the stage to elicit a behavior (Chance 2006). **Stimulation** can initiate behavior so that we are able to reinforce wanted behavior or to ignore or punish unwanted behavior.

Generalization, a subset of stimulation, is a process in which an animal takes a learned behavior and performs that behavior to criteria in new environments and situations (Ramirez 1999). It may take relearning a behavior from scratch in many new situations and environments before a dog will understand that sit means sit, no matter where they are or what is going on.

Generalization is the backbone of building self-control. The more distracting situations and novel environments the behavior is correctly performed in, the stronger or more fluent it becomes. As the behavior gets stronger we say it gains mass (Farhoody 2018).

• •

> **Sally says**
>
> *Renn is now 7 years old but it's only in the last couple of months that I've asked myself why she "refuses" to comply with my sit cue. After all, she'll lie down on cue while 300 metres away. I then noticed that she sits instantly when asked to if she's within a metre of me. So it isn't that she doesn't know the cue, she just hasn't been taught that it means "sit even if you aren't near your trainer". A great example of the trainer failing to generalize a cue …*

• •

All five principles have their place in getting and building behavior. First, we need to get a behavior initiated through stimulation. Then we can provide a consequence such as reinforcement, punishment, or extinction to increase or diminish the behavior. Once we have the final behavior we want, we can strengthen it using generalization.

• •

> **Sally says**
>
> *I was lucky enough to once own a border collie (Tin) who was so willing and honest that if she wasn't doing what I wanted, I knew that I needed to look at my training. One of my dumbest moves, which I shall never forget, involved teaching Tin to drop an object into another object, for example a ball into a bucket. We started training, as we usually did, in my office. Tin caught on really quickly and would reliably retrieve a tossed ball and place it in the bucket. Time to up the ante I said*

to myself. So I moved our session outside, exchanged the bucket for a low basin and replaced the ball with a small toy. I looked at Tin expectantly and she looked back puzzled, as if she'd never once seen this task before. And of course, in a way she hadn't because I had changed three variables at once. So once again I reached for the rolled-up newspaper and whacked myself about the head and shoulders, promising to remember to generalize in small steps in the future.

• •

Building behavior

We will primarily use operant conditioning, which includes extinction, as the basis of our training. As we train using operant conditioning, classical conditioning is also happening and Conditioned Emotional Responses are being developed. My goal is to use primarily positive reinforcement to build wanted behaviors as well as some negative punishment and extinction to eliminate unwanted behaviors.

Directionals (left and right) can be started in your front room and grown into flanks or circling of stock. To watch a video of directionals that have been grown into useful herding skills visit https://www.youtube.com/watch?v=WiC_C-SaPZ0

To build behavior using positive reinforcement you have to know what is reinforcing for your dog. What is reinforcing is determined by the dog, not the trainer. Reinforcers for your dog may include treats, tugs, flirt poles (a toy attached to a pole with a string), petting, praise, balls, Frisbees, a stream of water from a hose, access to livestock and many, many others. All of these reinforcers will not be reinforcing to all dogs, nor will they all have equal value to your dog. Your job is to find out what is highly reinforcing to your dog and use that to build behaviors. In my training I use primarily treats, bungee tugs, and flirt poles.

One critical aspect of reinforcers is that their value may change in different environments. Some dogs that will happily gobble treats or tug enthusiastically in most environments may refuse them in the presence of livestock, at least initially.

Reinforcers I use: food treats of all types, toys (which could mean anything from an expensive rubber toy to a nearby stick or anything to hand which the dog might fancy, such as my hat), tug activity, a back scratch, another (more desirable) cue, permission to do something the dog really wants to do, like chase a bunny in the field or stare at sheep ... Anything the dog wants can be used as a reinforcer. If the dog desperately wants to charge out of the gate when you open it, you teach him that the only way to get to charge out of the gate is to wait politely for permission. When I was training Renn to stop, I would use her desire to be closer to the sheep as the reinforcer. If she stopped when cued she was immediately given a walk-in cue and permitted to approach the sheep. If she didn't stop, she was asked to return to me and away from the sheep. Reinforcers are everywhere once you start looking.

Dogs do what works for them, what they find reinforcing. They do *not* hold grudges or act out of spite *nor* do they work to please us. We may incorrectly attribute human traits to dogs, but as we learn the laws of behavior we deepen our understanding of why our dogs behave the way they do. Being a keen observer of our dogs, ourselves, and our environments is one of the best ways we can build our understanding of our dogs and how best to train them.

In this chapter, we have touched on only the most basic concepts of how all animals learn. As we move through our training other important science-based principles will be introduced but all of these concepts will rest firmly on the foundations of operant and classical conditioning.

Rewards vs reinforcers

Just a quick word on why I will be using the term reinforcer rather than reward. Many people use the terms interchangeably but a reinforcer is not the same as a reward. A **reinforcer** is anything that strengthens a behavior. A **reward** is something given in return for wanted behavior but a reward is not necessarily reinforcing (Chance 2006).

An example of a non-reinforcing reward might be a promotion for exceptional work. If the person getting the promotion does *not* want the added responsibility that comes with the new position they may find the promotion punishing. Thus the "reward" is not reinforcing at all. Rewards, as well as reinforcers, are determined solely by the receiver.

In this book, we will stick to the terms *reinforcer* and *reinforcement* to be clear that we are referring to something that causes behavior to increase. We will not be rewarding our dogs, instead, we will be reinforcing our dog's behavior.

Does the past predict the future?

All training is based on the idea that past experience predicts future behavior. If this were not true we would have no hope of changing the behavior of our dogs through training. Operant and classical conditioning are always in play, but how *exactly* do we use them to create the behaviors we want?

In the next chapter we begin to answer the questions of not only *how*, but *why* we train herding as we do. We will be using science-based **marker training** to get and build behaviors we want. Marker training may also be called clicker training, but I prefer marker training because we will be using primarily verbal markers. A clicker is certainly a valuable tool we will be using at times, depending on which type of marker serves us best in a given situation. Once you understand and learn to use marker training proficiently you will suddenly see your dog's behavior in a whole new way. Your training will immediately advance faster and be a lot more fun!

CHAPTER 5

Getting behavior

Behavior is ever-changing. It is either getting stronger or weaker, it is never static. We all want to control the behavior of our dogs, our spouses, our bosses, and sometimes our friends but the only behavior we truly control is our own. To get our dogs and other people to change their behavior we have to change our behavior. Since we are going to concentrate on using positive reinforcement to affect behavior we need to have a thorough understanding of reinforcement.

Reinforcers increase behavior (Ramirez 1999). They can be anything an *animal* wants and is willing to work for. We will be working with primary and secondary reinforcers. A **primary** reinforcer is something that your dog is born wanting, such as food, water, or sex. In the case of herding dogs, movement of livestock or motion that mimics

Ignoring Sir's unwanted behavior of biting my pant leg and reinforcing interaction with me by tugging.

livestock movement is also inherently reinforcing (Burch and Bailey 1999). Secondary reinforcers gain their importance to your dog by being associated with a primary reinforcer. Thus secondary reinforcers are conditioned, learned by association. **Secondary** reinforcers are something your dog learns to want, such as tugging (Burch and Bailey 1999).

To use reinforcement effectively you have to identify what behavior you want to reinforce and then ignore any behavior you do not want. Once you can look at your dog's behavior in this way you will find plenty of behaviors you would like to see more of and thus will want to reinforce. But how exactly do you do this?

You build behavior by reinforcing it

One way to build behavior is by giving your dog food or starting to tug the moment your dog exhibits the behavior you want. If your dog sits and you immediately give a treat, the consequence of sitting is positive (the treat) and strengthens the sit behavior. Each time you give a treat or tug when your dog sits you increase the likelihood that your dog will sit again, provided your dog finds treats or tugging reinforcing.

Directly reinforcing a behavior works well for some behaviors such as static behaviors, a sit or down, but may not work well for a moving behavior. Suppose you are working on a sit and you hand your dog a treat at the instance that they sit but, as they take the treat they flop into a down and eat their treat. You have now reinforced both the desired behavior, the sit, and the undesired behavior, the flop down.

To make your training more exact and give you time to deliver reinforcement you can use a marker to pinpoint the correct behavior and allow you time to present the reinforcer. A marker is a **bridging signal**, a signal that pinpoints the exact behavior that is being reinforced (Bailey and Farhoody 2013–2015). The mark tells your dog exactly what they did to earn the reinforcer. This type of training is known as marker training. Before discussing markers, let's spend a bit more time familiarizing you with the ins and outs of reinforcement.

Using positive reinforcement training builds a great relationship with your dog! I believe you are not limited to being stoic and mechanically delivering treats as reinforcers. You may also use play, praise, petting, and even laughter as reinforcers. Good mechanics are important but being an automaton is not!

Types of reinforcers

The use of reinforcement is the most important part of positive training. If your dog does not find the reinforcers you are using motivating, they will not get into the training and work to earn those reinforcers.

Reinforcers I use for dog training fall into three main categories:
1.   Food and play – What I primarily use, depending on the dog's preferences.
2.   Praise and petting – Can be used alone or in conjunction with food and play.
3.   Cues and markers – These become reinforcers by being associated with reinforcement.

One big advantage of using treats is that they can be given quickly, so more repetitions (reps) can be included in a shorter time frame. This increases how much reinforcement your dog can earn in a given amount of time, also known as the *rate of reinforcement* (ROR) (Garrett 2005). Plus treats may lower arousal for your highly aroused dog as they sniff them out in the grass or conversely may raise it if you throw treats and have your dog run to get them.

Although tugging or using a flirt pole may slow down your training because they increase the time spent reinforcing, they are great for raising arousal levels. A flirt pole is excellent at bringing out your dog's herding instinct as dogs tend to view the flirt pole toy or "rat" as prey (Laurence 2008).

---

*A **flirt pole** is a pole with a string tied to one end and a toy attached to the other end. I use a lunge whip with a toy or "rat" attached to the end of the whip. The handler can make the rat dance to imitate the movement of prey. Using a flirt pole is one of the few ways that a handler can control a dog's access to prey.*

We will use both toys and treats as the situation warrants. I also like to use praise as my dogs find it reinforcing and so do I. I love telling them they are doing a great job! I believe sincere praise and petting bolster the other types of reinforcers when used in combination with them.

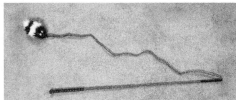

This small flirt pole is great for indoor work.

Cues become reinforcers when the behavior they name is taught positively (Bailey and Farhoody 2013–2015). They can then be used strategically as reinforcers. Just remember that repeating a cue when a behavior was not performed, or performed incorrectly, reinforces that unwanted performance. *Don't do it!* What is sad is that we think we are helping our dogs by repeating cues when we are actually building the exact behavior we don't want.

Value of reinforcement

As mentioned earlier various reinforcers have different values to your dog (Farhoody 2018). Kibble will usually not have as high a value as liver treats, but each dog determines what is most valuable to them. Also, the value of a reinforcer is often affected by your dog's level of arousal. A high value treat in your training room may have no value out in your yard if your dog is excited to be outside.

You can often tell how aroused your dog is by if and how they accept treats or play tug. When overly aroused they may take treats roughly or not accept them at all. They also may lose interest in tugging or only tug half-heartedly when highly aroused.

The reason praise and petting may be reinforcing to your dog is that dogs are social animals and through experience praise and petting often become positive consequences.

Quantity of reinforcement

Once you have determined the reinforcer you will be using in a certain training situation you also need to determine the quantity you will use. There are two times you should vary the amount of reinforcement. Firstly, you should increase the amount of reinforcement during initial training of a new behavior. Secondly, you should match the amount of reinforcement to the effort your dog puts into performing a behavior (Bailey and Farhoody 2013–2015).

When teaching a behavior, you want your dog to get into the training and the easiest way to make that happen is to pay extremely well, especially at the onset of training a *new* behavior. Unfortunately, we tend to be stingy and this is especially detrimental at the onset of teaching a new behavior. When starting a new behavior your dog may be uncertain what you are working on so any behavior that they do that is heading in the right direction is highly reinforceable.

*Giving a considerable amount of reinforcement just as your dog begins offering the behavior you want tells them: **Yes! That's it!***

As you train every day you also want to match the amount of reinforcement with the effort your dog is putting out (Bailey and Farhoody 2013–2015). If your dog only has to stand in one place and swing their head to touch a nose target you may feed just one treat but, if they have to run 20 feet to touch that same nose target you need to up the compensation by feeding several treats. The more effort your dog expends, the more you need to raise their pay.

Both the value and quantity of reinforcement used are important. Your dog determines what you use as a reinforcer and how much you need to use in any given situation. As your dog learns a behavior it becomes easier and the amount of reinforcement necessary usually declines. Always lean toward more generous reinforcement rather than minimal pay.

Placement of reinforcement

As you plan and rehearse a training exercise *without* your dog you will want to decide the best place and way to deliver reinforcement to your dog (Bailey and Farhoody 2013–2015). If you are using a treat, will you hand it or throw it? Where you deliver it should be either where the dog is doing the behavior, to build value for that place, such as on a mat, or where you want the dog to reset to repeat the behavior, off of the mat so the dog is ready to start the behavior again.

Generally, I like to deliver the reinforcer where I want the dog to perform the behavior, on the mat, in the sit, or near the nose target to build value for the position or the prop I am using. Then how do you get your dog off of the mat, out of the sit, or away from the nose target to reset the behavior?

Sir receives multiple treats while on an elevated dog bed to build value for it while sheep are present.

To reset you can either get your dog to come back to you by patting your leg, using your recall cue, or throwing a much lower value treat to get your dog to change their position. You need to experiment and see what works best for you and your dog.

Reinforcement can change arousal level

We will talk a lot more about arousal but for now, I just want to mention that there is an optimal level of arousal for training. Too little and your dog may be easily distracted. Too much and your dog may be laser-focused on livestock or, at the other extreme, so out of their mind with excitement that they may not even know you exist.

• •

Sally says

Barb's idea worked well for her dogs but my experience with Renn was that she was way too aroused by the sheep to even think of eating. Renn really enjoyed getting rid of some pent-up emotion by having a good tug between bouts of engaging the sheep. I found it calmed her down rather than winding her up, but if you have a dog which is not as calm, you would want to work on reducing the arousal level another way.

• •

Reinforcement can be used to raise or lower arousal levels, to a certain extent. If the dog is under-aroused, tugs and play can be used to get them excited and raise their arousal level. If the dog is over-aroused, but can still eat, I find that if I spread treats on the floor or in the grass, the action of sniffing to find the treats will slightly lower arousal levels and help the dog to calm themself.

I have coined the terms active and passive reinforcers. When I train *without* livestock I usually use **active reinforcers**, which are reinforcers that include movement such as tugs, flirt poles, or thrown treats, to build arousal. But when I get my dogs on livestock I use **passive reinforcers**, which are reinforcers that include less movement such as handing my dog treats. I use passive reinforcers almost exclusively when my dog is already highly aroused at just the sight and smell of the stock. Although handing my dog treats may not significantly lower their level of arousal, at least it doesn't raise it. Plus how they take treats, with a soft or hard mouth, indicates their current level of arousal, for most dogs.

Cues and markers as reinforcers

As your dog learns the cue for a behavior through positive reinforcement, the cue itself becomes an opportunity to gain reinforcement (Pryor 2005). Over time this association with reinforcement conditions the cue as a secondary reinforcer. The *upside* of the cue as a reinforcer is that you can eventually use the cue for the next behavior, to reinforce your dog for doing the first behavior. For example, if you cue sit and your dog sits, then rather than reinforcing with a treat or tugging, you can cue your dog to come. The recall cue reinforces the first behavior, the sit.

As mentioned earlier the *downside* of the cue as a reinforcer is that if you cue your dog to sit and they don't sit, you may automatically re-cue the sit. The second sit cue reinforces the behavior of remaining standing, something you want to avoid at all costs. Instead of immediately re-cueing the sit you can pause for 10 seconds and then re-cue the sit, to break the association of reinforcement between the non-sit and the next sit cue. Pausing 10 seconds is the general rule that I use, but you may adjust the time to fit your situation. I would suggest waiting at least 5 to 8 seconds before re-cueing a behavior. If your dog still struggles performing the behavior, try breaking it down into smaller steps or cue a different, easier behavior.

Markers or clicks also become conditioned reinforcers when they are consistently paired with primary reinforcement, food or play. Markers will only retain their value as reinforcers if they are followed by reinforcement relentlessly (Chance 2006).

---

*The **only** time you don't follow a mark with reinforcement is when you have marked an unwanted behavior. Then, and only then, you may skip reinforcing it since you don't want to increase the unwanted behavior by reinforcing it with a primary reinforcer. If you find yourself marking unwanted behaviors often or consistently, you need to work on your observation skills and timing. Not reinforcing a mark should be the rare exception, not the rule!*

The Premack principle

This principle was proposed by David Premack and states that more probable behaviors will reinforce less probable behaviors (Ramirez 1999). You can use this concept in many ways, such as by asking your dog to perform a controlled behavior, a sit, prior to opening the gate into your herding training paddock. Your dog would rather go into the herding training paddock than sit, so going into the paddock after a sit reinforces the sit.

Basically, all positive reinforcement training is based on the Premack principle. Working to gain reinforcement, eating or playing, is the more probable behavior that reinforces all other less probable behavior: sits, nose touches, stops, etc.

Sir is asked to sit on his way to get the tug.

The verbal cue to get the tug is a positive reinforcer for the sit.

The less probable behavior, sit, is reinforced by the cue for the more probable behavior, getting the tug.

If your dog only has interest in tugging or eating treats you can build mass on the less likely behavior by reinforcing the less probable behavior, tugging for example, with the more probable behavior, eating treats. Thus if your dog doesn't like tugging you can use treats as the reinforcer for tugging and slowly build up the strength of the tugging behavior.

I have touched on using markers. Next, we will look at how to use marker training in much more detail. Marker training allows you to communicate cleanly and clearly with your dog by telling them exactly what they did that earned reinforcement. Your dog will soon love to hear your marker and will work to make you mark!

What is marker training?

If you are familiar with clicker training then you understand a type of marker training. A marker is used to capture a slice of behavior similar to how a camera captures an image. We mark when our dog performs the exact behavior we are looking for. An example would be, verbally marking or clicking just as your dog plants their rear end on the floor, when you are looking for the sit behavior. The mark says: ***That's it!***

Imagine if your dog, or chicken, was as thrilled to hear your click, or verbal marker, as you are to hear the tone on your phone indicating an incoming call or message!

A box clicker is one of the most popular markers used for positive dog training. It makes a loud click and is especially useful outside and at a distance from your dog.

If you reinforce consistently after marking, your dog will soon learn that the mark means reinforcement is on the way! The mark tells your dog which behavior you are looking for and the paired reinforcement strengthens that behavior and makes it more likely to happen again. The mark signals reinforcement is coming so we call it a bridge. A **bridge** is a marker that "bridges" the *time* between the marking of the correct behavior and the reinforcement that is to follow (Bailey and Farhoody 2013–2015).

Although you are always looking for behavior to mark and reinforce, your dog will sometimes offer behaviors you don't want. In this situation, your options are either to ignore the behavior or to give a no reward marker (NRM), pause 10 seconds and then go back to work. I will discuss when ignoring a behavior is preferable and when using a NRM may be the better option. No matter which option you use, your dog should not lose enthusiasm for working with you. If training is not fun for you and your dog you are doing something wrong!

Types of markers

Some of the markers that can be used successfully with dogs:

- Whistle
- Verbal – word or sound
- Clicker or pen click
- Finger snap
- Mouth cluck or pop
- Light – for a deaf dog
- Hand signal

Some people like to use a clicker all of the time and others don't like to use one at all. I like using a clicker when I need a very precise marker or when I am working outside at a distance from my dog. When outside, the clicker is very **salient**, stands out as a completely different and noticeable sound, and clickers can be heard at great distances, especially box clickers.

I don't always use a clicker because I don't always need the precision of a click. Sometimes a click is almost too precise. For example, if my timing is a bit off when using a clicker, I can end up with my dog's rear end hovering slightly off the floor instead of sitting. As savvy animal trainer Bob Bailey is fond of saying, "You get what you click, not what you want". With a verbal yes as the marker, I am marking a slightly larger slice of behavior. Also, it is often not handy to have a clicker in my hand when I am working with a flirt pole or tug, so during those sessions I usually use a word as a marker.

Bob Bailey was Training Director for the Navy in the mid-1960s where he worked primarily with dolphins. During that time he met Keller and Marion Breland who had been graduate students of BF Skinner, the father of operant conditioning. Bob joined Keller and Marion at their business, Animal Behavior Enterprises (ABE), in 1965. ABE trained over 15,000 animals and over 140 species during their 40 plus years of existence. After Keller's death in 1965, Bob married Marion. Chicken training workshops were started by the Brelands in 1947; later, around 1990, Bob and Marion began to offer Chicken Workshops to the public under the name Bailey & Bailey. In 2013 Parvene Farhoody joined Bob to form the Bailey–Farhoody Chicken Workshops which ran through the summer of 2015.

*A good rule of thumb for marking is "better **never** than late"* (Devon Gaston, Chicken Workshop, nd). *If you miss the moment to mark you are better off waiting for it to come around again than to mark a behavior you don't want.*

Does the mark end the behavior?

This is ultimately up to the individual trainer, but I do *not* use the mark to end the behavior. Instead, I use a release word to end the behavior. If my dog has just sat and I say *yes*, my dog will continue to sit until I say *free*, my release word. Many people use a verbal marker, such as *yes*, as both the marker and the release word.

I *always* use a release word when I train with a tug or a flirt pole. I may be teaching walk in, walk toward the toy on the ground as if it is prey. When my dog is walking nicely I want to be able to mark that behavior. I do not want my mark or click to automatically release my dog to grab the tug or flirt pole toy, their reinforcer. Thus, I mark with *yes* and then release them to grab the toy with *get it*. This becomes important when I take my dog to sheep. If my dog walks in at a nice pace, I want to be able to mark that behavior but not have them grab or lunge at the stock after the mark.

Sir will walk in to the flirt pole prey but will wait for his release cue, get it, to grab the "rat".

If you have been using a marker to end the behavior, it is fairly easy to change the rule so the mark does not end the behavior. My dogs figured out that the rule had changed during the *first* flirt pole session using the new rule. The keys to changing a rule are for you *to know* exactly what the new rule is and *to be consistent* using the new rule to define when your dog is correct and has earned reinforcement.

Schedules of reinforcement

A *schedule of reinforcement* is the pattern and rate of reinforcement (Chance 2006). There are many schedules of reinforcement, but I use a fixed-ratio schedule of 1:1. This means that I reinforce *every* correct response. For each correct response given, my dog receives reinforcement. For example, I may give one or several treats for a correct response but I always reinforce each correct response, even if it is by giving another cue. I do this because we are not only building but also maintaining behavior. Any behavior not being reinforced will decrease. Over time I may use fewer or lower value treats or less tugging until I eventually transition to using cues and access to livestock as my principal reinforcers when herding.

*Many people advocate reinforcing every mark or click. I do not. Since the mark is a secondary reinforcer, just marking an unwanted behavior reinforces it. This is enough damage to your training! Feel free to **not** reinforce a bad mark or click with a primary reinforcer. A few bad marks will not hurt your training or break down the value of your bridge signal. If you find yourself in this situation often, you need to re-evaluate what and when you are marking (Bailey and Farhoody 2013–2015).*

Capturing, luring, and shaping

The three basic ways to get behavior are **capturing**, **luring**, and **shaping** (Fisher 2009). There is a fourth way, which is physical manipulation, but that is almost always aversive and not something I use in positive reinforcement training.

Capturing behavior: In their everyday life, our dogs are constantly performing behaviors and thus provide us with many opportunities to select a behavior that we prefer more often. You can capture *any* behavior that your dog performs. Usually a mark, followed by a reinforcer, is used to alert your dog to which behavior you want them to notice and repeat.

Capturing is one method to increase everyday behaviors that can be used as tricks such as yawns, bows, or tail wags. More importantly, you can catch and reinforce your dog for behavior that pleases and makes your dog enjoyable to be around, such as lying quietly while you work on your computer or waiting calmly as you work another dog on livestock. Capture and reinforce wanted behaviors to see them repeated often.

Luring and prompting behavior: Holding a reinforcer, usually a treat but sometimes a toy, to guide your dog to perform a desired behavior by following that reinforcer is known as **luring**. Lures are particularly useful to give your dog the general idea of the behavior you are looking for, especially if it is a new type of behavior that your dog is not familiar with. Lures should be used sparingly and faded quickly. I usually use treats for luring and only lure three times.

After a few reps with a lure, you can transition to no longer holding a treat while continuing to move your hand *as if* you still held the treat, called fading the lure. Using a hand movement that imitates the luring motion, but *without* holding a treat, is one type of **prompting** (Burch and Bailey 1999).

Even without ever using a treat or toy, our dogs quickly learn to follow our body indications such as the direction our shoulders or eyes are pointing, a hand sweeping, or a step back to draw our dogs forward. Dogs are brilliant at reading our body language and interpreting what we are saying to them before we even open our mouths. All of these movements, even some that we do unconsciously, can prompt our dogs to perform behaviors.

Shaping, free shaping, and targeting behavior: Almost all behavior is built using shaping, usually defined as building behavior by successive approximations. **Shaping** is splitting the desired behavior into small pieces and using the timing of your mark and the placement of your reinforcer to guide your dog toward the wanted behavior. The goal of shaping is to start with a slice of behavior in your dog's repertoire and mold that behavior to create a totally new behavior.

Whenever you are with your dog they are learning from you, whether you are "training" or not. When there is any interaction between animals, one animal is always shaping the other. What is your dog learning from you?

Even when we start with capturing or luring, we usually shape the initial behavior into a form of the behavior that we find more desirable. For example, I may capture a bow. Once my dog is offering bows frequently I will start reinforcing only the better bows, maybe those that are deeper. Similarly, if I have lured a behavior to get it going, I will quickly switch over to shaping to mold that behavior into the exact behavior I have in mind.

Free shaping is a training term for a form of shaping that depends on your dog *offering* behavior. No **props**, something in the environment that prompts or elicits a behavior, are used in free shaping. It's just you, your dog, your marker, and your reinforcers. You start by marking and reinforcing any slice of desirable behavior and slowly, incrementally building on that behavior.

Let's say you capture a slight left head turn with your first few clicks and want to shape that behavior into a full spin to the left. As your dog offers more left head turns to earn reinforcement, which you strategically feed to your dog's left, you begin to select only the more pronounced head turns in that direction. You continue to do this until your dog starts shifting their weight on to their left front foot, and then maybe your dog offers a tiny step to their left. You continue in this fashion and eventually shape a spin to the left from a slight head turn in that direction. This will probably *not* be a smooth or stepwise path. Your dog is trying to figure out what you will mark and reinforce and they will make mistakes. Allow your dog to work things out and keep sessions short. This is *very* hard mental work for your dog!

Another type of shaping is **targeting** which involves using a prop (Bailey and Farhoody 2013–2015). There are a multitude of props that come in an infinite variety of colors, sizes, shapes, and textures. Often props for dogs are used as nose, paw, or body targets, but not all props are targets. Some props are used as barriers to help guide our dogs as they learn new behaviors (Bailey and Farhoody 2013–2015). In herding, we can even include livestock and you, the handler, as targets or barriers.

A few *common props* used in dog training include:
- small ball on the end of a stick (target stick)
- piece of carpet or tile
- raised platform
- Frisbee or bowl
- cones (target or barrier)
- livestock
- handler (you)

In targeting, we draw our dog's attention to a certain prop, the target. For example, a target stick is a small ball on the end of a stick. One way to use a target stick is to shape your dog to touch the ball and then move the ball while holding onto the stick. Next, you shape your dog to follow the moving ball. You then can use the behavior of following the ball to shape a spin as well as many other behaviors. As in luring, you want to fade targets as soon as possible, if they are not part of the final behavior.

Targeting takes on a critically important role in herding when teaching certain skills:
- driving (taking the sheep away from the handler)
- fetching (bringing the sheep to the handler)
- flanking (circling the stock)
- off-balance flanking (circling past the point of balance; where the dog would turn in to control or fetch (bring) the stock to the handler)

There are times when we *want* our dog to use us as a target and other times when we absolutely *don't want* to be the target. Too much practice of the dog targeting the handler while fetching the sheep can make it extremely difficult to get our dogs to drive the sheep away from us. The problem is that we are now asking our dogs to take the stock *away* from us instead of bringing them to us, a behavior that has a lot of mass or strength. Plus our dog's herding instinct is to bring the sheep to us, adding tremendous amounts of mass to the fetch behavior. To keep our training balanced, we will include behaviors that have us as the target and those that do not.

On a fetch, the dog brings the stock to the handler, Sir is targeting me with the stock. The sheep are Sir's primary target and I am his secondary target.

If this sounds terribly confusing, don't worry as it will all be explained in far greater detail later. Just remember that targeting is *very* important in herding. *You* are the second most important target in herding, right after the sheep. Your dog should constantly be looking at the stock, their primary target.

Getting behavior is our main goal and capturing, luring and shaping give us the means to accomplish this goal. I don't shy away from using any of these methods to get and then grow behavior since all of these methods are based on positive reinforcement. Each trainer and dog have different learning experiences and individual strengths and weaknesses. I encourage you to experiment and use what works best for you and your dog. If you are making progress and having fun, you are on the right track to getting and building behavior.

We all want our dogs to succeed, but we can handicap our dogs by helping them too much. Failure is just information for you and your dog, so allow your dog to fail as well as succeed. We are all learning all of the time and mistakes are just part of life. Relax when training so that your dog can relax too (Fisher 2009).

Fundamentals of shaping behavior

We are going to use shaping to build behavior almost all of the time. Since shaping is such an integral part of training let's look at some of the basics I find helpful:

☐ Start shaping *only* after your dog is comfortable with the marker you are using and has had experience having it paired with great reinforcement. (Some dogs are fearful of clickers because they produce a novel alarming sound.)

- ☐ Practice without your dog to get comfortable with your mechanics.
- ☐ Keep your sessions short since shaping a new behavior is mentally exhausting for you and your dog. (Sessions of 2 to 5 minutes are sufficient.)
- ☐ Reinforce *generously* and *often*, especially to get the behavior started.
- ☐ Relax and have *fun* watching your dog figure out how to make you mark.
- ☐ Video you *and* your dog. (You'll be amazed to see what you *actually* did as compared to what you *thought* you did.)
- ☐ Stay quiet and motionless and allow your dog to think.
- ☐ Start with shaping a simple behavior while you and your dog learn shaping.
- ☐ Use a prop the first time or two you try shaping to get the behavior started quickly.
- ☐ Plan your training so you know what you are looking for and what your next step in growing the behavior will be.
- ☐ Plan where you will reinforce and what reinforcers you will use.
- ☐ Plan how you will reset your dog for the next trial.
- ☐ Plan where you, your dog, and the prop, if you are using one, will be positioned.
- ☐ Use barriers, when possible, to guide your dog and reduce errors.
- ☐ If you lure to jump-start a behavior, fade the lure after 3 or 4 reps.
- ☐ Split the behavior into thin slices to make it easy for your dog to be right, split – don't lump steps.
- ☐ Start with a slice of behavior that is already in your dog's repertoire.
- ☐ Be ready to mark and reinforce the *moment* your dog offers any behavior that could lead to your goal behavior. Don't miss your dog's first notice of or interaction with a prop. *Be prepared!*
- ☐ Move to the next step of your plan when your dog is performing the current step correctly *80%* of the time.
- ☐ Know where you are going with the behavior so if your dog makes a leap several steps ahead you are prepared to jump ahead in your training plan, especially if you have an experienced dog.
- ☐ If you are late marking, don't! The behavior will surface again.
- ☐ If your dog gets stuck you can *always* break the behavior down even further to the point it becomes micro-shaping, marking a muscle movement or just the slightest movement.
- ☐ If your rate of reinforcement (ROR), the number of times you reinforce in a minute, is low, you need to slice the behavior thinner to help your dog succeed and keep them working.
- ☐ Don't be in a hurry to help your dog.
- ☐ If you get stuck, stop the session, re-think, and re-plan.
- ☐ Don't be afraid to go back a step if you get stuck, but this should not become a habit. If this happens often, you need to look at your criteria-setting skills.

☐   Write down how far you got building the behavior in the session, note how you want to start your next session, and jot down anything else you want to remember.

☐   Videoing your sessions allows you to go back and look at your timing, criteria, and rate of reinforcement; the keys to good training. *Feel free to check any boxes that indicate practices you would like to emphasize or struggle with.*

*Remember that shaping is a skilled use of **reinforcement** and **extinction** (Farhoody 2018). You mark and reinforce successive slices of the behavior you are building and ignore the slices offered that do not move you toward your goal behavior. Thus you are increasing the wanted behavior with reinforcement and decreasing the unwanted behaviors with extinction.*

One way to learn about shaping, when not training, is playing a game to improve your timing. There are simple games for improving timing such as dropping a tennis ball and marking just as it hits the floor. You can find computer games to hone your timing.

Also, try playing the training game Genabacab with a friend. This game was developed by Kay Laurence and involves props to clicker train your friend or have them train you. Mary Hunter now has the PORTL manual, which teaches a similar activity, available at: *behaviorexplorer.com*. You can also gather game pieces and put your own game together. Training another person or being trained by another person is guaranteed to be an eye-opening experience!

*If you are working with a **crossover dog**, a dog that has been traditionally trained using primarily positive punishment, you may find your dog offers very little behavior (Fisher 2009).*

When initially training a crossover dog, I suggest beginning with a unique prop that you believe your dog will be comfortable with. Place the prop on the floor a few feet from your dog and mark any movement your dog makes to orient toward or investigate the prop, such as a head turn, step, or sniff. Your goal is to get your dog offering any behavior.

Shaping a valuable herding skill

Most people think that if their dog has herding instinct their dog knows instinctively how to handle all common situations with livestock. Although our dogs do come with amazing abilities to read and handle livestock, they sometimes need us to step in and help them learn how to use their instinctive skills.

My young dog Hart of Gold was just getting started on sheep many years ago. We ran into trouble when I tried to get Hart to go between the sheep and the fence. She would get close to the fence, but as she approached the sheep she would remain hooked up, staring at the sheep, as she tried to get between them and the fence. Her staring locked the sheep in place and prevented them from moving away from the fence. Thus as she walked forward, she pushed the sheep along the fence in front of her instead of moving the sheep off of the fence.

Note the difference in Sir's head and body position: holding rams in place (left) versus indicating going around them (right). A dog can hold stock in position with only their eye. If Sir had turned his body but kept his head and eyes focused on the rams they would be reluctant to move out of the corner even as he flanked into the corner.

One way traditional trainers deal with this is to take the dog by the collar and pull or drag them between the sheep and the fence a few times. Eventually, the dog gets the idea and starts going between the stock and the fence. This was not an option for me since I no longer force my dogs to perform behaviors.

After watching Hart struggle for a few moments I stopped her and waited, meanwhile pulling my clicker from a pocket as I stood off to the side of the action. I had previously flanked Hart and she had taken a few steps in the correct direction so I knew she had some idea of what I was asking her to do. After a minute or so of Hart staring at the sheep, she looked to me for direction. I did nothing, but as she turned her head back toward the sheep and the fence, I clicked. This was followed by another lengthy pause until she looked back at me. Again I clicked her head movement as she turned away from me and toward the fence. Since I had previously shaped spins with Hart, she understood the value of head-turning and offered a bit more of a head turn toward the fence. Now she was no longer staring at the sheep but looking between the sheep and the fence.

At this point I cued the flank, Hart offered a step forward along the fence, and she received a click. She then offered three steps forward and got another click. Since the sheep had not slid down the fence this time, but had moved slightly away from it, after the next step Hart took off and flanked between the sheep and the fence. *Success!* I repeated the two-part shaping of first head turning toward the fence and then walking forward, needing far fewer clicks to get the desired behavior of Hart flanking between the sheep and the fence each time. From that point on Hart never had trouble going between stock and a fence.

You may think that I was doing a *lot* of clicking with no mention of reinforcement, treats or toys, following the mark. In fact, one of the most valuable reinforcers for a herding dog is access to livestock. Just allowing Hart to continue interacting with the sheep after the click, instead of calling her off, was the most valuable reinforcement that I could give her, bar none!

Reinforcement reigns

Markers paired with reinforcers provide an extremely powerful way to get behavior. We all do what works and avoid what doesn't, and our dogs are no different as they seek reinforcement and avoid punishment. Although we use primarily positive reinforcement, we still have to have rules and boundaries to keep our dogs safe, make them respectful members of our families, teach them self-control, and train them to perform our chosen sport to the highest standard. Positive should not be permissive!

To train our dogs to exacting standards we need to hone our training skills to the highest level. The key training skills we must master are *timing* of the marker, monitoring and controlling the *rate of reinforcement*, and setting, observing, and marking *criteria* (Bailey and Farhoody 2013–2015). These skills can make communicating with our dogs precise and clear. I refer to **T**iming, rate of **R**einforcement, **a**nd **C**riteria as the **TRaC** skills.

Let's get on TRaC!

CHAPTER 6

Building behavior

The more clearly we communicate with our dogs, the easier it is for them to develop the precise behaviors we need for herding. To tell my dog what gains reinforcement and what does not, I rely on timing, rate of reinforcement, and criteria (Bailey and Farhoody 2013–2015). I also use no reward markers and time-outs, negative punishment, to decrease inherently reinforcing instinctual behavior, such as chasing livestock.

I call these important training tools the TRaC skills. **TRaC skills** include timing, rate of reinforcement, and criteria. When I use these skills wisely my dog should make few mistakes because my communication is crystal clear. But my dog is going to make mistakes and certainly some of these mistakes will be due to my less than stellar use of timing, rate of reinforcement, and criteria. If I trained perfectly then my dog would respond correctly almost 100% of the time. Figure those odds!

Since mistakes are going to happen, I can usually choose to ignore them and allow extinction to eventually eliminate the unwanted behavior. So why not just do that? The reason I use no reward markers is that many of the herding skills, such as flanking and walking in to stock, are inherently reinforcing for herding dogs. I also use time-outs for big infractions such as chasing, lunging, or flagrant biting of stock. Since time-outs are similar to no reward markers, I will discuss them in this chapter.

Before we worry about telling our dogs that they are not heading toward reinforcement with a no reward marker or time-out, we need to hone our TRaC skills and become very good at telling our dogs what does earn reinforcement.

Timing, rate of reinforcement, and criteria are critical to good training but they will do you no good if you don't have a clear idea of the behavior you are training. Before you begin a training session you need to define the behavior you want to train. If you can define your goal behavior in one simple sentence, you are good to go.

TRaC Skill # 1 – Timing

Precise **timing** is crucial for telling your dog what behavior you want more of. The smaller the movement you desire, the more critical good timing becomes. You get what you mark, not what you want (Bailey and Farhoody 2013–2015).

*To have good timing you have to anticipate movement. If you can determine the behavior that your dog does just **before** the behavior you want, you will be ready to mark the wanted behavior. If you wait to see the wanted behavior you will usually be late marking it. Observation is the key!*

When herding livestock, anticipation becomes even more important than when training pre-herding skills. Good timing in the field can make herding look effortless and bad timing can lead to train wrecks. I cannot tell you how many times I was told I was late giving cues during the years I took traditional herding lessons! Eventually, I figured out that to give cues in a timely manner, I had to anticipate the movement of both my dog and the livestock. Another simple, but not easy, concept to implement!

An example of anticipation is when my dog is flanking around to start a **cross drive**, driving stock in a line perpendicular to the handler. I know the spot where my dog needs to stop and walk into the stock, but since my dog is probably running, I have to give my cue to stop *before* my dog reaches that spot. If I wait until my dog is at the correct place to turn in before I give my stop cue, my dog will over-run the correct point because it will take them a few feet to get stopped. Herding is a game of anticipation and angles, so any time you invest honing your observation and timing skills will be time well spent.

A big part of timing is observation. You can only mark what you can see. Closely watching your dog and learning to anticipate how livestock respond to a dog's approach will help you develop a feel for how animals move and react. It is this *feel* that will help you improve your timing when herding. Spend time watching livestock as they move and interact. If you don't have access to stock you can go onto the internet and watch videos of sheep, cattle, goat, and duck herding. Closely watch how the stock and the dog interact. Can you anticipate how the dog's movement will make the stock respond? When you gain confidence anticipating how stock will respond to your or your dog's movement, we say you can **read livestock**. Being able to read livestock is crucial to herding success and comes with observation and experience.

*When your dog is moving fast you need to keep in mind how long it will take them to perform a stop or walk in cue. In this picture, I am sending Gold out even with the sheep to **cross drive**, drive the sheep from side to side in front of me, rather than having him go to balance and fetch them.*

Eventually, you will practice picking a point in the paddock where you want your dog to stop and see how close you can get to having them stop exactly at that point. It won't take long for you to get a feel for how quickly your dog will respond to your cues when running.

*The ability to read livestock is the foundation of stockmanship. **Stockmanship** is the knowledgeable and skillful handling of livestock. You use stockmanship every time you interact with livestock, be it at a trial or in your backyard. Good stockmanship is based on gentle yet efficient handling of livestock. Entire books have been written about stockmanship, but we will only be able to scratch the surface of the art and science of good stockmanship in* Positive Herding 102.

Because timing is so crucial in herding, you will want to develop precise timing. When you get outside with a dog and livestock there is a lot to think about and keep track of, so having good timing makes the experience a little easier and sets you up for success.

TRaC Skill # 2 – Rate of reinforcement

To me the key concept concerning reinforcement is generosity! Three ways to super-charge reinforcement are by increasing the value, amount, or frequency of treats or tugging.

Rate of reinforcement (ROR) is the number of reinforcers earned and delivered in a set amount of time (Fisher 2009). For example, if you train for 5 minutes and deliver 65 reinforcers your rate of reinforcement is 13/minute. Calculating your rate of reinforcement in different training sessions can give you the data necessary to spot and fix a problem caused by a low rate of reinforcement.

If your rate of reinforcement drops too low, your dog will no longer want to work to earn reinforcement. Your dog may sniff, walk away, lie down, or in other words – stop working with you, game over! Before it gets to that point, your dog may lose enthusiasm for training and respond without speed or precision. If you want a dog that is happy and engaged you need a high ROR. You can think of your rate of reinforcement as your dog's paycheck. If the pay gets too low your dog will quit showing up for work!

To raise your rate of reinforcement you need to slice the behavior you are teaching into thinner slices, split not lump. By asking for less behavior to earn a mark you are making it easier for your dog to be successful. This change means your dog will earn reinforcement more often and your rate of reinforcement will increase.

There are two ways that your ROR can be fairly low and not necessarily derail your training:
1. Tug or flirt pole use can slow down your training and cause your rate of reinforcement to be quite low. (A rousing game of tug, used as reinforcement, may take 20 seconds.)
2. Training behaviors that involve distance or duration can cause your rate of reinforcement to plummet.

If you are using a tug or flirt pole you need to match the length and intensity of your play time to the amount of effort your dog invested to gain the reinforcement. If your dog's enthusiasm or attention starts to wane, then ramp up the amount of treats or the time and/or the intensity of the play. Similarly, when you train duration or distance, the amount of time playing or quantity and/or value of treats given as reinforcement needs to increase so that your dog's pay is commensurate with the work they performed. Try to match the amount and/or quality of the reinforcement to the effort your dog puts out to earn it. More effort = more pay.

A jackpot, giving a large quantity of treats for exceptional performance, may be especially useful when starting to train a new behavior.

Being around livestock is super reinforcing for herding breeds. When your dog is around sheep they are highly reinforced just by looking at the sheep. For most dogs, there is *nothing* that compares in reinforcement value to getting to interact with stock. Sheep = jackpot!!!

TRaC Skill # 3 – Criteria

Criteria are the parameters that define a behavior. (Bertilsson and Johnson Vegh 2010). Almost every behavior is composed of many criteria. The criteria you use for a behavior determine what you will mark and reinforce. A behavior has many criteria but you should focus on only one criterion at a time.

For example, a flank has many criteria or aspects:
- Direction
- Speed
- Squareness (When starting a flank your dog should turn at a 90° angle to the livestock so no pressure is put onto the stock, which may cause them to move.)
- Distance from the stock

All of these criteria determine the dog's effect on the livestock, each in its own way, as we shall see. To mark a criterion, it must be observable and definable in one short sentence.

In the flanking example you might determine the first criteria to train are directionals, *come bye* and *away to me*. In doing that we will first break the behavior down into something as simple as an *eye flick to the right*, for the *away to me* direction. Then we might mark a *slight head turn to the right*. Next would be a *farther head turn to the right*. All of these slices of behavior fit our criterion, what we will mark.

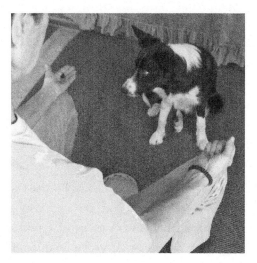

Sir during the first stages of learning directionals. In this photo we are working on away to me or counterclockwise. Directionals are initially taught inside with minimal distraction. Later, directionals will become flanks and the training moved outside. Eventually Sir will flank around livestock in a pen and then loose stock.

Only work on one criterion or aspect of a behavior at a time. If I determine that my dog is flanking too slowly and too close to the stock, I have to decide which of these criteria to address first. I can work on speed or distance, but not both at the same time. So if I decide to work on speed and I get my dog to really run while flanking, I will mark that even if my dog is still too close to the stock. After I have trained one aspect of the behavior to criterion I can begin to address the other.

Shaping is all about setting criteria, usually in thin slices, and then growing that behavior by building those thin slices into a complete behavior. We often talk about setting criteria low or easy when starting a behavior, think of the eye flick in teaching directionals. We want it to be easy for our dogs to be successful, especially when starting a new or potentially difficult exercise. When our dog is successful about 80% of the time, we increase or raise our criteria to move toward our goal behavior.

You don't want to wait for your dog to be 100% correct before increasing your criteria since you will be extinguishing parts of the developing behavior as you move toward the final behavior. When shaping, you are always moving the behavior toward your goal behavior by reinforcing wanted behavior and extinguishing unwanted behavior.

Since you have to identify and observe the criterion you are going to mark, you must remain vigilant during training. The longer the training session, the more difficult it becomes to stay focused and maintain criteria and mechanics, so keep sessions short.

Criteria and rate of reinforcement are related

Criteria and rate of reinforcement are inversely related, in other words, as you raise criteria your rate of reinforcement will likely fall, and as you drop criteria, a slippery slope, your rate of reinforcement will rise (Bailey and Farhoody 2013–2015). If you are asking more from your dog you will likely have slower or more incorrect responses. Thus your rate of reinforcement will drop. As your dog figures out the next step, they will respond correctly more quickly, thus raising your rate of reinforcement. If your rate of reinforcement goes through the roof, you probably need to up your criteria.

- Criteria **increase** = rate of reinforcement *decrease*
- Criteria *decrease* = rate of reinforcement **increase**

Setting criteria is an art as well as a learned skill. Experience will teach you when you have set criteria too low and your dog leaps ahead, or too high and your dog struggles or quits. All dogs are different and you will need to adjust criteria for each dog as an individual. As you train different skills on different days, you again will have to adjust to how your dog is performing. Over time you will get a feel for how fast to raise criteria, taking into account the behavior you are shaping and your previous experience shaping your dog.

Cover your TRaCs

Bob Bailey says that almost all training problems are related to either timing, rate of reinforcement, or criteria (Bailey and Farhoody 2013–2015). When struggling with your training, start by looking at the one brief sentence that defines your goal behavior. Are you clear about your training goal? If you don't know where you are going, how can you expect your dog to figure it out? This is one time that help from a more experienced trainer or viewing video of your training can be priceless. Remember you get what you mark, not what you want!

Covering your TRaCs includes looking for:
- Timing that is late, early, or erratic
- Rate of reinforcement that is too low or too high
- Reinforcing inconsistent criteria
- Reinforcing multiple criteria
- Marking and/or reinforcing behavior that you *don't* want

No reward markers (NRMs)

Many instinctual herding skills are inherently reinforcing for dogs. Herding breeds love to flank. Just ask any agility enthusiast with a border collie about the problems that can arise when their dog wants to flank or curve between obstacles instead of running straight to them. For a dog with herding instinct, flanking around an obstacle or cone circle is not just inherently reinforcing, it is *very* inherently reinforcing!

A **no reward marker** (NRM) is a word, a verbal cue, that tells a dog they are no longer heading toward reinforcement, in other words, they are wrong (Alexander 2003). NRMs are negative punishers, used primarily with behavior chains and inherently reinforcing behaviors. I use a couple of different no reward markers, such as *oops* or *I don't think so*.

I used to use *okay* as an NRM, but don't anymore because I found myself using it too often in my everyday speech, so it just became part of the blah, blah, blah my dogs heard in the house. Plus I used to have "okay" as my release word with previous dogs, so I am prone to saying it in the wrong situation. Rather than have to think about when to use "okay", I decided it was easier to just drop it.

The way I use a *no reward marker* is:

1. Say the *no reward marker*
2. Behavior stops (dog stops)
3. Break eye contact and pause 10 seconds (*Response cost*)
4. Re-cue the behavior

Using a No Reward Marker to stop Sir chasing a tractor, a very inherently reinforcing behavior.

This video shows the use of a no reward marker: https://youtu.be/B9TXeQ3uN6o

Response cost

The withholding of reinforcement for the 10-second pause is the **response cost** for performing the incorrect behavior (Burch and Bailey 1999). During this pause, the handler removes their attention from the dog to stop any reinforcing interaction, thereby decreasing the undesired behavior. I feel using the no reward marker pause also gives my dogs a moment to breathe and think, as it breaks the flow of training. Often the mistake seems to have happened because my dog is a bit over-aroused and this brief pause helps them to calm down.

The *most important part* of the no reward marker procedure is the response cost pause. It is this short, but noticeable, pause that punishes the incorrect behavior. It is also this pause that breaks repeated cues apart, *away to me, away to me*, so that when you do re-cue the behavior you are not reinforcing the earlier incorrect behavior. Cues are reinforcers, so if you quickly re-cue an incorrect response you are reinforcing that incorrect response with the repeated cue.

I say my no reward marker in a matter of fact or happy voice, and although my dogs usually stop immediately I have not seen their enthusiasm to continue training wane. Certainly, you don't want to use a no reward marker often or your rate of reinforcement is going to drop like a rock. If you find yourself in this situation you need to go back and re-train the behavior. No dog will do well on a steady diet of no reward markers.

I find using no reward markers work well for me. Many trainers do not use NRMs. (I think Sally is one of them.) If you find your dog losing enthusiasm or shutting down when using an NRM, then NRMs may not be for you.

Some dogs find being wrong upsetting and a no reward marker punishing. My dog Qwest is very sensitive, but I use no reward markers occasionally without reducing his enthusiasm for training. Other dogs find no reward markers very punishing and they will shut down or quit working. Let your dog tell you if no reward markers should be part of your training. Just be sure to give your no reward marker in a neutral or happy voice so that the tone or delivery of the cue is not punishing.

Before you start – No reward marker (NRM)

If you or your dog need to have a specific skill in place before you begin training an exercise, it will be covered in the section: **Before you start**.

A no reward marker needs to be taught to your dog before it can be used to interrupt an incorrectly performed inherently reinforcing behavior. It is easiest to teach an NRM using a non-inherently reinforcing behavior and then transfer its use to inherently reinforcing behaviors.

To teach a no reward marker your dog needs to have at least one obedience behavior, such as down or sit, trained to fluency. If your dog does not have a fluent obedience behavior skip ahead to Chapter 12, Obedient RAMs *and train sit to fluency before training a NRM. Your dog also needs to be toy or tug motivated with a good release behavior.*

For this example, I use sit as my obedience behavior, but any fluent behavior can be used. You will need a toy or tug with a 6-foot string attached and some high-value treats.

NRM – Step by step

1. Set a timer for 3 to 5 minutes.
2. Your dog is positioned about 10 feet away from and facing a toy on the floor.
3. You stand 5 feet to one side of and facing the toy, while holding the string attached to it.

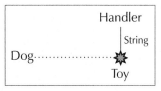

4. Release your dog to get the toy and have a short tug session.
5. Repeat step 4 until your dog trots or runs to grab the toy or the flirt pole toy.

---

6. Release your dog to the toy, but give your sit cue as soon as your dog starts to move.
7. If your dog sits, mark and release your dog to the toy for a tug session.
8. If your dog continues toward the toy, give your NRM (such as 'oops') and whisk the toy back into your hands before your dog can grab it.

---

9. Repeat step 6 until your dog stops immediately when you give your NRM. Now be ready to mark the stop and toss a treat to your dog.
10. Reset and release your dog to get the toy and have a short tug session. Repeat this step until your dog is again trotting to get the toy.
11. Reset your dog but this time allow your dog to get halfway to the toy before giving your NRM. Again you will mark and reinforce your dog with a treat if they stop immediately or you will quickly pull the toy out of their reach.
12. Stop when your timer sounds and take a break. Work this exercise over several short sessions.

It doesn't take dogs long to figure out that the NRM means they no longer have access to a reinforcer and that stopping at that point is reinforced.

Troubleshooting
*   ***Dog gets sticky*** – Many dogs will slow down to a hesitant walk after the toy has been pulled away a few times. If your dog slows down significantly, return to releasing them to get the toy, allow them to grab it, and have a tug session. Repeat this as often as necessary to keep your dog trotting toward the toy when released to it.
*   ***Dog heads to handler instead of stopping*** – If your dog comes to you rather than stopping, you need to get the toy off the floor and into your hands much more quickly. The toy should fly from the floor to your hands as quickly as possible. Practice getting the toy back to you without your dog present until you can smoothly make it almost seem to disappear.
*   ***Dog doesn't stop when given NRM with inherently reinforcing behavior*** – Later, suppose you are working on flanks around a cone circle and your dog takes the wrong flank. You give your NRM, that you have trained previously, and your dog continues to flank in the incorrect direction. At this point I cue my dog to stop since allowing them to continue in the wrong direction is inherently reinforcing. I realize that my stop cue also reinforces the dog going the wrong direction but

I believe allowing the dog to continue a highly inherently reinforcing behavior, the flank, is more reinforcing than a stop cue.

Once your dog has learned the correct response to a NRM, stop and wait, there will be very few times that they will continue the incorrect behavior instead of stopping immediately.

I am usually working with a flirt pole when training inherently reinforcing behaviors such as directionals and flanks. A flirt pole is perfect for whipping the toy attached to it back to me before my dog can grab it.

When I use NRMs in my training I no longer reinforce my dog stopping with a treat, as I did while teaching the cue. Instead, after the pause, I immediately reset for another trial and continue with my training.

Example using NRM

If I am working with a flirt pole and cone circles to teach my dog flank cues, *come bye* for clockwise and *away to me* for counterclockwise, I need a way to tell my dog when they have chosen to go the wrong direction.

I cue *come bye* and my dog starts to flank *away to me*. I then have a choice to make. I can either do nothing or give a NRM which interrupts the flanking motion and stops my dog, pause for 10 seconds, and then resuming training. If I do nothing, my dog is going to continue to flank since flanking is very inherently reinforcing for my dogs. Thus the incorrect behavior is being reinforced by allowing it to continue. If I give a no reward marker, *oops* or *I don't think* so, my dog will immediately stop because they know continuing the behavior will *not* earn reinforcement.

In this scenario there are two reinforcers in play. The first is the flirt pole toy, which I control. The second is the behavior of flanking, which is inherently reinforcing for my dog and which I cannot control. When I add livestock to the situation, then flanking becomes even more inherently reinforcing as my dog will *really* want to get to the head of the livestock to control them. If an inherently reinforcing behavior is in play, doing nothing will only increase that behavior because just performing the behavior is reinforcing.

Time-out (TO)

I only use time-outs for major crimes such as flagrant biting or lunging at livestock. A **time-out** is another type of negative punishment in which the dog is removed from the scene of the crime for a few minutes (Garrett 2005).

I use time-outs most often when I still have sheep in a small pen and my dog is working outside of the pen. This is when my dog is quite new to having access to livestock. If I have any concerns that my dog is going to lunge at the sheep in the pen, I will have them drag a light 10-foot long line. If I am having my dog flank around the penned sheep and my dog lunges toward the pen and attempts to bite the sheep, I will initiate a time-out.

The steps for a time-out are:
1. Calmly pick up the long line.
2. Gain control of the dog, but don't jerk them to interrupt the behavior.
3. Say your no reward marker.
4. Quietly walk the dog away from the stock and out of the paddock.
5. Position the dog behind a barrier or otherwise prevent the dog from looking at the stock.
6. Wait 3 to 5 minutes and return to work.

The *most important* aspect of implementing a TO is remaining calm and quiet throughout the procedure. If you yell at or chase your dog, their arousal will skyrocket and *increase* the reinforcement they derived from trying to attack the sheep. In addition, your arousal/excitement will peak when your main job is to remain calm and think, even if your dog cannot. A calm TO helps to lower your dog's level of arousal.

*Please **do not resort to positive punishment** when your dog attempts to attack penned stock as it will tend to increase your dog's arousal. Yelling at your dog only increases the likelihood that your dog will continue to repeat or escalate this unacceptable behavior. Instead, if the TO did not eliminate the unwanted behavior, work with your dog on easier exercises to build self-control near stock.*

Again, time-outs, by definition, are negative punishment. What you are teaching your dog by using them is that lunging and flagrant biting lose them access to livestock, their top reinforcer. As with no reward markers, if you find yourself using time-outs often, something is wrong. Negative punishment should be used sparingly, if at all. Another way to look at time-outs is that they are *time-out* from positive reinforcement.

Sir has been placed in "time-out" behind a visual barrier. Just looking at stock is reinforcing for herding dogs.

An alternative time-out

If removing your dog from the sheep for a time-out is not decreasing the unwanted behavior you can try an alternative time-out.

For an alternative time-out the steps are:
1.   Calmly pick up the long line.
2.   Gain control of the dog, but don't jerk them to interrupt the behavior.
3.   Say your no reward marker.
4.   Quietly walk the dog away from the stock and out of the paddock.
5.   Tie or crate the dog so that they can see the stock.
6.   Calmly work another dog or an imaginary dog on the sheep for 5 to 10 minutes.
7.   Remove the second dog, if you are using one.
8.   Bring your dog back into the paddock.
9.   Return to work.

Work the second dog calmly and quietly. Move the sheep around and have fun! You want your dog to see what fun they are missing. If you are using an imaginary dog, move the stock around yourself while giving cues to your imaginary dog. You want the stock to move calmly while you give cues. If you cannot think of what cues to give, imagine yourself as a dog and cue yourself to move the sheep around the paddock.

Your dog should remain calm while they watch the second or imaginary dog work. If your dog cannot remain calm while watching, you will not be able to use the alternative time-out. You want your dog to remain calm at all times while watching livestock, even if they are being worked by you or another dog.

Getting on TRaC to build behavior

Growing behavior is all about seeing, marking, and reinforcing wanted behavior. Timing, rate of reinforcement, and criteria are the skills that allow you to communicate with your dog. If these skills are well-honed, your communication will be clean and clear, if not, your dog will struggle and your training will flounder.

Once you get basic behaviors built, the next step is to strengthen them. We will briefly look at the four stages of learning and how to generalize, proof, and build fluency. Then we will discuss when and how to add cues, deal with mistakes, and solve major problems. The coming chapter will be our last important stop before getting into the nuts and bolts of training your dog to herd.

CHAPTER 7

Strengthening behavior

Once we get and build great herding behavior away from livestock, we still have a lot of work to do to get it into a usable form for herding. A dog that knows its flanks only indoors or in the backyard will not be much help around sheep in a pasture. We need to build really strong behaviors that can stand up to massive distraction – livestock!

Adding strength to a behavior can be illustrated by thinking about going bowling. Imagine the difference in how many pins will fall when you roll a Wiffle ball, which weighs less than an ounce, down the alley instead of a bowling ball that might weigh 13 pounds. Your score would definitely suffer!

Behavioral momentum, a theory dealing with the mass and velocity of a behavior, was developed by John A Nevin (Farhoody 2018) to explain why behaviors differ in strength. Momentum or behavioral strength under pressure from distraction, can be illustrated with two balls. Similar to the Wiffle ball, a behavior may stand up to very minor pressure or distractions, such as a change in trainer position or moving from the backyard to the front yard, but it will soon break down when faced with more intense distractions. A behavior with bowling ball mass will be stronger and much more robust. This behavior will hold up even under intense distractions, out in the front yard with fast and loud traffic.

I thought I had a handle on how much mass a herding dog's behaviors needed to withstand the tremendous distraction of livestock. Only after getting my dogs to the point of working sheep did I come to understand the degree of distraction livestock presents for dogs. The best way I can explain it is that you don't need herding behaviors that are bowling ball strong, you need behaviors that are *wrecking ball* strong. Think in terms of *tons* rather than pounds of mass! Almost all problems you encounter teaching herding to your dog will come down to your dog not having enough mass on behaviors when faced with the ultimate herding distractors – livestock.

Sheep may be just another distraction, but they are a HUGE distraction!

Four stages of learning

To have behaviors strong enough to withstand the distraction of moving livestock, we need to grow our fledgling behavior through all four stages of learning (Reid 1996):

1. Acquisition – (acquiring) learning the behavior and putting it on cue
2. Fluency – (automatic) perfecting the behavior
3. Generalization – (application) taking the behavior on the road
4. Maintenance – (always) keeping the finished behavior usable

Shaping is the primary way our dogs learn or acquire trained herding behaviors. Anything we do to teach a skill, including shaping, luring, or capturing, is part of the **acquisition** stage of learning. Our dogs are acquiring a new behavior from the time we start teaching it until the behavior meets all of our criteria.

Once our dog has acquired the behavior and we have it on *cue,* we start working on perfecting it. **Fluency** builds the behavior to the point that it is easily and accurately performed. This is when we really start building velocity and mass on the behavior. After covering the stages of learning we will dive into cues and cueing, but first we need to finish our discussion of stage two, fluency.

The elements of **fluency** include (Luck 2015):

1. Precision – accuracy of the behavior
2. Latency – time between when the cue is given and when the behavior is performed
3. Speed – how quickly the behavior is performed (*Final cue is added at this point although a temporary cue may be used until this point.*)
4. Distraction – making it harder for the dog to perform by adding novelty to the environment (different movement, sounds, smells, objects, available treats or toy, etc.)
5. Duration – how long the behavior lasts
6. Distance – how far away from the handler the dog performs the behavior

Duration is very important in herding so be sure and train stationary behaviors to a length of 3 to 5 minutes. When you take your dog to sheep, you will need them to hold a sit, down, and stand for a considerable length of time. If your dog is used to popping out of position after a few seconds, they will struggle later.

Now that we have a strong behavior, we are ready to generalize it. **Generalization** simply means training the behavior in different places or changing the environment. Just moving from in front of your dog to beside them can cause a behavior to temporarily disappear.

Generalization can take many forms. In this example, the chicken is learning to generalize the color of the **hot target***, target choice that gets reinforced, no matter where it is positioned. Targets are moved while the chicken is being reinforced from a cup.*

In a new place, you may need to set your dog up for success by reducing your criteria. For example, you may lure the behavior once or twice before presenting the cue or reduce the distance or duration. Once your dog learns that *sit* means *sit* no matter where they are or what is happening, they will become more adept at generalizing other behaviors. An important aspect of generalization is salience. **Salience** means noticeable, important, or stands out from the environment. For humans the salient element may be color or shape while for dogs, it may be movement or scent.

Dogs are great at discriminating, telling the difference between two stimuli (objects or situations), but not so great at generalizing.

Maintenance is the last stage of learning and is simply continuing to reinforce the behavior enough to keep it stable and usable. Once you have herding behaviors trained to this stage, just working stock will provide enough reinforcement to maintain the behaviors, if you maintain criteria.

Watch behaviors closely as they will degrade if you allow your criteria to slide. You may start with solid, quick stops yet over time find your dog gliding to a stop or not stopping at all. Usually these problems sneak up on handlers because they develop slowly. Your dog may start out taking one extra step when stopping and before you know it they are taking five!

To get behaviors wrecking ball strong we need to build them through all four stages of learning. It is this complete training that develops our dog's self-control and confidence, which is vital for all herding dogs.

Right on cue

So now we know how to build a strong behavior, but unless it is on cue it does us no good. A **cue** is a *discriminative stimulus*: a stimulus, an event, or thing that elicits a certain reaction, that when present, the behavior will be reinforced (Bailey and Farhoody 2013–2015). In other words, the cue tells your dog that if they perform the cued behavior *now,* they will earn reinforcement.

We attach the final cue when the behavior is shaped and strong, in the middle of the fluency stage of development between training speed (3) and distraction (4). We want the behavior to meet all of our criteria before we attach the final cue so we may *not* use the final cue while we teach the behavior.

You may use an intermediate cue while training a behavior. This cue may be a gesture or word that prompts the behavior or gives the dog permission to perform the behavior. Once the behavior meets all of your criteria, you want to install the permanent cue that will be associated with only the finished behavior.

Adding a cue

You are at the point of reinforcing when your dog offers the sit behavior without any luring or prompting. When do you start adding a cue, either a verbal or hand signal? You want to wait until your dog is offering the new behavior reliably, meaning you can predict when they will perform it. The cue should be added when your dog is performing the behavior as you want to see it *and* you are willing to bet $100 that you can predict when your dog will offer the behavior. Your goal is to get your dog to associate the cue with the behavior, so you need the cue to come *before* the behavior.

This video shows chicken training using different colored cones as cues for different behaviors: https://www.youtube.com/watch?v=Atl9xtvRRtg

The following example works best if you have reinforced your dog for standing in a few previous sessions to build a little mass on the stand. Okay, in this training session you are willing to bet $100 that your dog will sit after being reset to a stand after their last sit. So you might toss a treat to get your dog out of the sit. As soon as your dog eats the treat and returns to you, cue *sit before* they have a chance to sit. Your dog sits, you mark and reinforce. If you are using a clicker and food you would click and treat. Yay! You have successfully started adding a cue!

Quite quickly it will look like your dog understands the cue, but if this is the first cue your dog has learned it is likely that your verbal *sit* is not salient to them. At this point, your dog will probably sit just as reliably if you don't say anything or say a completely different word. For your dog to notice the cue, they have to learn that the sit will *only* be reinforced when cued with the word 'sit'. Now you need to extinguish the sit unless you cue it. You knew there was a catch, didn't you?

Dogs are visual learners, so movements, hand signals or body motion, are much more salient to them than verbal cues. Dogs often are responding to our body movement when we think they are taking our verbal cues. Viewing video is the easiest way to see if you are inadvertently cueing with your body movement.

Now throw a treat to reset, say nothing, and your dog will return to you and most likely sit. *Do not mark or reinforce!* Instead back away from your dog to get them up and moving toward you. Repeat this process. It will take several trials, but eventually your dog will pause before they sit. They are trying to figure out why you are no longer giving treats for the sit. *Be ready!* At the moment your dog pauses you want to *immediately* give your *sit* cue, while your dog is still standing. Now your dog sits, gets marked, and earns a jackpot!

You are halfway home! Your dog is just starting to learn that what you say is important enough for them to pay attention to it. Congratulations! Unfortunately, it can take a long time for your dog to figure out that your verbal cue is a green light that means reinforcement is available for a specific behavior … *now*. From here on you will *no longer* mark nor reinforce uncued sits.

The next time you reset your dog you will *not* give your sit cue and most likely your dog will offer the sit anyway. You are back to moving away from your dog to get them to stand and waiting for that ephemeral pause again. After more **aborts**, resetting your dog without marking or reinforcing them, your dog will eventually pause again. This pause gives you the opportunity to cue the sit. If your dog sits, mark and heavily reinforce it. Over time your dog will connect the cue to the opportunity to perform the behavior and earn reinforcement, which means your dog will not offer the sit unless you have cued it. Don't get discouraged! This process takes as long as it takes. Your dog will eventually catch on to how cues are added and this process will become much quicker and easier as your dog generalizes the process.

If your dog throws behaviors at you, the behaviors are not under stimulus control. In other words, your dog has not learned that the behavior will only be reinforced when cued. No cue = no reinforcement.

Extinction is necessary

Extinction may be your friend, but it is a love-hate relationship. You use extinction to add a cue, but it can be difficult to watch your dog struggle through extinction. Adding a cue for the first time can be especially frustrating for both you and your dog because you have to extinguish the behavior of sitting when *no cue* is given. Going through extinction is frustrating for your dog because behavior that used to earn reinforcement no longer does. Just to repeat, as your dog learns cues for more behaviors, they will start to generalize the process and will learn new cues more easily, so hang in there!

Changing a cue

There are times you will want to change a cue on a behavior. Three times you may want to change or add a cue are when you want:

1. A new cue for a final version of a behavior (changing from an intermediate cue to a final cue)
2. A different version of a behavior (tuck vs drop back sit)
3. A different cue (either a different verbal, whistle, or hand signal)

In the first two situations, wanting a more precise version of a behavior, you can re-train the behavior using added or changed criteria and then attach a different cue. The new cue will then be associated *only* with the new behavior. If *sit* is associated with a drop back sit, the dog goes into the sit by walking their front feet backward, and you want a tuck sit, the dog keeps their front feet still and tucks their rear end up under them, you can teach the tuck sit, without using your sit cue, and then add a new cue such as *tuck*. If the drop back sit is your dog's default sit you will have to remain vigilant to mark and reinforce only tuck sits when you cue *tuck,* as the drop back sit has a lot of mass and is probably inherently reinforcing.

If you find yourself in the third situation, wanting to change or add an additional cue, feel free to do so. To add a new cue, simply give the new cue, pause for a second, and then give the known cue. It won't take very long for your dog to anticipate the old cue, when you give the new one, and respond to the new cue. Once your dog is responding to the new cue, the old cue is dropped. Eventually, we will add whistles to our herding cues in this manner, but we will start out using only verbal cues.

I was taught to use verbal cues for close work, penning and shedding, and whistle cues for distance work, outruns and driving. I have seen people use only verbal cues and others who use only whistle cues. I like verbal cues for close work because I feel I can modulate them more precisely than I can my whistle cues and thus give more precise information to my dog.

---

*You can use **different cues for one behavior** but **not** one cue for different behaviors. You can cue the same sit behavior with a verbal cue, hand signal, and whistle as long as all cues are associated with the exact same sit behavior.*

Stimulus control

To really get control of a behavior you need your cue to meet four requirements (Pryor 1985). Let's use the sit as an example behavior with the verbal cue *sit*:

1. Your dog readily responds to *sit* **every** time it is given by sitting.
2. Your dog does *not* sit without the cue *sit* being given.
3. Your dog does *not* sit when you cue *down* or *bow.*
4. Your dog does *not* down or a bow when you cue *sit.*

Getting true stimulus control takes work, but when you are putting sheep into a pen and cue your dog to *walk in* to the sheep you don't want your dog to flank. When you are trying to complete a precise maneuver with touchy sheep, your success or failure can be determined by mere inches. One false step by your dog and you can have a sheep explosion on your hands.

It doesn't take much to cause a train wreck. Quest looks innocent, but he definitely was the cause of the sheep and I nearly colliding!

Building strong behavior

Before you start training a new behavior you need to have established your criteria and have a plan in place as to how you will develop it into a skill that your dog is confident performing. At first you want to make it easy for your dog to succeed and difficult for them to fail. This is known as setting your dog up for success. As your training progresses and your dog gains confidence, you slowly start making it easier for your dog to fail and more difficult for them to successfully perform the skill.

For example: Once I get my dog walking in confidently to sheep I challenge my dog by asking, *Can you walk in if I* …

- march in place?
- swing my arms?
- clap my hands?
- walk away, perpendicular to you?
- walk in the opposite direction you are walking?

If your dog can confidently walk in to the sheep while you try to distract them, you will know you have grown a strong behavior. Since you will usually be standing still and calmly cueing your dog, you know that if they can handle these tough distractions there is a good chance that they will be able to handle almost any distraction when they are walking in. If you are at a trial and a horn is honked, a paper blows across the field, or people clap, you will be glad you took the time to elevate or proof your dog's performance.

Don't train until your dog gets it right, train until they can't get it wrong!

Sir, can you hold your down when temptation is everywhere? Start early to build strong behaviors.

Strong behaviors lead to a confident and relaxed performance. Your dog will not herd to their potential unless they are relaxed. A dog that lacks confidence will not have the suppleness of mind or body to think and react with the speed, precision, and power necessary for brilliant performance. If you think about your own performance, you will find that if you are confident of success you can relax and do your best, maybe even have fun!

Chains and sequences

Now that we have super strong behaviors we need to be able to put them together in order to herd. The two main ways we do this are through chaining and sequencing. A behavior **chain** is a series of behaviors that *always* follow each other in the *same* order (Chance 2006). The chain is initiated with one cue and the following behaviors are automatically cued by the behavior that came directly before them.

A good example of a chain is a dumbbell retrieve. The retrieve is many behaviors chained together. A *retrieve* may consist of the dog setting up next to the handler, starting on a cue from the handler (start of chain), going out to the dumbbell, picking up the dumbbell, returning to the handler with the dumbbell, sitting in front of the handler, while still holding the dumbbell, (end of chain), and finally releasing the dumbbell when cued by the handler. Each of these behaviors can be taught separately and then put together in a chain with only one cue given to perform the entire chain. Only the last behavior in the finished chain needs to be reinforced with a cue or a treat.

An example of a chain in herding is the silent gather. A **silent gather** is one in which the handler sends their dog to fetch the flock and remains silent until the sheep are at their feet. This chain consists of the dog being set up, a cue being given (start of chain), the dog flanking out around and behind the stock, the dog lifting the stock, and the dog driving the stock to the handler (end of chain). The only cue given is the initial cue to tell the dog to fetch the livestock.

In a chain one behavior automatically cues the next and the order of behaviors always remains fixed. If the order of behaviors varies, then you have a sequence and not a chain.

A **sequence** is a series of behaviors that follow each other in *no particular* order. A common example of sequences is found in agility. An agility run may consist of many numbered obstacles but each run is unique in terms of the order of the obstacles. In one class there may be three jumps in a row and in the next class there may be a jump, a tunnel, and then weave poles. Each agility obstacle may have been taught as a chain, but since they are completed in a different order on every run, the entire course is a sequence and not a chain.

Other than the silent gather, most herding maneuvers are sequences. Your dog may start out with a fetch but needs to be stopped, walked in, and then given a flank to get the sheep back to you. The sequence of the cued behaviors depends on what the sheep are doing, what the dog is doing, and what the handler is trying to accomplish, such as turn the post, drive or cross drive, or negotiate an obstacle such as a chute, pen, or shed.

Back chaining and forward chaining

There are two ways chains are usually taught, back chaining or forward chaining. **Back chaining** is teaching the *last* behavior of the chain *first*, then the next to last, etc. until you have trained the first behavior of the chain (Burch and Bailey 1999).

To back chain the dumbbell retrieve you would first train the dog to hold the dumbbell while sitting in front of you, the last behavior in the chain. The idea is that you build greater mass on the last part of the chain. As you grow the chain your dog repeats and is reinforced for the last behaviors many more times than the first behaviors. Thus, when your dog does the entire chain they are always moving toward more familiar and more highly reinforced behaviors.

In **forward chaining** the *first* behavior of the chain is taught *first*, then the second, and so on until you get to the end of the chain (Burch and Bailey 1999). Most chains taught in dog training are usually back chained, but as in most aspects of training, this is not a hard and fast rule.

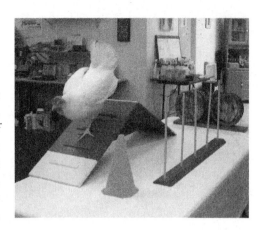

In this chicken agility chain, the A-frame may have been the first obstacle trained, but it would be the last obstacle of the course or chain. The entire course was always completed in the same order, with the A-frame as the last obstacle, making this mini-course a chain instead of a sequence.

Dealing with mistakes

Mistakes happen. You make mistakes and your dog will too. Mistakes are just information that tell you what your dog is struggling with and what skills you need to work on (Bertilsson and Johnson Vegh 2010). You will want to deal with mistakes as neutrally as possible. Remember that your dog is doing what you have trained (reinforced) them to do. What behavior you have trained is what you have reinforced and not always what you wanted.

There are many ways to deal with a mistake:
1. *Repeat* the exercise three times, if you believe your dog knows the behavior. If your dog is still incorrect break the behavior down and make it easier for your dog.
2. *Ignore* the incorrect behavior: extinguish it through the absence of reinforcement.
3. *Change* the environment to make it easier for your dog to be correct.
4. *Interrupt* the behavior, this is especially important for inherently reinforcing behaviors.
5. *Use a NRM* (No Reward Marker) and pause 10 seconds, especially for inherently reinforcing behaviors.
6. *Stop*, so you don't get farther off track.
7. *Question* why the mistake happened. Think!
8. *Plan* how to deal with the mistake.

Mistakes are MAJIC: Mistakes Are Just Information so Chill

Mistakes are often due to your dog being overwhelmed. If you have upped your criteria too quickly or jumped ahead too far, your dog may struggle. Again, the answer is to split not lump. Make the steps of learning smaller for your dog and your rate of reinforcement will soar.

As much as you want to see your dog be successful, you need to allow your dog to fail. Instead of trying to micro-manage your dog, allow them to respond without prompting. Sometimes your dog will learn a lot by finding out what does *not* earn reinforcement (Luck 2015). That is the beauty of using positive reinforcement. If your dog fails and nothing happens, your dog is not positively punished, they will keep working and no harm is done. Importantly, you have no fallout from punishment to deal with.

This is one of my favorite sayings about the effects of positive punishment from Police K9 trainer Steve White: **"Punishment is like a nuclear bomb. If the blast doesn't get you, the fallout will."**

Punishment has consequences that will affect future training. One reason this happens is that punishment only tells your dog what not to do, which leaves a lot of options open, while reinforcement tells your dog what specific behavior you will pay for. Punishment also may elicit negative emotion in your dog, a negative Conditioned Emotional Response (CER). This negative feeling may be attached to the trainer, a prop or piece of equipment, a place, or something in the environment such as livestock.

When your dog is over-aroused or distracted, mistakes are bound to happen. At these times you will see one or more of these responses: tenseness, shutting down, or the zoomies. Around livestock you may also see: lunging, biting, freezing, barking, or staring.

Don't spend a lot of time trying to figure why your dog does something. Instead, analyze what went wrong in your training and plan to change it. No one can know what their dog is thinking, but a lot of time can be wasted guessing!

If you have a training session filled with mistakes and problems, it is easy to get down on yourself, your dog, or both. If a session is not going well, it is best to stop and take a break. Both you and your dog will just become frustrated if you keep failing.

• •

Many's the time I spent an agonising and sleepless night worrying about a problem which had appeared during that day's session, only to discover the next day that the problem had disappeared – it was a once-off, never to be seen again. An example springs to mind – I had been invited to train at a friend's place and was working alone with a small group of sheep. Suddenly the usually reliable Renn cut off a single ewe and chased her a hundred metres, ignoring all my demands that she stop and return to me. I have no idea what that ewe said to enrage Renn so, but I am happy to report that it's never happened again.

Sally says

• •

Although it does not seem to matter to your dog if you end on a successful or failed trial, it probably will matter to you. I suggest you end your less than stellar sessions with a successful easy exercise for your own satisfaction.

Problem-solving

Remember that almost all major problems are caused by getting off TRaC with timing, rate of reinforcement, or criteria (Bailey and Farhoody 2013–2015). These are the touchstones you need to come back to time and time again to solve your training problems.

The steps I suggest to use to figure out **major problems** are:
1. *Stop* if you are off track or are no longer having fun.
2. *Take a break* for minutes or hours, but a day is even better.
3. *Forget about training* during your break.
4. *Review video*, if you have it.
5. *Enlist a friend* or coach to watch you train, if you don't video.
6. *Pinpoint the problem* to get back on TRaC.
7. *Go back* to the point where your training was successful.
8. *Formulate a training plan* to move forward.
9. *Modify your environment* if need be. Change the exercise, location, type of stock you are using, add or take away barriers, or move from working livestock back to foundation exercises without stock.
10. *Work your **new** plan*.
11. *Repeat*, as necessary.

Never be afraid to split a behavior or exercise down into thinner and thinner slices. Feel free to go back to where you were successful and start from there again, hopefully with a good idea of what went wrong and a new plan in place. Never be afraid to give yourself and your dog a break from training when you are stuck. Some of my best insights have come to me in the middle of the night! Finally, don't be afraid to ask for help. Positive training is positive training. If you know a good positive agility, obedience, or trick trainer, ask them for help with your problem, even though they may not know anything about herding. You may find they are extremely helpful if they can see your training as simply positive training instead of positive *herding* training.

We have briefly covered a lot of material in this Getting and Building Behavior section and have not scratched the surface of the knowledge and skills you need to be a proficient positive trainer. Check out the Resources at the back of this book, take online classes, and go to seminars to improve your knowledge of science-based positive training. Spend a lot of time working with your dog to implement what you have learned and your skills will skyrocket. Your dog will be your best teacher!

Conclusion

We have covered, what I consider to be, the basics for starting, building, strengthening, and repairing behavior. You have also met Sally, Renn, and me. You now have a framework in place to start training herding! From now on it's less reading and thinking and more planning and doing. It's time for you and your dog to get started in your training room so you can eventually move to your outdoor training room, known as a paddock, where the sheep and the real fun are!

Section 2
Foundation, Foundation, Foundation

CHAPTER 8

Tools of the trade

Finally the time has come to begin training! You can start training your dog in your house or backyard and eventually move on to working with livestock. Before you start training you need to gather some equipment. You also need to grow your knowledge and skills in order to train your dog. If you are unsure about what you are teaching you are setting your dog up for failure. Let's jump right in with a look at the tools needed to train herding.

Equipment needed

In addition to your dog, you will need some training equipment to teach herding. The tools and facilities needed include:

- Marker (such as a clicker) + a verbal marker
- Reinforcers
- Treat holders
- Cones
- Crook or stock stick
- Long line
- Pens and barriers
- Livestock (eventually)
- Training areas
- Whistle

Markers

In addition to a verbal sound or word, a mechanical **marker** such as a clicker can be used. Be sure and test your mechanical marker *before* you start training with it. Some dogs are afraid of unique sounds and some are very sound sensitive. You want your dog to have a positive association with your marker and not associate it with fear. If your dog startles or runs away when you click, try to mute the sound such that your dog responds with curiosity, rather than fear, to the click.

Above: The box clicker is widely used and makes a rather loud click. It is especially useful outside where it makes a unique sound that is very noticeable or salient to your dog.

Above: The i-Click is a quiet clicker that is great for use inside or with dogs who are sensitive to the louder click of the box clicker. This clicker may also be placed on the floor and clicked with your foot.

The two types of clickers widely available are the box and i-Click. Box clickers are quite loud while i-Click clickers have a muted click. If your dog is sensitive to the loud click of the box clicker you can hold the clicker behind your back or put a piece of tape on the metal tongue to dampen the sound. Karen Pryor developed the i-Click clicker and it works well for sound-sensitive dogs. You may even use a retractable pen click or other sound as your marker for very sound-sensitive dogs. The advantage of the louder box clicker is that you can use it out in the field when your dog is working at distance. Clickers have a distinctive sound that stands out from environmental noise making them salient to your dog.

Karen Pryor has been a leader in the introduction and spread of positive dog training. She started working with dolphins in the 1960s and has never stopped advocating clicker training. She is known for her well-written books, including Don't Shoot the Dog! *and* Reaching the Animal Mind, *and for starting and hosting ClickerExpo for the past 15 years. Karen has been instrumental in promoting positive training methods for over 40 years!*

You can **load** a marker, a click or word, by pairing it with treats 20 to 30 times. Randomly mark and then deliver a treat to condition the mark as a secondary reinforcer. Loading a marker is not mandatory. You can just start using a mark followed by a reinforcer and your dog will quickly come to positively associate it with the treat. You now have a secondary reinforcer!

When you are working outside with a clicker use a yellow, orange, red, or pink one in order to make it easier to find if it should fall out of your pocket or treat pouch into the grass.

Reinforcers – Food, tugs, balls, flirt poles

The reinforcers used for primarily training fall into two main categories: food and toys. You can use any **food** your dog finds reinforcing and that is easy for you to handle and deliver. It should be cut into appropriately sized pieces depending on the size of your dog but don't be stingy!

There are many toys that you can use as reinforcers for your dog but they fall primarily into three categories:
- Tugs
- Balls
- Flirt poles – these are lunge whips or light, flexible poles with a toy added to the end of an attached line

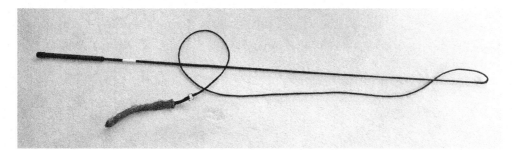

This large flirt pole is a lunge whip, with a 6 foot shaft. A toy or "rat" is attached to the end.

Tugs are great reinforcers. If your dog is trained to bring them back you can throw them to reinforce stationary and moving behaviors. **Balls** can also be used if your dog will retrieve them. **Flirt poles** (FPs) are my reinforcer of choice for working with my dogs on stop and walk in, as well as on flanks using cones. Flirt poles can be made or purchased. You can buy shorter ready-made ones from dog equipment suppliers but for a longer one, you will probably have to buy a lunge whip at a farm store and add your own toy to the end of it.

No matter what reinforcer you are using, remember to match the value of that reinforcement to the effort your dog is putting out to earn it. For harder work your dog should get more pay; better and/or more treats, more time tugging, more reps/farther thrown balls, or more time tugging on the FP toy. I often use a homemade liver cookie and break off a bigger or smaller piece depending on how much reinforcement I want to provide.

I like to use homemade liver cookies when I am out in the field training. They are soft and about 3 inches in diameter. I put them in a pocket and break off a small piece as needed. This eliminates wearing a treat bag. The recipe can be found in the appendices on page 318.

Treat pouches, bags, and vests

You can buy many types of **treat bags** or **pouches** to carry treats and small tugs or balls in as well as a clicker, if you are using one. You can also use your pockets but be sure you can get the reinforcer out of your pocket quickly. Reinforcement is a process and you reinforce *everything* from the time you mark until you deliver the reinforcer. The longer it takes you to deliver your reinforcer the more likely you will be reinforcing additional behavior that you do *not* want.

In addition to pouches or bags, there are also **vests** that can be used to carry your training supplies. Try out a few options and see what feels right and works best for you and your dog.

I prefer treat bags that have a waistband and a metal spring closure that is easy to open and close. I often bend over and need to close the bag in order to keep the treats from falling out.

Cones

You will need at least 8 to 10 traffic **cones** to set up cone squares and circles. I like the heavier rubber ones because they do not blow over when it is windy. The cones should be 12 to 18 inches tall and all of one color. I use orange cones because they are readily available and easy for dogs to see.

I have also used small buckets turned upside down as ground markers. You can use many different types of ground markers as long as you or your dog will not get hurt if you run into them. You may use Frisbees for ground markers but I tend to reserve them for use as targets. You can use Frisbees for ground markers *or* targets but not both since they would then be one prop that cues two different behaviors.

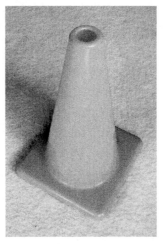

For outside use, you will need some 12 inch heavy cones. Lighter cones work well inside but are easily blown over by the wind. Orange cones are the easiest to find in many sizes and weights.

Orange cones will quickly fade if left out in the sun so be sure to pick them up and store them under cover when not in use.

Crooks and stock sticks

Traditionally shepherds have carried **crooks** while herding and I like to have one in hand when I am working my dog on livestock. Many handlers now prefer to carry a **stock stick** and it is used exactly as you would a crook.

Basically, I use a crook as an extension of my arm. A crook or stock stick is a *portable barrier*. They can be used to block livestock at a chute or pen or help set up a shed, separating one or more animals from a group. They are to be used only as barriers and are *never* used to hit your dog. The *only* time they should be used to hit livestock is if the stock is attacking the handler, which is a very rare event.

I prefer to use a traditional lightweight crook. Many people now use stock sticks instead.

Carrying a crook or stock stick feels awkward at first but the more you do it the more comfortable you will become with it. After you have carried one for a while you will feel something is missing when you don't have it in hand when you go out to herd.

Long line

I use a light long line to interrupt unwanted behavior around livestock such as lunging and flagrant biting. The **long line** should be a cord 10 to 15 feet long, lightweight, and have a large knot at the end so it can easily be stepped on or picked up and not slide out from under your shoe or through your hand. Do *not* tie a handle at the end of the line as it could become caught on something while your dog is working. If your dog is very fast you may want to wear light leather gloves to prevent a rope burn when you pick up the line while your dog is running.

A long line is used as an emergency brake, not as a replacement for a stop or as a positive punisher. It should be used temporarily and then removed. If you find yourself depending on it you need to go back and build mass on your stop and other behaviors to increase your dog's self-control.

I usually use a long line while the stock is in a pen and will also put it on my dog when I first start working loose sheep. I attach the long line to my dog's flat collar but it can also be attached to a harness. If you are not comfortable using a long line then don't! You can often hold on to a leash to give your dog some freedom but still maintain control. The important thing is safety first! Dragging a long line allows your dog to work farther from you without you losing total control of the situation.

If your dog currently is not trustworthy while off-leash, they will be by the time you can reliably call them off of livestock.

Pens and barriers

You will need at least 5 or 6 small corral panels or other barriers to form a **pen** about 12 feet in diameter, if you will be working sheep or goats. If you train on calves you will need a pen about 18 feet in diameter and if you use ducks you can use a cage, X-pen, or a sturdy metal dog crate as a small pen. Besides cattle or hog panels, you can use gates or build a pen with posts and woven wire.

Your dog should be able to see the livestock through the pen but not get to them. The pen is the first step you as the gatekeeper will use to control your dog's access to livestock. Panels that can be hooked together and then easily taken apart are ideal.

These panels work well because they easily connect and form a free-standing pen. They are small enough to move and climb over yet keep sheep contained. Also pictured are some light 18-inch cones that I use.

Other **barriers** you may find helpful include:
* Fences
* X-pens
* Your body
* Crook or stock stick
* Trees or other natural obstacles

Livestock

Initially, you won't need any livestock for your training but you will need some down the road. Sheep are my favorite stock to train on but you may also use cattle, goats, or ducks. You can try chickens, geese, or pigs but they may not be ideal. You want calm, non-aggressive, and fairly small stock to work. Usually, I use 3 to 5 head of sheep in basic training situations. You will need more livestock for some of the advanced training in the future. The larger the flock or herd, the calmer the individuals in the group tend to be. Remember, you don't need *any* livestock to start training herding.

Rams or bucks are not suitable for training as they can butt each other, your dog, or you. Also be careful when working livestock guarded by a livestock guardian dog (LGD), as the guard dog may attack or run your dog off if they perceive your dog as a threat to their flock.

If you are using cattle, dairy calves between 500 and 800 pounds are preferable. Beef calves are usually less calm than dairy steers or heifers. Hair sheep are **lighter**, more flighty, than wool sheep and lambs lighter than ewes, wethers (castrated males), or rams. Rams or bucks are prone to butting other rams and possibly humans so for safety's sake avoid training on them. Any livestock with young at their sides are *not* suitable for training. Mothers will often try to attack dogs that they perceive are threatening their young. Even if the livestock is in a pen I would not use stock with young at their sides. Again, safety first!

Training areas

Training locations that will be useful:

*   Training room – a room in your house or nearby building where you initially train
*   Other indoor rooms
*   Deck or patio outdoors
*   Fenced yard
*   Outdoor training area – a fenced paddock or yard suitable for livestock

You will start training in the training room in your home and then move to other rooms, a deck, a fenced yard, to the outdoor training area without stock, and finally to the outdoor training area with livestock to generalize your training.

The outdoor training area should be about 20×30 feet for sheep or goats and appropriately fenced for the livestock you will be working. You will need a larger area for cattle and can get by with a smaller area for ducks. For all livestock, you will need an area that is fairly flat and has good footing.

The closer your training areas are to your house the more likely you will be to train in them. If you have to walk or drive any distance to get to where you will train you will most likely be limited in the time you can spend training. If there is any way you can obtain some stock to train at home you will be glad you did. If you do have some livestock close at hand, take every opportunity to observe them. Watch how they interact with each other and how they respond when you feed, clean their area, or move them. Do they notice your dog even if your dog is outside of their paddock and at a distance?

We will talk more about the stock training areas you will need as you get farther in your training. As you learn what you will be doing with the livestock you will begin to have a better feel for the livestock area that you need.

Caution: If you have livestock at home, do not allow your dog to stare at them for hours on end or run the outside of the fence where the livestock are kept. You can take your dog near the paddock with the livestock while on leash and eventually you will do some exercises around and in the corral with your dog. Your dog should never have access to the livestock, or to staring at the livestock, without you in the picture. You are the gatekeeper of your dog's access to livestock and access definitely includes the watching of stock.

Whistle

Eventually, you will want to augment your verbal cues with whistle cues. Your dog will be able to hear a whistle more clearly when they are at a distance, working in tall grass, or when the wind is blowing toward you and away from your dog. I usually use a whistle when my dog is at a distance but I use verbal cues when my dog is working close to me, such as while penning or shedding. It is easier for me to control the speed and pitch of my voice when I have to give cues quickly or when I need to finesse my cues. Whistle cues are great when your dog is far away as you don't have to shout.

Some people whistle using their fingers but there are several types of metal and plastic whistles used for herding. You will need to try a few and experiment to see which type you prefer. If you use a whistle it is best to put it on a lanyard so you don't lose it. Learning to use a whistle is *not* easy. You will want to start learning long before you plan to use whistle cues with your dog.

To learn to use a **whistle**:
- Start early since it takes time to become proficient
- Practice where your dog *cannot* hear you
- Consider buying a CD that teaches herding whistles

CDs that teach herding whistles are available at a reasonable price. A CD can also give you ideas on what whistles to use for which cues. Whistling is another skill that can take a long time to learn but, will pay big dividends when your dog starts working at a distance from you.

A positive training test run: Rear-end awareness

Let's start our training with a test run by teaching a skill using positive reinforcement. Teaching rear-end awareness is not mandatory but helps your dog to build rear-end strength and proprioception which can help to keep your dog injury-free.

Proprioception is the knowledge of where an animal's limbs are in space. In other words, a dog with rear-end awareness not only knows where their rear feet are but realizes they have rear feet!

Training rear-end awareness gives you an easy, fun introduction to shaping a behavior that is not crucial to herding. If you are unfamiliar with positive training you can use this training to gauge how skilled you and your dog are at using positive methods. If you or your dog struggles with this exercise I suggest you work building your positive training skills by working on exercises from a book listed in the Resources or take an introductory class on positive training. There are also many on-line positive reinforcement classes currently offered.

Teaching rear-end awareness can be started early in your puppy's life or at any time later. It is really fun to see your dog realize they have back legs!

By having Sir get on the bowl perpendicular to me he naturally pivots his feet around in order to orient toward me. This gives him the idea of what I am looking for (rear-foot movement) and gives me the opportunity to mark his rear foot movement as he pivots.

To teach rear-end awareness you can use a low, wide bowl turned upside down or right side up and shape your dog to stand with their front feet on or in the bowl. I use high-value food as the reinforcer for this exercise. Start with marking and then reinforcing your dog for looking at the bowl, then moving toward it, placing one front foot on it, and then standing with both front feet on the bowl. Feed your reinforcers near the bowl and then directly to your dog as they stand on the bowl.

Once your dog has their front feet on the bowl lure (3 times or less) with a treat placed to the side of their head such that they pivot their rear feet to get the treat while keeping their front feet on the bowl. Mark any movement of rear feet and grow that movement until they can pivot 360° around in both directions with their back feet while their front feet remain on the bowl.

Once your dog is giving you some rear foot movement you can stand up and use the placement of your body to encourage pivoting.

Be sure to fade your body movement (begin to stand still) or your dog will become dependent on your change of position to initiate movement of their rear feet.

Rear-end awareness is important for herding dogs because they often are moving quickly and turning sharply over rough or irregular terrain.

Onward

Now you know what equipment, facilities, and livestock you will need. Next, we will look at the foundation skills your dog will need to maintain self-control around livestock. We start teaching some basic obedience, add arousal, and build some major mass on those basic behaviors. Your training success will depend on your dog's behaviors having wrecking ball mass but those behaviors begin in the comfort of your own home.

CHAPTER 9

Instinct and arousal

In many ways herding behaviors are no different from obedience behaviors. The main difference is that obedience behaviors are generally *learned* while many herding behaviors are *innate*. **Innate** behaviors are inborn and in herding breeds, these behaviors are what we base herding upon. In herding breeds, we call this specific type of complex innate behavior **instinct**.

A dog having or not having herding instinct is the difference between herding and what I call "obedience around livestock". A dog with herding instinct may naturally read, rate, and control their stock while a dog without this instinct has little if any natural ability to handle stock and instead listens for cues to tell them when and where to move in the presence of livestock. Both types of dogs can herd but herding breeds usually have an instinctive drive to read and control their livestock which is both a blessing and a curse.

Most border collies have herding instinct or "eye". Here Qwest is hooked up on the sheep, reading the movement of the group and individual sheep. He is also keeping track of me! There is a lot for your dog to pay attention to when near livestock, so have patience when they struggle to listen to cues and perform behaviors.

A big part of what you will learn in this book is how to take obedience behaviors and build those behaviors into skills that you can use to gauge your control of your dog and your dog's self-control around livestock. Once you have that control in place you will be able to bring the herding behaviors that you taught away from livestock, to stock and begin herding.

Often the first sign of instinct you will see in your dog is the "eye" or hook up. **Hook up** is what you see when herding dogs look at and immediately lock onto their prey with laser focus. So what do you do when your dog stops and locks onto prey, be it a tug in your hand or sheep in a field? You may need to add some OIL to get them moving.

OIL behavior – Override Instinctual with Learned behavior

Upon seeing sheep your dog may **lock up**, which means their movements slow down or stop completely. You might cue your dog to perform a well-known behavior, such as *down*, but instead of downing they stand stock still and just stare at the sheep. In this case, your dog's instinct to "eye" prey is overriding their operantly conditioned response to down.

Instincts are innate behaviors, meaning that animals are born with these behaviors and do not have to learn them. A simple innate behavior is a reflex and a complex innate behavior is a modal action pattern or MAP. We will go into much more about modal action patterns because in herding breeds they form the instinctive framework for herding behaviors: orient, eye, stalk, and chase.

Instinctual behaviors generally override learned behaviors. Fortunately, you can teach your dog to perform trained behaviors such as down or sit even when they instinctively want to just eye, stalk, or chase. If this were not true you would not be able to train your dog to herd! Herding is combining the use of your dog's innate herding skills (instincts) with your trained direction (cues).

From now on as we talk about instinct or instinctual behavior we will be referring to herding instinct or instinctual herding behavior. Dogs have many other instincts, from caring for their pups to wagging their tails, but we will be concerned only with herding instincts.

I worked on self-control behaviours with Renn from about 6 weeks of age. None-theless, transferring trained behaviours to sheep wasn't as easy as I had naively assumed it would be. Once Renn got into stalk mode it sometimes seemed impossible to communicate with her and there was nothing to do but take a break. We can teach our dogs to break out of the trance and become responsive herding partners but it does take time. To stay sane during this period of training I recommend you remind yourself that it's not that your dog is refusing to comply with your cues, but most likely they are simply unable to, in that moment.

It is easy to find out if your obedience behaviors have enough mass to override your dog's instinctual herding behaviors. You can use sit, stand, or recall, among other behaviors, to test your dog's skills and self-control or cue-responsiveness around livestock. Two nice things about starting with obedience behaviors are that you may have some basic obedience behaviors already trained *and* you won't mess up your herding skills if you first learn how to positively train basic obedience behaviors. If you have never trained using positive reinforcement, start by training behaviors that aren't important for herding such as a sit, nose touch, or bow. If you struggle and end up with sloppy behaviors, they will not be behaviors that are really important for herding.

Applying OIL to herding breeds

If you have a herding breed you will want to start dealing with your dog's tendency to eye and lock up on anything that they perceive as moving prey as soon as possible. Be aware that chasing cars is just a different expression of the herding instinct. When chasing, your dog is engaging the chase part of their instinctual modal action pattern.

You can easily test your dog's tendency to lock up on stock inside your house, if your dog tugs. Start by asking your dog for a fluent behavior such as sit, using treats as reinforcers. Once your dog has correctly performed the behavior several times, pull out a tug and ask your dog to sit while they look at the tug. Watch to see if the latency, the time it takes your dog to respond, increases noticeably. If your dog is still responding immediately you can increase the difficulty by asking your dog to sit with the tug slowly moving and eventually with it moving quickly. Does your dog still sit quickly, no matter how fast the tug moves?

If you find your dog locking up instead of responding to cues, you need to train them to override their instinctual behavior with learned behavior. Go back to the point with your tug where your dog performed the sit immediately. Now move forward one step

*Sir sitting on cue
while hooked up.*

to where they struggled and slow down the movement of the tug until your dog can again perform quickly. Your goal is to reinforce the quick sit, at each level of tug movement, until your dog can perform quickly no matter what you do with the tug and eventually the flirt pole rat.

What you are doing is shaping the sit from scratch using latency, how quickly your dog responds to the cue, as your criterion. Remember that you want a quick start *and* finish to the sit. Your dog may start to sit as soon as you give the *sit* cue but then sit in slow motion or get stuck partway down. Your first criterion is for the sit to start immediately and your next is for the sit to finish quickly. Work on the first criterion alone until your dog can start to sit quickly. Then work on the second criterion of finishing the sit quickly. After you get your dog sitting with low latency, while you move the tug quickly, you can move on to doing the same thing with other obedience behaviors such as the stand and down.

Once your dog has mastered responding to these cues while you whip the tug around, get out your flirt pole. Now go through the same procedure as you did with the tug until you can flip the flirt pole rat around in front of your dog and have them respond immediately to your sit cue. Finally, re-work your other obedience cues, such as stand and down, while you flip the rat.

OIL training is important!

If your dog cannot sit while you twirl a tug in front of them, they will not be able to sit with sheep in front of them. If they cannot sit in the presence of sheep, they will certainly not be able to listen for or perform herding cues around livestock. Each dog is different. Some dogs will fly through this procedure but most with herding instinct will struggle. It takes as long as it takes and your dog will tell you when they are ready to move on.

When your dog is responding well away from livestock you are ready to take them to penned stock and see what you have in terms of mass on your behaviors and self-control. It takes tremendous self-control for your dog to override their instincts and perform behaviors you have trained.

Testing engagement

When you take your dog to livestock remember to be as calm and relaxed as possible. Have the stock in a pen or behind a fence so your dog does not gain access to them by accident. Safety first! Also, have your dog on a leash and use super high-value treats or toys as reinforcers. If you have an area where the livestock has been kept for some time, you should first take your dog out and let them explore the area, off-leash if possible, with no livestock present. Often just the smell of livestock and the presence of manure is enough to get your dog over-aroused and unable to respond to cues. If your dog can respond to sit, down, stand, and recall in a paddock where livestock have been kept, you are one giant step ahead!

Now you are ready to take your dog to see stock! Before you try asking for a sit in the presence of sheep, let's see if your dog can eat or play with sheep in the picture. Keep your dog on a leash or long line to prevent them from leaving you and approaching the stock. Can your dog engage with you? Your dog likes to tug, really likes to tug! Your dog will tug on cue and meets all of your criteria in your training room, other rooms in your house, on your deck, in your front and back yards, and even in your outdoor training area without sheep. That is one strong tug behavior!

At the start of this session, I had Sir on a long line to prevent him from dive-bombing the sheep. Once he showed me he was able to control himself, even though his tugging was not great, I removed the long line and worked at engaging him with the tug. What else could I have done if he continued to be distracted from tugging by the presence of the sheep?

You are confident that you have lots of mass on your tug and are ready to try it around livestock. Next, have your sheep in a small pen, put your dog on a leash or long line, move to where your dog just notices the sheep, and ask your dog to tug. Make sure you keep your dog on a leash or long line for this exercise to prevent your dog from charging the sheep. If your dog immediately begins tugging, despite livestock being present, you have jumped a major hurdle!

If, and this is more likely, your dog stares at the sheep and totally ignores your attempts to get them tugging, you will know your dog is too distracted by the sheep to tug. Move farther away from the sheep until your dog is able to tug with you. Now you can begin to understand what mass wrecking ball behaviors must have to compete with sheep!

Quick test: Pull out one of your dog's favorite reinforcers, a treat or tug, and hold it 2 inches from their nose. Can they sit? Down? Stand? You may be surprised!

Follow the same training procedure with treats, making sure to keep your dog on a long line or leash. Can your dog eat treats in the presence of sheep? How close can your dog get to the sheep and still eat treats? Let's find out. At this point you will pull out the super high-value treats you brought along because you know your dog is a real chowhound. Offer your dog that piece of steak. Can your dog eat? Many dogs cannot initially play or eat in the presence of livestock, even if the sheep are quite far away and behind a fence. Before you ask your dog to perform any obedience behaviors you need them to engage with you and be able to eat and/or play.

If your dog cannot engage with you by playing or eating, both highly reinforcing behaviors, within sight of sheep there is not much chance that they will be able to sit or do any other cued behaviors, yet! Now you need to move your dog farther away from the sheep. Back away and keep asking your dog to eat or play until you get to a place where your dog can respond. This is the distance from sheep that you will initially start working with your dog.

Go out to the sheep, at the distance you determined previously, as often as possible and encourage your dog to eat and play. Once you have your dog eating and/or playing, it is game on! You may find that your dog can eat but not tug or tug but not eat. Your goal at this point is to get your dog to engage with you by either eating treats or tugging. For most dogs that is a huge first step! If your dog can engage with you around livestock they will eventually be able to take obedience and herding cues too.

Before we get into building the foundation behaviors for herding we need to take a closer look at the action patterns that form the basis of the herding instinct and how arousal plays into the herding equation. If you want to understand herding you need to understand modal action patterns.

Modal action patterns

Modal action patterns (MAPs) are a set of instinctive behavioral sequences that usually run to completion (Coppinger & Coppinger, 2001). They have also been called fixed action patterns (FAPs) but since scientists are now finding that these patterns can be somewhat flexible the name has been changed to MAPs. Some predators can stop and re-start the sequence when interrupted and some cannot.

The wild *hunting or predatory* modal action pattern has many variations but all are based on the sequence of: **orient > eye > stalk > chase > grab–bite > kill–bite > dissect > consume.**

Different types of dogs have been bred to eliminate certain parts of the predatory MAP in order to be useful as hunters or guardians. Livestock guardian dogs (LGDs) no longer have the dissect part of the sequence and thus will usually not consume prey or dead livestock that has not been dissected, torn open. They will consume a carcass once it is cut open. This is why LGDs may be seen lying near a dead lamb. They are not protecting the carcass. Instead, they are simply unable to consume it until it is torn/cut open. Once the carcass is opened they will eat it.

The instinctual *herding* sequence is based on a truncated predatory or hunting pattern:

The typical *herding* MAP is: **orient > eye > stalk > chase > (grab–bite).**

(Grab–bite is desirable since we need our dogs to bite when threatened or cued, but kill–bite is never acceptable in herding dogs.)

Modal action pattern (instinctual) behaviors found in the herding breeds:
- Orient – search and approach (outrun)
- Eye – hook up (lift)
- Stalk – walk toward prey while hooked up (fetch and drive)
- Chase – circling (flanks)
- Grab–bite – bite (bite acceptable in certain situations)
- ~~Kill–bite~~ – killing bite (unwanted)

Herding breeds, especially gathering breeds as compared to driving breeds, use primarily the orient, eye, stalk, and chase instinctual behaviors in herding. The grab–bite is necessary for protection and confidence when dogs are facing large or aggressive livestock. In most herding breeds, kill–bite has been selectively bred out.

In order for the herding instinct to manifest or be displayed in your dog, it must be released. There are two types of **releasers**, a stimulus that releases or initiates instinctual behavior. The first type is the *initial* instinct releaser. Herding breed puppies are not born exhibiting instinctual herding behaviors. They need a releasing stimulus at the appropriate time in their development to trigger herding instincts. This is called **turning on** to livestock. A dog that has turned on wants to control movement. Because livestock moves they want to control stock. Some puppies are triggered at a very early age,

4 to 6 weeks, but for other dogs it may not happen until years later. Some dogs never have their herding instincts released and are never turned on to herding livestock. There is no guarantee that a herding bred pup will ever exhibit herding instinct! You can encourage the turning on of herding instinct by exposing your dog to moving livestock. Many dogs are turned on by almost anything that moves quickly, such as a passing car or other dogs running nearby.

• •

Sally says

I was never concerned that Renn wouldn't herd – even at a few weeks old she was completely transfixed by movement. I found it difficult to keep her attention on the task at hand, especially if another pet went by (the cats did this on purpose of course, once they realised they could incite a reaction). But she hadn't shown any special interest in the sheep until about 3 months old when she unexpectedly leaped through a gap in a gate and chased the ram. From then on she had to be watched very closely to ensure that she was prevented access to the stock and did not get to rehearse any unwanted chase'n grip behaviours. It's impossible to overstate the effect sheep have on a border collie.

• •

The *second* type of releaser relates to the initiation of a modal action pattern. Most MAPs in *nature* are true chains. There is a releaser that starts the chain of behaviors and the previous behavior releases the following behavior until the animal completes the chain. For predators, completion of the chain is usually consumption of prey, provided they catch it. Some predators *have* to follow the chain from start to finish or they cannot consume their prey. If the chain gets interrupted, the prey does not run so there is no chase, they must start over from orient again and cannot go straight into grab–bite, even if their prey is standing helplessly in front of them.

This is not true of the herding dog MAP. Amazingly, herding dogs can mix and match instinctive behaviors and not miss a beat. If they could not, all we could do with them is a silent gather: outrun, lift, and fetch (orient and eye-stalk). In herding, we usually start with the outrun (orient) but often stop the dog on top, then ask them to walk in (eye-stalk). Next, we may flank the dog (chase) before asking them in again (eye-stalk).

For more information on dogs' instincts and evolution I highly recommend Dogs: A New Understanding of Canine Origin, Behavior and Evolution *by Raymond and Lorna Coppinger.*

Herding dogs do *not* herd to consume prey. They find engaging in instinctive herding behaviors inherently reinforcing. For this reason, once your dog is working stock you do not need to use treats or toys as reinforcers, although you still may wish to. Once working sheep, your reinforcer list grows from toys, treats, and cues, to include allowing your dog to continue to work stock. Be aware that your dog also finds staring at stock inherently reinforcing. If you don't use a no reward marker and just stop your dog when they are incorrect, they will still find watching the livestock inherently reinforcing.

States of arousal

Levels of arousal are important in herding training. **Arousal** is the state of being alert, awake, and attentive. We often think of arousal when our dogs are overly aroused or excited but arousal levels can also be too low and under-aroused dogs may be inattentive or fearful.

The **arousal bell curve** is based on the Yerkes–Dodson Law, which states that there is an empirical relationship between arousal and performance and was originally developed by psychologists Robert M Yerkes and John Dillingham Dodson in 1908. The idea is that performance and arousal are linked and that there is an optimal range of arousal for peak performance for a given behavior. If arousal is too low the dog is under-aroused and may have scattered attention or be fearful. If arousal is too high the dog is over-aroused and may have laser focus or lose self-control. The goal is to have your dog at the optimal level of arousal.

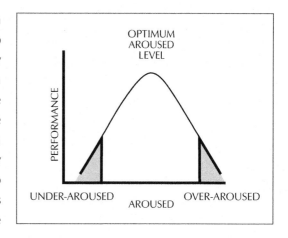

With herding dogs, we tend to have more problems with our dogs being over-aroused than under-aroused, since livestock and livestock movement are inherently stimulating to dogs. It is for this reason that all herding behaviors should be taught away from stock, where arousal levels can be optimized. It is much easier for our dogs to think and learn when they are not over-aroused. Thus, we first need to build strong herding behaviors away from stock and then introduce them around livestock.

Teaching herding behaviors around stock, as is traditionally done, sets your dog up for failure because your dog will usually be over-aroused when first introduced to livestock. When your dog is over-aroused their ability to think and learn is impaired. You want to get your dog near stock *as soon as possible* but rather than starting with herding behaviors, work on recalls and other non-herding behaviors as their initial training around livestock. Obedience behaviors such as sit, stand, and down work great to help you gauge your dog's level of arousal near livestock.

Raising arousal

If you do need to raise your dog's arousal level you can try vigorous tugging, working with a flirt pole, or raising your own level of excitement by moving and talking quickly. If your dog freezes while staring at stock they may appear under-aroused but are more likely over-aroused.

Although I find tugging raises my dog Sir's arousal level, Sally found that tugging allowed Renn to dissipate energy and build focus. Experiment to find out what works best for you and your dog.

Lowering arousal

Since you will usually be dealing with arousal levels above optimal, let's take a closer look at over-arousal. The important thing is to be observant and know what is normal for your dog.

Signs your dog is over-aroused may include:
- Tense muscles
- Staring
- Freezing
- Barking
- Lunging
- Shivering
- Not playing
- Not eating

When Sir is over-aroused he will bounce his left rear foot while standing.

There are several ways to lower arousal around livestock. One easy way is to feed treats in the grass. As dogs use their nose to scent out treats on the ground they naturally begin to relax. Another way to lower arousal is to take short breaks when near livestock to let your dog relax and watch the stock without having to be attentive to you. If you have a dog that is highly over-aroused you may need to get a chair and sit a comfortable distance from livestock with your dog on leash. Start from quite a distance away and work closer as your dog relaxes.

To foster lower arousal levels, mark and reinforce any signs of relaxation such as:
- Laying down
- Rolling onto a hip
- Sitting
- Putting head on ground while lying down
- Relaxing muscles
- Standing quietly
- Giving attention to handler: an ear flick, look, or movement toward handler

This procedure, *systematic desensitization*, may take a long time but is well worth the time invested, if your dog is extremely over-aroused by the sight of stock. I am not going to go into detail about *desensitization* or *habituation*, which are both forms of classical or Pavlovian conditioning, but you may want to explore them further.

One other thing you can do to calm your dog is to send them calming signals. Your dog is an excellent reader of your body language, mood, and state of arousal. Some calming signals you can send your dog are:
- Moving slowly and calmly
- Cueing using a low pitched voice
- Breathing slowly and steadily
- Cueing in a quiet voice
- Cueing slowly
- Smiling

Desensitizing Sir with sheep at a distance.

If you are calm you will help your dog to calm down. Taking breaks during exercises is especially important if your dog is over-aroused. There is no point continuing to train until your dog drops back into the optimal arousal zone. By setting up the environment, such that your dog cannot get to livestock, you will be able to relax knowing that you, your dog, and the livestock are safe.

Over-aroused or fearful?

Some dogs are afraid of livestock. They may overcome their fear or they may not. These dogs may display some of the characteristics of over-aroused dogs, such as muscle tenseness, barking, lunging, freezing, shivering, etc. To figure out if your dog is fearful rather than just over-aroused, note how your dog carries their weight as they move toward stock. Fearful dogs tend to shift their weight back onto their rear ends while overly aroused dogs keep their weight shifted forward. Does your dog want to escape from or engage with the stock? Listen to your gut and don't force your dog to engage or go near livestock if they are afraid.

My friend Alesia brought Sir's sister Liz over because she seemed afraid of sheep. Once Liz was allowed to freely move the sheep, while on a long line, she went from apprehension to confidently controlling the sheep in just a few minutes!

One way to decrease your dog's fear is to increase their arousal. Allowing a dog to move and interact with small, calm livestock, while on a long line, can raise their level of arousal and increase their confidence. Often getting the livestock moving engages your dog and raises their arousal level enough to overcome their fear. Most importantly, don't put your dog in harm's way by allowing them to get chased or hurt by the livestock. One bad experience, especially if a dog is new to working livestock, can affect their lifelong confidence around stock.

Note to new positive reinforcement trainers

Herding is extremely complex with much to learn and many skills to master. As you learn about herding you will also need to grow your positive training skills. Learning positive training is not quick or easy. The sooner you start learning positive training methods, the more prepared you will be to master the exercises that come later in this book. Don't wait to master positive training, start now! You must be a competent positive trainer before you attempt to train herding using positive methods. Otherwise you are attempting to learn two difficult skills at once, which sets you and your dog up for failure.

Thus, if you are new to positive reinforcement training I suggest you take time to become familiar with it by training several non-herding behaviors before you attempt teaching any herding behaviors. There are several good books in the Resources section at the back of this book that you will find helpful. Both herding and positive training are art forms based on science. Only through education will you grasp the science and only through experience will you develop the art.

You will know you are ready to dive in to training herding using positive methods when you feel comfortable and confident teaching non-herding behaviors using positive methods.

Positive training is simple but it is not easy! The best guarantee of success in training positive herding is to have a strong foundation in positive training. If you are not comfortable and confident training a sit positively, you will certainly struggle training herding behaviors using positive reinforcement. Positive training is the foundation that positive herding stands on.

Calm and collected

The goal of this chapter has been to help you get your dog comfortable and relaxed around livestock. To get the best out of your dog and yourself, you both need to be confident and relaxed. The first step to achieving these goals is for you and your dog to feel safe. Do whatever it takes to secure safety for all parties involved. If you are nervous your dog will become anxious and if your dog is fearful or over-roused you will become anxious. Using penned stock and/or moving farther from your livestock are options you should always consider if you find you or your dog becoming anxious.

Instinct and arousal are double-edged swords. Instinct instills the wonderful herding behaviors that we want, yet instinct can also make it difficult to harness those behaviors. Arousal can work for or against us. We want our dogs in the optimal arousal zone but can sometimes find them under and more often over-aroused. Your job is to observe where your dog is and work to move them to where they need to be. Remember that you are the gatekeeper. You decide when and how your dog gains access to livestock and that access is the key to your dog's level of arousal.

CHAPTER 10

Planning to succeed

Some of the simplest and best advice for making the most of your training time comes from Bob Bailey, "Think, plan, do." Because there is a lot to teach your dog, you need to think about what you want to train, plan your training session, train, figure out what went well and what not so well, and jot down some ideas for your next session. Several short sessions are better than one long one but I tend to work in longer sessions that I divide by taking short breaks as I go. For me, the most difficult part of training is getting started!

There are several parts to a training plan. You can write down your plan or formulate it in your mind but you need an idea of how you are going to train every session.

Your **plan** should include:
- Length of session – no livestock: 5 to 10 minute sessions, using livestock: 3 to 10 minutes initially and later 10 to 20 minutes
- Props needed
- Location of training
- How to start and end the session – start = *ready?* end = *that'll do*
- Practice without dog
- Decide how and where to present reinforcer
- Resetting procedure
- Video or note-taking – video is strongly suggested
- Data recording – even if just notes on the session
- Ideas for next session – jot ideas about what you want to work on next time
- Review of session – review video or notes
- Plan for next session

If you are like me, you will struggle to limit the length of your training session. Once I get started I have so much fun that I don't want to stop, and neither does my dog!

I provide training plans for each exercise as we go along. My plans are for the actual shaping of the behavior and are followed by troubleshooting suggestions for when things do not go exactly as planned. Feel free to use my plan or modify it to better suit you and your dog. At some points, you may be able to skip steps, and at others, you may need to add additional steps. Let your dog show you what works for them.

Session length
Suggestions for limiting the length of a training session:
- Count out a set number of treats and stop when the treats are gone.
- Set a timer – Start with sessions of only 20 or 30 *seconds* and grow the seconds into minutes as you and your dog gain experience and skills.
- Use a large treat and break off pieces so that when the treat is gone the session is over.

Almost all training is shaping. You start shaping a simple behavior and build it into a skill. This progression is constantly repeated. You can start most behaviors in your training room and will eventually use them out in big fields with sheep or other livestock.

Here is a sample shaping progression for flanks (*come bye* and *away to me*):
1. Directionals taught indoors with dog sitting in front of handler
2. Directionals expand to targets on floor
3. Directionals become flanks using mini cone square indoors
4. Flanks taken outside using mini cone square
5. Mini cone square becomes mini cone circle
6. Flanks expanded by increasing size of cone circle
7. Cone circle taken to new areas
8. Cone circle taken to livestock paddock – no livestock
9. Cone circle placed around small pen – no livestock
10. Cone circle enlarged around small pen – no livestock
11. Dog on long line flanking and livestock in pen – cones present
12. Dog on long line flanking and livestock in pen – no cones
13. Dog on long line flanking and livestock loose – no cones
14. Dog flanking loose and livestock loose

This is the basic progression for moving all obedience and herding skills from indoor training exercises to outdoors, working livestock in real-life situations, be it trials or farm work.

When making your training plan, especially once you are working with livestock, avoid getting your dog into a situation you are not in control of. If you are not sure your dog can successfully handle a situation, restructure your plan or the environment so you are setting your dog up for success. Be sure to put safeguards in place to prevent your dog from practicing unwanted behavior.

Some ways you can help your dog succeed are by putting your dog on a long line, moving your position closer to your dog, or breaking down the exercise and making it easier. If you don't have confidence your dog is going to be successful, listen to your instincts and change your training plan.

Record keeping

Keeping records helps you to remember what and how you trained, gives you insight into how you might train faster and more efficiently, and helps you to overcome training problems. Most people do not like to keep data but it can be quite easy and painless.

I have tried *many* different types and forms of record keeping. I always start with great intentions to maintain records but usually stop within weeks, if not days. I now use two types of records that I enjoy keeping and find very useful, a journal and a form that I developed.

My journal is just a blank, lined journal that I use after every training session. I usually do not take notes during the session but rely on my memory and video. In my journal I may write:

1. Dog's name
2. Date
3. Place
4. Skill trained
5. What went well
6. What went *not so* well
7. What insights I had – if I had any!
8. What I want to work on next session
9. How I felt about the session

My journal entry may be anywhere from a few paragraphs (normally) to a page (occasionally). I usually don't spend more than a few minutes on the entry but it comes in very handy if I have a break of several days in my training or if I look back months later to see how I trained some skill. The journal also really helps when I am feeling discouraged because I can look back and see just how far we have progressed.

It is easy to get discouraged and feel like you are not making progress. If you keep a journal or other records you can look back weeks or months and realize just how far you have come. I tend to get mired in the present, especially if I am dealing with a training problem, and forget all of the progress we have made previously.

When recording thoughts in a journal or on a form, be kind to yourself. Record your mistakes as your best friend might. We are our own worst critics!

If you are going to keep hard data, you can track any element that you can count or quantify that you think will be helpful to you. Although I keep a journal and a record sheet, I depend primarily on video of a session if I am struggling with teaching a behavior. On video I can step back and watch myself train almost as if I am watching a stranger or student train. By just being an observer I often can spot where my training has broken down. Plus I can watch in slow motion or re-watch a troublesome area several times to see what really went on. Only keep records that are meaningful to you or you will end up keeping no records at all!

I have developed a simple form that I like to use because it is short, simple, and easy to use. Besides lines to record my thoughts and observations it also has a blank traffic light on it that I use to gauge how much fun I had during my session. I do this by coloring in one circle of the traffic light: red, yellow, or green.

When I work away from livestock I have no trouble keeping my training sessions fun but as a crossover trainer I tend to revert to a more serious state of mind when I get out in a paddock with my dog and livestock.

I color in one section of the form per session, adding notes about some of the items on the list below. This form could also be used to track other criteria that you are struggling with such as taking breaks, holding criteria, low rate of reinforcement, late timing, or any other general topic you want to keep track of. Eventually you can stop using the form or switch to monitoring a different skill or criterion.

1. Date
2. Dog
3. Skill trained
4. High points
5. Low points
6. Insights
7. Plans for next session
8. Color in the traffic light:
   Red = stop!
   Yellow = caution
   Green = full speed ahead

If I decide the session was Green I move forward as planned, if Yellow I think about what went wrong or why it was not much fun, and if Red I stop and do not train again until I have a plan for making the next session fun for me and my dog. When a session is no longer fun something is wrong. This form prevents me from going too far off track and doing damage to my relationship with my dog.

If you are not a crossover trainer you may not need to use the traffic lights to track if you are having fun but you could still use them for monitoring if your session went as planned:

Red = road closed – stop
Yellow = delays ahead – caution
Green = no delay – go for it

What is nice about this form is that you can see at a glance if your training is progressing as you planned or if problems are creeping in. If you see two yellow or a red light on the form, it is a warning that your training is getting off track and you need to re-think and re-plan future training sessions. A copy of this form is found in the appendices on page 319.

Coaching and video

Having a good coach is a tremendous asset. They can watch your training or a video of your training and give you vital information that will allow you to proceed smoothly or help you understand what you need to change to overcome problems. A knowledgeable and compassionate coach is priceless! Unfortunately, positive herding coaches are scarce. Fortunately, you may be able to get some coaching from another positive dog trainer and this coaching can be extremely helpful.

If you cannot find a coach, the next best thing is to take video and coach yourself. Today video cameras and smartphones provide high-quality video. You can purchase a tripod fairly inexpensively and it will make videoing your training much easier.

When you set up to video be sure and capture both you and your dog in the frame. When you start working livestock be sure they are in frame too. Having video of a session allows you to go back and look at your timing, rate of reinforcement, and criteria. If possible, save all of your video so you can go back and see what progress you have made. I have hundreds of videos of my training from over the years.

Training and then watching the training session gives you two completely different perspectives. After training a session you will remember what you *think* you did but the video shows what you *actually* did. It is amazing how much more objective you can be when you are watching yourself train. You can step back and watch yourself almost as if viewing another person doing the training.

Frame your videos such that you capture you, your dog, and the livestock. Try to zoom the video in as far as possible while still capturing all of the action.

Your video may not be perfect but it will still be invaluable as a training record.

Some of the great things about video:

- Non-judgmental
- Accurate
- Slow-motion available
- Replay as necessary
- Share online with coaches or teachers

Once you get to working livestock, it will *really* be helpful to see what you, your dog, and the sheep did in a certain situation. When you are just starting out, it is often difficult to keep track of everything that is going on around you at the same time. There is so much interrelated movement among you, your dog, the sheep, and the environment that it overwhelms your ability to see and process what actually happened. If you can go back and look at the situation, without the pressure of having to participate in it, you can see much more and usually learn a lot.

It's your choice

No one gets up in the morning and finds that they can't wait to plan, keep record of, and review video of their training. At least no one I know! Often planning is minimal and record-keeping and videoing are non-existent as we train. If you take the time to plan, keep consistent records, and use a coach or self-coach using video, I promise you will be happy that you did. By following these steps you are training yourself to become more adept at avoiding problems and solving them when they appear. We all owe it to our dogs to become the best trainers that we can be. Will you become the person your dog thinks you are?

Section 3
Basic Herding Skills

CHAPTER 11

Herding in a nutshell

Herding is all about control: the dog controls the livestock and the handler controls the dog. It is a dance that uses the dog's natural herding instincts to read and respond to stock and weds that inborn ability with the cued herding skills that the handler has trained. The difficult part is knowing when to honor the dog's instinct by allowing the dog to decide what moves to make and when to override that instinct by asking the dog to respond to cues.

There are some truly excellent handlers but none read livestock as well as a good dog. A great handler uses their dog's ability to read and control livestock. They do *not* tell their dog every move to make but know when to take control of their dog and when to give control back to their dog.

It has been said that when herding, a dog has one ear on the livestock and one ear on the handler. In effect, your dog's attention is split between you and the stock while herding.

Stockmanship

The goal of herding is to move, sort, or confine livestock in the most efficient and least stressful way possible. The art and science of reading and gently handling livestock is known as **stockmanship**. Good stockmen are kind to and care about the welfare of the stock they handle. Stock at trials should be handled with the same compassion and concern you would have for your livestock at home.

If safety is your first concern when herding then good stockmanship should be your second.

Herding and stockmanship are inextricably entwined. Every time you allow your dog access to stock your dog interacts with that stock from the time they go in the gate and look at the stock until you take them back out the gate. It is your responsibility to not allow your dog free access to stock until you can control your dog and ensure the safety of your livestock. A young dog turned loose with sheep may go nicely around and bring them to you but more likely will chase and run them into a fence.

Stockmanship will be taken up in more detail in a chapter in *Positive Herding 102* but remember that every interaction you or your dog has with livestock is determined by your knowledge, experience, and intentions. Good intentions amount to little if you don't have the knowledge or experience to fulfill those intentions. One of the primary concepts you will need to understand to become a good stockman and help your dog handle stock correctly is the flight zone.

Flight zone versus fight zone

The **flight zone** is an imaginary bubble or distance around an animal that, when entered by a potential predator or threat, makes the animal uncomfortable such that they either move away from or toward the animal or object that has approached too close. Most people think of a flight zone as an area that when entered will provoke the animal to flight but if it is a ewe with a lamb it could become a **fight zone**. Also if an animal cannot flee, they may fight. I will refer to it as the flight zone but remember it can easily become a fight zone when an animal feels trapped or has young at its side.

The flight zone is often represented in drawings as a circle around the animal but that is an oversimplification. The flight zone is usually closer to the side of an animal and

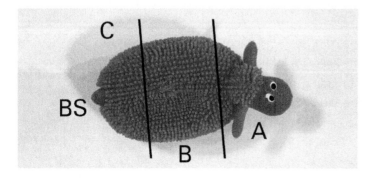

Different parts of the flight zone determine how an animal will be affected by pressure on the bubble.

A – Position to stop or turn animal
B – Position to move animal forward or slight turn
C – Position to move animal forward
BS – Blind spot

larger in front and behind them. A flight zone is *not* a fixed distance for an animal or group of animals and depends on many variables. In herding, the variables we are most concerned with are our and our dog's interaction with the stock's flight zone.

No two dogs and no two people have the exact same effect on an animal or that animal's flight zone. One dog can work very close to their stock and the stock will remain calm and responsive. Another dog must work at two or three times the distance away from the same stock in order to keep them relaxed and comfortable. It is the same with people. You will find that around one stationary person the stock will come quite close while they will keep a much greater distance from another standing person.

It is said that herding dogs, as predators, are tremendous readers of their livestock. To survive predator attacks, livestock, especially smaller and more vulnerable stock, must be just as good at reading predators if they are going to survive on the range or in the pasture.

The easiest way to learn about flight zones is to move some sheep or goats *without* a dog. Go into a pasture, with permission of course, and try to move some sheep from one place to another. You will be amazed at how much you learn! There really is no substitute for experience. Now bring your dog into the pasture on a leash and move the sheep again. How does the reaction of the sheep change? I would guess that you do not need to get nearly as close to the sheep to initiate movement when you have a dog along. If you took a different dog along you would see that the sheep react a bit differently to this dog. Sheep are excellent at reading predators and predators' intentions!

The handler as the dog

One of the very best ways to learn about flight zones and how livestock reacts to different types of pressure is to work some stock without a dog. Locate some docile sheep, goats, cattle, or ducks and move them. You will want to watch the stock's heads since their body motion will follow in the direction they are facing.

How much pressure does it take to move them? How close do you need to be to get movement? How do they react when you walk toward them, slow down, speed up, raise your arms out to your sides, speak or make other noise, clap your hands, jump in place, run at them, crouch down, hop toward them, move your arms, slap your leg, back away from them, kick dirt at them, go to one side of them, move through the middle of them, and perform any other maneuver you can think of? How do they react differently when you use a crook or stock stick to extend your reach? Now move them next to a fence or away from a gateway or feeder. How do they react differently in these situations? More details on handler controlling and moving livestock exercises can be found in the chapter on stockmanship in *Positive Herding 102*.

You should now have a good idea of how this group of animals reacts to you. If there happen to be any herding obstacles in the paddock that you can use, try penning or putting them through a chute as well as driving them from one point to another in the paddock. If there are some trees, try driving the stock between the trees or through a shallow creek. Try driving them uphill, downhill, or across a hill. The more experience you get handling stock the better you will be able to see the interaction between you, your dog, and the livestock.

The more you know about how livestock respond to you and your dog the better equipped you will be to help your dog when needed, such as when penning stock.

I am applying pressure by raising my arm and stepping into the sheep to turn them back toward the mouth of the pen. Note the direction the sheep are looking.

My pressure has changed the entire scenario. At this point, I am holding pressure by keeping my arm extended and standing still but not applying more pressure.

Now the sheep have turned away from me, are on the move, and Sir is flanking out around the sheep to catch them and keep them in the mouth of the pen.

If you have a friend along, you can learn a lot and have some real fun when one of you becomes "the dog" and the other the handler. The handler cues the "dog" just as they would a real dog. Can the handler put the "dog" in the necessary place and have the "dog" apply the correct amount of pressure to drive the sheep to a point only known to the handler? How about the challenge of penning the sheep or putting them through a chute, gateway, or between trees? These exercises are guaranteed to have you laughing as you learn! And isn't that what positive reinforcement training is all about?

Balance

Positive training may be about fun but herding is all about balance. **Balance** is the point your dog instinctually goes to bring the livestock straight to you, the point of control. When a dog goes out around livestock their instinct tells them where they need to turn in to bring the livestock to you. If your dog does not have herding instinct you will need to tell them where to turn in to their stock to bring them directly to you.

Many people think of balance in terms of the face of a watch. If you think of the handler at 6 o'clock and the sheep in the center then the dog would have to run to 12 o'clock and turn in to start driving the sheep straight to the handler. When a dog flanks out to 12 o'clock and turns in to the stock we say that the dog has gone to balance.

Balance is essential to a good herding dog. Because you want to encourage your dog to go to balance you do not want to allow your dog to continuously circle stock and never get to balance. Flanking around and around stock is known as **orbiting** and should be avoided. A dog with good balance is easy to teach flanks, but more difficult to teach off-balance flanks. **Off-balance flanks** are flanks where the dog goes beyond balance and continues to flank beyond 12 o'clock toward the handler, thus losing control of the stock. Many dogs find it very difficult to override their instinct to go to balance and flank toward the handler.

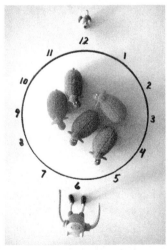 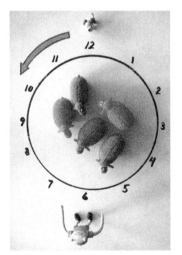

In a perfect world, balance would always be exactly opposite of the handler. If the handler is at 6 o'clock, then balance for the dog would be at 12 o'clock. Balance is the point at which the dog controls the stock or would need to apply pressure to bring the stock directly to the handler.

Once a dog is at balance and starts flanking toward the handler, in the direction of the arrow, they are going off-balance or performing an off-balance flank. Most dogs don't like to go off-balance because they lose control of their stock when they are not at balance.

Pull

There is another factor that comes into play with balance and that is pull. **Pull** is the pressure livestock feel to move toward a safe area. Stock feel pulled toward safety and away from danger. Pull is always thought of in terms of where the livestock want to go or where they perceive safety is. It is because of pull that the balance point is often *not* 12 o'clock, per the above example.

You can usually anticipate where the sheep will pull to. Sheep will usually pull toward an exit gate or other sheep that they can see. Sheep like to flock and stay together for safety. Goats and ducks flock well but cattle tend to have less instinct to stay together. Most animals will pull toward other stock or the area that they came from.

At trials, stock tends to pull toward the set out and exhaust pens, once they have been exhausted previously. The **set out pen** is the pen holding livestock before a run and the **exhaust pen** is the pen holding stock after a run. Fortunately, your herding breed dog is an expert at reading pull and will adjust where they turn in to bring the stock directly to you. Sometimes it looks like they could not possibly be correct but allow them to bring the stock and you will find, more times than not, they are spot on. Thus the balance point is not a set place but moves depending on where the stock perceives safety is located.

When working in a paddock or pasture the gate through which the stock entered the area is usually a strong pull. Animals realize that the gate is their best escape route.

In this picture, the sheep are now in a fenced area with the gate, striped fence section, at the upper left. The pull is indicated by the circled P in the arrow near the gate. Your dog would have to come into the stock between 10 and 11 o'clock to bring the sheep directly to you.

If your dog does not have herding instinct you will have to tell them where to turn in to bring the stock to you. You will have to read the pull in the scenario and adjust where you ask your dog in accordingly. Having to read the livestock to determine when and where to ask your dog in as well as adjusting your dog's position behind the stock as they bring them to you are just a few of the determinations you will have to make for your dog if they do not have herding instinct.

We also say that a dog has **pull on their stock** if they can draw the stock back to lean on them such that the sheep allow themselves to be directed by the dog almost as if the dog has a set of invisible reins on them. Dogs with pull can change stock's direction without perceptibly flanking to hold a line or can get sheep to slow down and almost magically get the sheep to depend on and trust them.

Forward-moving versus sideways-moving dogs

Dogs tend to fall into two groups; sideways-moving or forward-moving. The difference between forward-moving and sideways-moving dogs is how comfortable they are approaching and entering the flight zone.

A **sideways-moving** dog tends to be more comfortable flanking and stopping. They often have a more crouched posture, more style, and tend to move less freely. They may be described as sticky or defensive type dogs. A dog with **style** is a dog that works with their head and front end close to the ground and their rear end up. A **forward-moving** dog tends to be more comfortable walking into and moving stock. They often have a more upright posture and tend to move more freely. They are often described as pushy or offensive type dogs.

The ideal dog is a balance of forward- and sideways-moving but most dogs tend toward one type or the other.

Forward- and sideways-moving dogs are at the opposite ends of a continuum. You can free up a sideways-moving dog and slow down a forward-moving dog but it will take constant vigilance to maintain your gains, as dogs always tend to move back toward the type of behavior that they find most comfortable. Hint, it's reinforcing!

You can use the knowledge of which type of dog you have to your advantage when your dog is herding. If you have a forward-moving dog that does not like to stop, you can cue your dog to walk in after a nice stop. If you have a sideways-moving dog that does not like to walk in, you can cue your dog to flank after a nice walk in. In each scenario, you are using a cue for a preferred behavior as a reinforcer for a less preferred behavior, the Premack principle.

You will also use your knowledge of your dog's type of working to manage how you handle your dog. If you have a sideways-moving dog you will want to ask for fewer stops and instead go directly from flanking to walking in, to avoid getting your dog stuck in the stopped position. If you have a forward-moving dog you will want to use more stops to get your dog to pause and think and you will need to monitor that your dog does not **slice in** on their flanks, wind in closer and closer to the stock rather than maintaining a fixed distance from the stock while flanking.

For a sideways-moving dog, your key cues may be *hurry* (speed up) and *close* (flank closer to the stock). For a forward-moving dog, your key cues may be *easy* (slow down) and *out* (flank farther from the stock). A good stop is key for all dogs!

Behavior around livestock

Herding is all about your dog reading and reacting to livestock while listening and responding to your cues. Your dog may provide the instinctual herding behaviors but you will train obedience behaviors and shape the herding behaviors. Both instinctual and trained behaviors are important for herding.

If your dog does not have herding instinct, they can still herd as long as they are not afraid of livestock and you tell them when and where to move. Your job as the handler becomes much more critical if your dog does not have the instinct to control livestock. You will still teach obedience and herding behaviors but may find teaching some herding skills, such as flanking, may require more time and effort to train.

If your dog does have herding instinct, you will also work first on training obedience-type behaviors and then on herding behaviors. Your challenge will be to have your trained behaviors strong enough to override your dog's instincts.

No matter what skills or instincts your dog brings to the table, your goal is to train all behaviors to competency so your dog can perform them with livestock in the picture. This is easier said than done!

Basic obedience behaviors defined

Although I have talked about herding and obedience skills, there really is no distinction between them other than that obedience behaviors are commonly taught as basic manners and herding behaviors are taught only for herding. The real difference is between trained behaviors and instinctual ones. You can shape and put many behaviors on cue but you cannot instill instinct in your dog, they were either born with herding instinct or not.

One great thing about obedience-type behaviors is that we can use them around livestock to gauge how much self-control our dog has. Just as we tested our dog to see if they were able to engage with us around livestock, we will use obedience-type behaviors to test their ability to think and respond to cues around stock.

Sir is heeling off-leash with me near my sheep. Heeling for herding is different from competition obedience heeling. For herding, I do not want my dog to look at me but instead keep track of me while focusing on the livestock. Another difference is that for herding we want the dog to heel on both sides of us as we always want to be between our dogs and the stock while heeling.

If your dog knows competition obedience heeling you can still train heeling for herding as long as you attach a different cue from what you use for obedience heeling.

The **core obedience behaviors** I especially like to have well-trained before going to livestock are:

- Recall
- Heeling – not competitive obedience heeling
- Sit
- Down
- Stand

Let's take a closer look at each of the basic obedience behaviors.

Recall: The recall is the same around livestock as it is in everyday use. A **recall** is the behavior of your dog coming back to you when cued. I use the cue *here* instead of *come* because the traditional herding cue for a clockwise flank is *come bye*. Make sure your criteria for recall includes coming all the way back to you and remaining with you. I like to have my dogs come back close enough that I can pet or put a leash on them. If you already use *come* as your recall cue then you will want to pick a different cue for your clockwise flank, such as *go-bye*.

Recalling your dog from livestock is important but difficult for most dogs. Remember that interacting with livestock is very reinforcing and coming back to you and away from stock should earn great treats or amazing tugging and loads of verbal praise.

Heeling: Heeling in herding is quite different from competition obedience heeling. If you have trained competition heeling you will want to start over with a new, separate heeling behavior especially for herding.

In herding, **heeling** has criteria that includes:
1. Dog's front legs stay even with handler's legs
2. *Dog looks at stock and not at handler*
3. Dog stays with handler – stops when handler stops and moves forward when handler moves
4. Dog sits when handler stops (optional)
5. *Dog heels on either side of handler*
6. *When heeling around stock, dog heels to the outside of the handler*

The criteria in *italic* are totally different from competition heeling. When heeling around livestock you want your dog to watch the livestock and yet keep track of you. This is the beginning of your dog learning to keep one ear on the livestock and one on you. During training, when we are circling the stock, we usually want to be between our dogs and the livestock so your dog needs to be able to heel on both your right and left sides.

When you start training your dog to heel using these criteria you will definitely want a new cue to differentiate herding heeling from competition heeling. I use the same cue for when my dog is on both my right and left sides but you may use different cues for each side.

Heeling is important around livestock because it challenges your dog to control themselves while watching stock *and* keeping track of you. Start heeling around stock with your dog on a leash and progress to off-leash heeling. A dog that can heel off-leash or on a loose leash around moving livestock has really started to gain essential self-control!

Sit, down, and stand: Your basic obedience behaviors of **sit**, **down**, and **stand** are no different around livestock than they are in your kitchen. You will eventually use these behaviors to test your dog's self-control and engagement with you around stock.

If you have not taught or don't know how to teach basic obedience-type behaviors using positive reinforcement, you need some new science-based training skills: refer to the Resources section at the back of this book for help. Please do not train any herding behaviors until you have the listed obedience behaviors solidly trained.

Basic herding behaviors defined

There is another completely different group of behaviors that you will need to train for herding.

The basic **herding behaviors** I want on my dog before taking them to stock are:
- Directionals/flanks
- Stop or down
- In and back
- Out and close
- Easy and hurry

Let's take a closer look at each of the basic herding behaviors.

Directionals: Directionals are simply the cues for right and left. In traditional herding *your dog's right* is known as **away to me** and *left* as **come bye**. Since directionals are the start of **flanks**, a dog circling the stock, instead of right and left I like to think of them as clockwise and anti-clockwise.
- **C**lockwise = **C**ome bye
- **A**nti-clockwise = **A**way to me

I especially like to think of flanks in this way because right and left change, from your perspective, when your dog is at your side versus when they are on the other side of the stock facing you.

The easiest way I have found to keep the flanks straight is to think of the flanks from above, as if you were looking down from a drone. In this way, the directionals don't

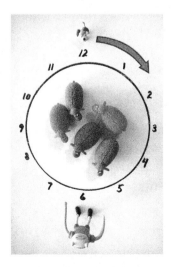 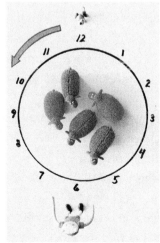

FAR LEFT: Come bye
LEFT: Away to me

Flanks can continue all the way around the livestock in a complete circle but more often are only a partial circle or just a few steps. While flanking, your dog should not put pressure on the stock. In other words, the stock should not move away from your dog as they flank around the livestock.

change, no matter where your dog is relative to your position. A dog flanking should not be putting pressure on the livestock so should maintain their distance from the stock as they flank, thus a dog flanking around sheep should not cause the sheep to move away from the dog.

Stop: A solid stop is a vital behavior for your herding dog. Having a stop behavior allows you to control your dog and the situation. **Stop** means that your dog stops quickly when cued and stays in that position until given another cue.

I use ***there*** as my stop cue. My dogs are allowed to choose their position; sit, down, or stand, when they stop. This means that if my dog immediately stops and stands, sits, or lies down and holds their position, they have met my criteria for a stop.

Teaching a down as a stop is easier than training just a stop. A *there* cue allows your dog to assume any position as long as they quickly stop and remain stationary until cued to move. A *down* cue has fewer criteria which makes it easier to train. Teaching both behaviors will be covered, so feel free to use either. Since many dogs already have been trained to down, there may be much more mass on the down behavior than there would be on a newly trained stop behavior. The real advantage to using *there* rather than a down is that it allows your dog to pick the most comfortable stationary position for them.

With a sticky dog, it can be difficult to get them up and moving once they clap down to the ground. If your dog tends to **clap**, drop down to the ground every time they stop, you may want to teach stand as your stop position. For a pushy dog, you may want to teach a down to anchor them when they stop.

In and back: To move livestock your dog needs to apply pressure to livestock. Most people use the cue ***walk in*** and it means walk directly toward the stock and apply pressure. The opposite of *walk in* is *back*. **Back** means back up away from the livestock while continuing to face the livestock and release pressure on the stock.

Out and close: Two more basic herding behaviors are *out* and *close*. **Out** means move farther from the livestock *while* flanking. Out is an essential behavior since most novice dogs tend to want to flank too tight or close to their stock and put unwanted pressure on it. Again ***close*** is the opposite of *out* and cues the dog to move closer to the stock *while* flanking. *Close* is very helpful if a dog runs too wide or far off of their stock and you need them to flank in closer. Often this cue is used if your dog has **lost contact**, and is no longer engaged with the stock.

In and back: *Your dog should walk straight into the stock when cued in. They should move the entire flock or herd, not just an individual or two, by applying pressure.*

The in cue sets the line that your dog is to hold with the stock. If you ask your dog in at 3 o'clock your dog should take the sheep off perpendicular to you and continue on that line until given a different cue.

If you need your dog to release pressure on the stock you can cue back which asks your dog to back away from the stock while still facing them.

Out and close: *If your dog is disturbing the stock as they flank, you will need to move them farther from the stock while they continue flanking. Many young dogs tend to flank too close to their stock because they do not realize that it is actually easier to control stock when they are off of them a fair distance.*

At first, you may need to ask your dog out often but over time they should realize that being off of the stock makes it easier for them to maintain control.

In the diagram, the dog is flanking away to me and is moving out or farther from the stock as they flank by following the path of the arrow.

Easy and hurry: The final two basic herding behaviors are *easy* and *hurry*. **Easy** means slow down, which I define as dropping down one gait. The four main dog gaits are run or gallop, canter, trot, and walk. If your dog is cantering they would slow down to a trot when cued *easy*. **Hurry** means speed up one gait. If your dog is trotting they would start to canter when cued *hurry*.

With these few herding behaviors, your dog can be placed anywhere in a field to approach or block livestock. Your dog can get around, walk into, circle both directions, drive, move closer to or farther from, speed up or slow down, and stop and hold position around livestock. This is when the fun begins!

The overarching principle of herding is to move your dog relative to the livestock and apply or release pressure. Herding is a game of angles using pressure and release on the flight zone. You decide where you want the livestock to go and your dog knows how to control and move them using instinctive and trained behaviors. You cue your dog and your dog responds to both your cues *and* the livestock. It is amazing that herding dogs can read and control livestock, yet perform our verbal or whistle cues with such precision, ease, and confidence.

Herding cues defined

Most people use the traditional verbal herding cues. If you ever work with a teacher or train with a friend, it will be much easier for them to relate to your herding performance if you both use the same cues.

Some **traditional herding cues** are:
- *Come bye* or *bye* – flank clockwise
- *Away* or *away to me* – flank anti-clockwise
- *There* – stop
- *Here* – come to handler
- *In* or *walk in* – directly approach stock
- *Out* – move away from stock (usually while flanking)
- *Look back* – look back for more stock
- *That'll do* – quit working and return to handler

There are many variations of these cues as well as others that are used in specific situations. Besides the different cues, each cue can be given quickly or slowly, high or low pitched, loudly or quietly. Each variation of how the cue is given tells your dog how you want them to carry out the cue. A drawn-out or slowly given cue usually causes your dog to respond with a slower behavior, as does a soft cue. A fast, loud cue usually gets a quicker behavior such as a faster flank. So how you say or whistle your cue can tell your dog almost as much as what cue you give.

More information on changing the speed of the walk in or flanks and training out and close will be found in chapters 21 and 22, where modifier cues are covered.

Three moving parts

Herding is quite simple in some ways and yet highly complex in others. The basic idea of herding is easy to grasp; the dog controls the livestock and the handler controls the dog. Most dog sports consist of a dog and a handler doing some activity together, two moving parts. What makes herding complex and addictive is the addition of the third moving part – the livestock. The more experience you have and the more you learn about herding, the more you understand the interaction between the dog, the stock, and you, and the more intriguing herding becomes.

You can immerse yourself in herding for decades and never stop learning. There is always a new scenario, a different set of livestock, a new location, or a different type of dog to spark a new insight that leads to a deeper and more profound understanding of herding. The best part is that your dog will not only work their heart out for you while herding but will also love every minute they are doing it.

Believe it or not, it's time to start training! If your dog needs more solid obedience behaviors, let's jump right in and get started.

CHAPTER 12

Obedient RAMS – from recall to stand

There are some important rules for training all behaviors that you should be familiar with. Since you will now be starting to shape behaviors, let's revisit them.

Training do's and don'ts
- Have fun.
- Plan.
- Start easy and build slowly – Shape behavior in slices not lumps.
- Start inside, move outside, then to stock.
- Ping-pong both number of repetitions and time of duration – As you grow steps of heeling or seconds of sitting, start small and don't keep asking for more and more. Instead start out with 1, then 2, 1, 1, 2, 2, 1, 2, 3, 2, etc. You do not want to continually make it more difficult for your dog to earn reinforcement.
- Don't repeat cues – If your dog does not respond to your cue, pause for several seconds or use your no reward marker and pause 10 seconds before starting again.
- Timing, rate of reinforcement, and criteria are key – If you have a problem in training go back and look at these essentials.
- Practice without your dog.
- Video – If possible.

The RAMs
In Chapter 2 you met the RAMs, the Rules and Mechanics, and now it is time to get acquainted with them using your obedience behaviors: recall, sit, down, heel, and stand. If you or your dog need to have a specific skill in place before you begin training an exercise, it will be covered before the RAMs and called: **Before you start**.

Since the recall is so important in building a good relationship with your dog, let's start there.

Recall

THE RULES

1. ***Goal*** – The goal is to have a dog that will come directly back to you in any situation, no matter what the distraction.
2. ***When to begin teaching*** – Start teaching a recall as soon as possible.
3. ***When to move on*** – Begin close and heavily reinforce *every* successful recall. Eventually, challenge your dog in safe places that are highly distracting. *Always* reinforce a prompt recall! A recall is essential around livestock so practice often and reinforce highly. *Never* scold your dog for not coming after you call them. If you scold your dog they will associate the verbal punishment of the scolding with being near you, essentially punishing the behavior you are trying to build.
4. ***Appropriate environment*** – Start inside, move outside, and finally work with your dog on a long line around livestock.
5. ***Setting up the environment*** – Initially, you want a distraction-free place but over time keep building mass and adding distraction as your dog continues to be successful. Start close and get in many reps with high-value reinforcement.
6. ***What props are needed*** – Tugs or high-value treats and eventually a long line. Marker use is optional.
7. ***Criteria in one sentence*** – The dog should immediately come directly back to the handler when called, such that the dog's collar or harness is within the handler's reach.
8. ***Reinforcement to use*** – Tugging or super high value treats. It is easier to get a fast recall if you engage your dog in a game of high energy tugging than using treats. Try both types of reinforcement and see what works best for your dog.
9. ***Cue to use*** – Use *here* or another word but avoid using your dog's name or *come* as your recall cue, since *come bye* is a traditional flank cue.
10. ***When to add the cue*** – Start by prompting your dog a few times by bending down, slapping your thighs, and using a temporary cue such as your dog's name or *pup-pup-pup*. Once your dog immediately stops what they are doing and comes to get the treats or tug, drop the prompts of bending and slapping your thighs and add your final cue. Then drop the temporary recall cue, if you used one.

THE MECHANICS

1. ***Your position*** – Stand near your dog while inside your house.
2. ***Your dog's position*** – Allow your dog to focus on something other than you and then prompt them to come to you by slapping your thighs and excitedly calling

their name or *pup-pup-pup*. After 3 trials start using your recall cue instead of pup or your dog's name. When your dog is immediately turning to come when called, drop the prompts of slapping your thighs and bending down.

3. ***What is marked*** – Mark the moment your dog turns toward you.
4. ***How and where the reinforcement will be delivered*** – Deliver the treat or begin tugging as soon as your dog returns to you.
5. ***How to grow the behavior*** – Do a lot of short, easy recalls until your dog is running back to you. Then start adding minor distractions. Eventually, move outside and finally work around livestock with your dog on a long line.
6. ***When to practice without your dog*** – No need to practice without your dog.

Initially, you will practice your obedience behaviors with little distraction but eventually you will take them near stock. Using a tug instead of treats encourages a fast recall. Hide the tug and bring it out just as your dog approaches you.

Sir recalling in the presence of sheep.

Troubleshooting

- ***Dog does not respond*** – If your dog does not respond to your recall cue, most likely because they are distracted, you will need to go get your dog, take them by the collar or harness, and gently bring them back to where you were standing when you called. Now you need to stop and think of a new plan that includes lowering the level of distraction, shortening the distance between you and your dog, and/or raising the value of your reinforcement.
- ***Dog responds slowly*** – If your dog returns to you slowly, turn and run away from them as soon as they start back to you. Your quick retreat should activate your dog's prey drive and kick them into chase mode. As your dog gets close to you, turn around and face them to begin tugging or to deliver a super high-value treat.
- ***Dog's response is variable*** – If your dog sometimes comes fast and other times dawdles, use differential reinforcement to match the amount and/or quality of the reinforcement to the effort your dog put in to earn it. Your dog comes straight and fast = long, intense tugging or several super high-value treats. Your dog meanders back = short, calm tugging, one treat, or just a verbal *good dog* and a quick pat.

Recalls are a good measure of your dog's self-control. Work them relentlessly!

You cannot do too many recalls or reinforce your recall too much. You will eventually be calling your dog off of a super high-value reinforcer – livestock. *Having a recall is non-negotiable.* You *must* be able to call your dog away from danger and off of moving livestock.

Once you go to livestock you will have your dog on a long line that is to be used only as an emergency brake to interrupt unwanted behavior. The long line is *not* to be used as a replacement for a solid recall.

Sit and down

The Rules

1. **Goal** – The goal is to have your dog sit or down immediately when cued.
2. **When to begin teaching** – Start teaching sit and down as soon as possible.
3. **When to move on** – You will pick either sit or down to work on. Once you have one behavior on cue, start working on the other. Again, start inside and once the cue is added work up to at least 30 seconds of duration with distractions before moving outside. Eventually, you will be working sits and downs around livestock.
4. **Appropriate environment** – Start inside, move outside, and finally work with your dog on a long line around livestock. Add difficulty by randomly cueing sits and downs.
5. **Setting up the environment** – Work inside in a distraction-free place to start. Build mass and move outside. Eventually move to training around livestock.
6. **What props are needed** – High value treats or tugs and eventually a long line. Marker use is optional.
7. **Criteria in one sentence** – The dog should immediately sit/down when cued.
8. **Reinforcement to use** – Treats are easiest to use for teaching sits and downs.
9. **Cue to use** – *Sit* and *down* are standard cues.
10. **When to add the cue** – When you are willing to bet $100 that your dog is about to perform the behavior, without any prompting, you may add the cue.

The Mechanics

1. **Your position** – Start facing your dog.
2. **Your dog's position** – Your dog should be standing, facing you.
3. **What is marked** – Mark or deliver reinforcement as your dog's rear end, for sit, or entire body, for down, hits the ground.

4. ***How and where the reinforcement will be delivered*** – Deliver the treat directly to your dog's mouth while in the sitting/down position. Initially give several treats while your dog is sitting or down. Move away from your dog to encourage them to stand again.

5. ***How to grow the behavior*** – Move around your dog so they learn to sit/down no matter where you are standing. Change positions such as sitting in a chair, lying down, or facing away from your dog when giving the cue. Also add distractions of clapping, running in place, etc. Then work on adding duration to the sit/down. Over time move outside and, as with other behaviors, eventually work them around livestock while your dog is on a long line.

6. ***When to practice without your dog*** – No real need to practice without your dog.

Sir is working on performing his obedience behaviors, sit and down, to criteria, in the presence of livestock.

Because Sir can become over-aroused, I am using treats for these stationary behaviors.

Troubleshooting

- ***Dog hovers instead of sits*** – If your dog hovers above the floor, instead of sitting, you are marking too soon. Withhold your mark until your dog has settled their rear end onto the floor. This is usually only a problem if you are using a clicker to mark the sit. You get what you mark, not what you want.

- ***Dog does not go all the way into the down*** – A critical criterion for the down is *elbows on the ground*. Many dogs will go down but will not settle all of the way into the down. Be sure to only mark and reinforce elbows touching the ground.

- ***Dog rolls on a hip in the down*** – Don't worry about how your dog sits, fold back versus butt tuck, or how they lie, sphinx versus rolling on one hip. You are only interested in having your dog sit or down in the way most comfortable for them.

To start the sit or down, lure your dog into position with a treat and **jackpot**, feed many treats one after the other, no more than three times. Then prompt your dog by pretending to lure but no longer have a treat in your hand. Do this three times. Then reset your dog to a standing position and wait. Your dog most likely will offer the down or sit, then jackpot. If your dog just stands and looks at you for 15 seconds, prompt them by using a hand signal or movement that is similar to the motion you used as a lure.

You can keep the hand signal and then add a verbal cue before the hand signal. Eventually drop the hand signal, or fade the hand signal, until your dog is offering the behavior. Then add the verbal cue. **Fading** is making a physical prompt, such as a hand motion, smaller and smaller until it is eliminated.

The key to teaching sits and downs is reinforcing heavily in place, while your dog is in the sit or down.

Sit and down are easy to teach and should be some of the very first obedience behaviors you work on, along with recalls. Save heel and stand for after you have a strong sit, down, and recall.

Heel
THE RULES
1. *Goal* – The goal is to have a dog that will stay by your side and keep track of, but not look at, you no matter what distractions are present.
2. *When to begin teaching* – Begin teaching heeling as soon as sit, down, and the recall are solid.
3. *When to move on* – Start heeling inside, move outside, and finally around stock on a loose leash. This behavior is never-ending. You will use it every day and its most important use will be gauging your dog's self-control around livestock.
4. *Appropriate environment* – Practice everywhere!
5. *Setting up the environment* – Start inside and keep building mass until your dog can heel on a loose leash around moving livestock.
6. *What props are needed* – All you need are great treats and a leash. A marker is optional.
7. *Criteria in one sentence* – The dog should walk beside the handler with their head looking toward the livestock while keeping their front legs even with the handler's legs.

8. ***Reinforcement to use*** – It is easiest to train this using treats.

9. ***Cue to use*** – I use one cue, *heel*, for heeling on my right and left sides but you may use a different cue for each side.

10. ***When to add the cue*** – You can start by using prompts such as *let's go* while slapping your leg. Once your dog has the idea and can heel a few steps, drop your leg slap. As soon as your dog is doing those few steps without the leg slap, change your cue to whatever you want your final heel cue to be.

THE MECHANICS

1. ***Your position*** –Stand inside your house.

2. ***Your dog's position*** – Your dog stands on either your right or left side, facing the same direction you are. Your dog will move forward with you and stop when you stop. Your dog will be looking forward, not up at your face. You may want your dog to sit when you stop, but the sit is optional.

3. ***What is marked –*** The initial position you mark is your dog standing (or sitting) next to you. Later you will mark your dog moving forward with you while staying even with you.

4. ***How and where the reinforcement will be delivered*** – Treats are delivered directly to your dog's mouth when your dog is in the correct position next to you.

5. ***How to grow the behavior*** – Initially you reinforce your dog for standing (or sitting) next to you. Then reinforce for your dog staying with you as you take one step. You slowly build the behavior until your dog can heel beside you, on either side of your body, for at least 30 steps for one treat. Grow the behavior slowly by ping-ponging the number of steps you reinforce.

6. ***When to practice without your dog*** – If you have never taught heeling, practice with an imaginary dog to ensure you know what you are looking for, when you will mark and/or feed, and how you will get a treat out and deliver it to your imaginary dog.

Sir heeling with me near sheep. Note that he is not looking up at me. I want Sir to stay with me while keeping track of the stock.

If I were heading the opposite direction Sir would be on my right side, the side away from the sheep.

Troubleshooting

- **_Dog forges_** – If your dog keeps moving ahead of you, cut down the number of steps you take, mark when your dog is in correct position, and feed _behind_ your dog.
- **_Dog lags_** – If your dog consistently walks behind you, cut down the number of steps you take, mark when your dog is in correct position, and feed slightly _in front of_ your dog. It may also help to walk a bit faster. Experiment to see what works for your dog.
- **_Dog stares at handler_** – If your dog tends to look at you when heeling, add the criterion of dog's head looking forward. Initially, you will mark and reinforce the forward head position while your dog stands (or sits) beside you. Also, be sure to feed directly in front of your dog instead of toward your body, to reinforce the correct head position.

A marker can become a crutch to "catch" your dog as they begin to forge or lag to prevent them from moving farther out of heel position. Thus you are marking exactly what you don't want, your dog moving out of position.

Since this is not competition heeling, you do not need nor want your dog watching your face. If you do heeling competitively be sure you train heeling as a completely separate behavior with a different cue. Also, practice with your dog heeling on both sides of you.

You may also want to teach a set-up cue which tells your dog to get into heel position and be ready to start heeling with you. I use the cue, set up, _while looking down to the side I want my dog to set up on._

Heeling is not easy to train because your dog probably has a lot of experience walking in front of you and possibly pulling. Although this is the best obedience behavior to gauge your dog's self-control around livestock you can move forward using other tricks or obedience behaviors to test self-control.

Watch Sir heeling around rams at https://youtu.be/ZKluD-FE6-o

Stand

Before you start – Hand target

To teach the stand you first need to train a **hand target**. A hand touch is easy to train and comes in handy. You can use either the palm or back of your hand. I use my palm and the following instructions assume you will be using your palm for the target. Most people use a clicker to teach a hand target but I often just use the marker word *yes*. You may substitute the use of a marker word for the click in the instructions below.

Watch Qwest learning the stand while facing me: https://youtu.be/Z1Vwxq6LsSc

Get a clicker and have several high-value treats ready. Hold out your hand, palm facing your dog, about a foot in front of them and be ready to mark. Usually, your dog will investigate your hand by coming up to it with their nose. As they touch your hand, click, and put the treat into your palm. Repeat dropping a few treats, one at a time from above, into your palm for your dog to eat out of your hand. Then move your hand about a foot away from your dog and repeat.

If your dog does not readily touch your hand then you will have to shape the hand touch. Move your hand so your dog will notice it. That movement may arouse your dog's interest in your hand enough to approach it. If not, mark and reinforce your dog looking toward your hand, then approaching your hand, and finally touching your hand.

Be sure and click just as your dog touches your hand. If you click too early you will get your dog putting their nose near your hand but not touching it and if you click too late you will reinforce your dog moving their nose away from your hand. Also, you want to make sure your dog is not touching with their open mouth instead of their nose. Sometimes it is better not to click than to mark the wrong behavior. Initially, the presentation of your hand will be the physical cue or hand signal for the nose touch. Once your dog is touching readily you can add a verbal cue such as *touch* or *nose*.

Work this behavior until your dog can touch your hand, held high or low, and even jumping off of the ground to touch it.

The Rules

1. *Goal* – The goal is to have your dog stand immediately when cued.
2. ***When to begin teaching*** – Start teaching stand once your dog has a strong hand targeting behavior.

3. **When to move on** – Again you will start inside and once the cue is added work up to at least 30 seconds of duration with distractions before moving outside. Eventually, you will be working stands around livestock.

4. **Appropriate environment** – Start inside, move outside, and finally work with your dog on a long line around livestock.

5. **Setting up the environment** – You must have a hand target on cue to teach the stand. Your dog should touch your hand with their nose when they hear the cue *touch*. Work inside in a distraction-free room to start. Build mass and move outside. Eventually move to working around livestock.

6. **What props are needed** – High-value treats or tugs and eventually a long line. Marker use is optional.

7. **Criteria in one sentence** – The dog should immediately stand and remain standing when cued.

8. **Reinforcement to use** – Treats are easiest to use for teaching stands.

9. **Cue to use** – *Stand* is the cue I use. I start with *touch* and once my dog is reliably jumping into a stand I change the cue to *stand* by saying *stand* right before I cue *touch*.

10. **When to add the cue** – When your dog is reliably moving into the stand, add the cue. First, use *touch* and the physical cue of a hand target. Then insert the verbal cue *stand* in place of *touch* before giving the hand signal. Initially, your dog will be cued with *touch*. Your hand then becomes the physical cue for stand. Finally, say *stand* before presenting your hand. In teaching stand, go from the verbal cue *touch*, to the physical cue of a hand presentation, to the final verbal cue of *stand*.

THE MECHANICS

1. **Your position** – Stand next to your dog inside your house. Use the palm of your hand as a nose target. Place your hand, palm down, next to the point of your hip and 6 inches to the right/left, depending on which side you are working on and how tall your dog is.

2. **Your dog's position** – Your dog will be sitting at your side, in heel position. Be sure to work both sides.

3. **What is marked** – Initially mark as your dog touches your hand. Then change to marking the moment your dog lands in the stand. First, your dog will jump up to touch your hand target, on the cue *touch*, and you will mark and reinforce the touch. Then wait until your dog lands in a stand to mark and reinforce the stand.

4. **How and where the reinforcement will be delivered** – Deliver the treat to your dog's mouth as they land in the stand.

5. **How to grow the behavior** – Start inside and work both sides of your body. Then start to slowly turn your body toward your dog such that eventually, you are

facing your dog. Finally, work the stand from all different distances and positions, relative to your dog.

6. ***When to practice without your dog*** – You definitely need to practice the stand without your dog. There are a lot of mechanics to get straight! You have to be quick to catch your dog in the stand before they sit, especially if you have done a lot of training your dog sit at your side for heeling.

Start with your dog sitting at your side. Present your hand as a target and cue touch. *Mark and reinforce the hand touch. When your dog is reliably touching your hand, change to the cue* stand, *followed by* touch *if your dog does not jump to touch your hand, and mark and reinforce when your dog lands in the stand. You may now fade your hand target by cueing the stand without the target. Reinforce any upward movement by your dog. Most dogs will quickly figure out to stand with only the verbal cue. If not, go back to using the hand target and bring it closer to your hip until your hand is resting flat against your hip. Then go back to just the verbal cue with the hand closest to your dog at your side.*

If your dog lands with their rear end away from you, feed to the outside such that they turn their head away from you to get their treat. Over time this will help move their rear end back in line with your body. If they land with their rear end curled behind you, feed with their head turned toward you to encourage them to land straight.

I often work sit, down, stand, *and* recalls *in the same situation. One way that I can gauge Sir's level of arousal is by how gently or aggressively he takes treats from my hand. If his arousal level is too high I will often throw treats into the grass for him to find. The behavior of sniffing for the treats lowers his state of arousal and gives him a break from performing cued obedience behaviors.*

Troubleshooting

- ***Dog sits after the jump instead of standing*** – If your dog sits before you can mark and get your treat delivered, you need to anticipate the stand. As your dog jumps up to touch your hand, get ready to mark. It is better to mark too soon, while your dog is in the air, rather than too late, once your dog lands and sits down.
- ***Dog is too small to use hand as target*** – If your dog is small you will probably have to teach your dog to target a target stick instead of your hand.

A **target stick** is just a stick with a ball on the end.

Teach your dog to nose target the ball on the end of the target stick using the instructions for teaching the hand target except have your dog target the ball instead of your palm. If you want you can start out holding the ball in your palm and then move your hand back up the stick as your dog continues to touch the ball with their nose.

Once your dog targets the target stick you can use it to teach the stand by holding the stick so that your dog has to jump up to touch the ball with their nose. It is the same procedure outlined above except using a different target. Hold the target stick by your side, such that your dog has to jump up to touch it, and follow the instructions as written.

The stand cue will come in handy around livestock. You can also use it to test your dog's self-control near stock. If you have a dog that tends to **clap** (often lies down quickly and is reluctant to get up and move), then having a stand cue is indispensable for getting your dog back on their feet!

Any training you do to help your dog overcome instinctual with learned behavior will help free up your dog. (See Chapter 9, Instinct and arousal.) You may not be able to get a dog that claps to jump to their feet but you can decrease the severity of them locking up and being unable to respond to cues.

From heeling to herding

Only after you have your dog engaging with you around livestock, eating treats and/or tugging, should you ask your dog for other non-herding behaviors such as sits, downs, or recalls around stock. Your obedience-type behaviors *must* be wrecking ball strong before you take them to livestock. Be sure to keep your dog on leash or use a long line to insure you are controlling your dog's access to stock. It is best to also have your stock in a small pen as an added safety measure. A small pen is also suggested because it prevents the livestock from moving around. Stock movement triggers instinctual behavior and usually raises your dog's level of arousal. Set your dog up for success!

• •

It might seem strange to use games with your puppy as herding training exercises. After all, most traditional training has usually been done with sheep in the picture right from the start. In fact, it is quite possible to teach many of the cues to your puppy long before they even know what a sheep is. I've occasionally used cues around stock that were never intended for stock use – one time Renn couldn't see our sheep which were in an unusual place. So I asked her to spin left on the spot, then stopped her when she was looking directly at the sheep before flanking her.

• •

Work on these basic obedience behaviors around livestock as much and as early in your training as possible. As your dog's ability to maintain criteria around stock and to move closer to them increases, their self-control and confidence will grow. Eventually, your dog will be able to do all of these cued behaviors within a foot or two of a pen holding stock. Finally, your dog will be able to do these cued obedience behaviors with livestock loose and moving.

Watch Sir heeling around rams at
https://www.youtube.com/watch?v=-vL8-MONK1w&feature=youtu.be

While working with your obedience behaviors around stock you will want to be training your basic herding behaviors away from stock. All behaviors, obedience or herding, should be initially trained away from livestock and taken to stock when trained to proficiency.

CHAPTER 13

Transitioning obedience skills to stock

Once you begin to work obedience skills around livestock you will realize how strong a behavior has to be to meet criteria near stock. Your herding skills will need to be even stronger than your obedience skills because then the stock and your dog will be moving. If your dog cannot perform a sit around livestock there is no way they will be able to stop or otherwise control themselves when their instincts are screaming – CHASE!! So, let's quickly review the skills your dog needs before they begin herding.

Skills necessary to start herding (performed near penned livestock):
- Eat or play with you (engage with you)
- Work for food, a tug, a ball, or another toy
- Perform sit, down, stand, recall, tricks
- Heel (optional)

When performing obedience behaviors near livestock, you always want your dog to be looking at the stock and not at you. Your dog should have one ear, and both eyes, on the stock and one ear on you.

If your dog *cannot* engage with you, perform basic obedience behaviors or tricks, and recall reliably off of penned stock your dog is *not ready* to move forward with herding. If you move forward before your dog has the skills and self-control necessary you are setting them up for failure. Do yourself and your dog a favor by working the above skills until you have confidence that your dog is capable of listening and controlling themselves near livestock. Time spent building mass on non-herding skills around livestock is time very well spent! Once your dog is ready, decide what stock you will use, set up a pen for the stock, and move your stock into the pen.

Getting your stock to your training area

There are several ways to move your stock from the pasture or dry lot where you keep them to your training area. How you accomplish this depends on your setup and how docile your livestock is. If you have another trained dog you will certainly use them to move the stock but if not, you need a safe, easy, and efficient way to get your stock into a small pen in your training paddock.

*Do **not** try to move the livestock from where they are housed into your paddock and small pen using your untrained dog on a leash as a helper! This may be your dog's initial introduction to livestock and should not include your dog lunging at stock or being jerked around while you yell and wave your arms.*

If you are going to be working your livestock in the paddock where they stay, you can set up your small pen in that paddock and feed your stock some grain or hay inside the pen every day. Place a tub or two near the pen and put a bit of feed into them. Call your animals and step back away from the tubs and pen. After a few days, the stock will start coming over to the tubs when they see you approaching with feed or when you call.

Slowly move the tubs into the pen and leave the gate open. You will move away from the pen as you call your livestock. Within a few more days your stock should be going readily into the pen to get the feed. Now start shutting the gate and leaving the stock in the pen for 10 to 15 minutes before releasing them. After a few days of the stock being shut in for short periods, you should be ready to work your dog outside of the pen.

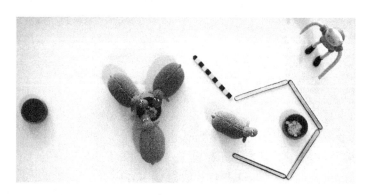

Another way to move your stock into a pen is to put out several tubs with a small amount of grain in each and have the stock move from one to the next, as they empty each tub, until they enter the pen.

Eventually, you can reduce the number of tubs. Be sure to have the last tub at the very back of the pen so you will not disturb the stock as you close the pen gate.

If you are not going to work your livestock in the paddock where they stay you will need to use barriers creatively. The most efficient, safe way to move stock to your training paddock is through a series of lanes, panels, or other barriers. You may have to set up some temporary electric fence or netting to efficiently move your livestock.

If you use electric fencing or netting be sure and train your livestock to it before you try to use it as a barrier. Contact a local farmer, your County Extension Service, or the manufacturer/seller of the electric netting or fencing for information on safe setup and use of electrified fence.

Warning! – Do *not* allow your dog to come into contact with "hot" electric fence! If livestock is present, your dog may associate the shock they receive from the fence with the livestock and develop fear of the livestock. Make sure the fencing is switched OFF before you take your dog near it! It is ***never*** a good idea for your dog to touch an electric fence!

Once you get your stock into your training paddock you can then use feed in tubs to get them into your little training pen as explained above.

Before you start

Before you start working with livestock allow your dog to explore the area, especially when going to a paddock where livestock have been held but are not present. If you allow your dog time to sniff and check out a new area they will be more relaxed than if you bring them in and immediately expect them to listen and respond to your cues. If the area is fenced such that your dog cannot escape, then turn them loose. If the area does not have a dog-tight fence, then keep your dog on a leash or long line but allow them to investigate the area to their heart's content.

Setting the stage for success

As stated earlier, when taking your dog to stock your most important job is to be the gatekeeper. You control your dog's access to livestock just as you control the *rat* when you train with a flirt pole. Unfortunately, you cannot flip the sheep, cattle, or even ducks up and out of your dog's reach at a moment's notice, like you can flip the flirt pole rat. Instead, you can use a long line to interrupt your dog when they display unwanted behavior such as lunging, chasing, or inappropriate biting.

Your dog may lunge at passing vehicles early in training. Deal with this lunging just as you would lunging at livestock; use your no reward marker and pause for 10 seconds. Work on reinforcing a non-compatible behavior such as sitting or lying down while vehicles pass nearby. Of course, all of this work is on leash!

As the gatekeeper, you control your dog's access to their highest level reinforcer – the livestock. To control access to stock, put your dog on a leash or long line *before* you open the gate to the paddock containing the livestock. Your dog will be on a leash or drag a long line until you are confident that your dog has enough self-control to perform cued behaviors fluently.

At this point, you will not be allowing your dog much access to livestock, yet you will need to upgrade the value of the food or play you will be using during the session. It's time to pull out the high-end, super high-value meat, tug, toy, or rat!

If you use both food and play around livestock, be strategic by using food if your dog is exuberant or confident and use toys if your dog is subdued or afraid. Usually, food helps a dog to calm down and play helps them to fire up!

If you do use treats, you can gauge how excited your dog is by how gently or roughly they take the treats from you. Usually, a calm dog takes treats softly and an excited dog takes them more aggressively. You can also gauge your dog's level of arousal by how they play. Are they really into it or barely engaging? You know your dog best so use that knowledge to your advantage.

The pen

The pen is one of the most important parts of setting your dog up for herding success. The pen should be made of panels that your dog can see through, yet are high and sturdy enough to keep your stock inside and your dog out. You also want a fairly small pen, just large enough to comfortably allow your livestock to turn around. The idea is to keep the livestock calm and stationary in the pen. Dogs tend to focus on prey movement and want to control or chase that movement. The less your stock move in the pen, the less distracting the stock will be to your dog. Just the sight, smell, and sound of the livestock will be a huge distraction for your dog.

The livestock

Now that you are ready to start training around livestock, which livestock is best? In Chapter 8, Tools of the trade, the discussion centered around different types of livestock and why one type might be better than another. Basically, you want to use 3 to 5 head of docile stock such as hair sheep, young wool sheep, goats, ducks, or calves. Avoid breeding age males of any species. It is ideal to have calm animals that want to stay together but will easily move off of pressure from you and your dog.

Another suggestion is to use the livestock that is handiest or easiest to get to and work. The closer and easier it is to train on livestock, the more you will tend to do it. Owning a few ducks, ones that work well for herding, might initially be better than traveling some distance to sheep and paying for their use. The more often you can take your dog to stock the better!

Another advantage of having stock close at hand is that you will tend to work more short sessions when you don't have to go very far to livestock rather than few, much longer ones.

Your dog's initial interactions with stock should be on a long line or leash, after they have displayed their ability to perform obedience behaviors within sight of stock. If your dog seems fearful or is not interested in stock you may want to allow them access, while dragging a long line, to loose stock. Often allowing some unstructured interaction with calm, non-threatening stock will trigger their herding instincts and build their interest and confidence.

*After just a few minutes loose on a long line, Alesia's dog Liz has **turned on** to the sheep and is covering, controlling and turning back a lamb that decided to break from the flock. **Turned on**, in this situation, means that her herding instinct has turned on and not that she has turned toward the sheep.*

Be extra careful to protect your dog from aggressive stock and help your dog by moving the stock for them. In this situation, you move the stock and verbally encourage your dog to interact with them. Your dog is allowed to interact in any way they feel comfortable as long as they do not chase, lunge, or bite unnecessarily.

Your dog may bark at stock. Barking at stock, for most breeds, is another sign of insecurity. Allow your dog to bark but move farther away from the stock until the barking diminishes. As your dog gains confidence the barking should fade.

Leash and long line use

A 6-foot leash and long line are means of controlling your dog's access to stock. Both should only be attached to either a flat collar or harness. Anytime you have a leash or long line on your dog, think of it as an emergency brake, not a steering mechanism or a replacement for a stop or recall. If you find yourself using the long line or leash for anything other than an emergency brake you need to add more mass to your foundation training.

The long line should be held with one hand so that if you need to turn and walk with your dog you can turn and face the direction you are walking. Extend your arm out toward your dog as you walk and try to maintain some slack in the line. You want the line to be off of the ground if you are walking with your dog. If your dog is on the outside of a cone square or circle and you are on the inside, you need the line high enough off of the ground so that it clears the cones as it passes over them.

Your dog will know you have a leash or long line on them but ideally the only time they would feel the line or leash pull tight is when they charge or lunge at the stock.

Heeling as a measure of self-control

Have your dog heel on leash as you approach the paddock gate. Most dogs will become aroused at the sight and smell of stock and may have trouble heeling. If your dog starts to pull on the leash or stops dead in their tracks, stop your approach to the gate, move farther from the paddock, and work on heeling. Your dog must maintain their self-control, as evidenced by being able to heel with you, right up to the paddock gate.

Once you get your dog up to the gate, cue a sit and shorten your 6-foot leash to 3 feet. Often you can shorten your leash by hooking the loop handle into the snap that attaches to your dog's collar or harness. Then use the large loop of the leash as your handle. Hold onto the leash the entire time your dog is around the livestock, from the time they approach the gate until they exit.

If your dog sits and waits, open the gate and go through it, having them sit just on the outside of the open gate. While still holding the leash, call your dog to you into the paddock and ask for another sit. Jackpot if your dog has successfully performed this behavior and is now sitting in front of you in the paddock! If your dog tries to break the sit and rush ahead of you toward the stock, take them back outside the gate and work coming through the gate until they can take your cues and calmly enter the paddock. You are setting the tone for all of your dog's future sessions around livestock so take your time and don't skimp on this training.

You will follow this procedure *every* time you take your dog to livestock. No exceptions! In this situation you are literally the gatekeeper. You not only control your dog's access to the stock but are setting them up to calmly take your cues and be responsive around livestock.

If you are changing to a long line you would do so at this point by attaching the long line first and then removing your leash. You must always maintain control of your dog to prevent them from practicing unwanted inherently reinforcing behaviors. The leash or long line allows you to quickly and easily interrupt lunging or other undesirable behaviors.

Open the gate and begin …

With stock in a small pen and your dog on a leash or long line, you are ready to start transitioning your obedience skills to stock. Once you enter the paddock your dog will always either be with you, tied up, or crated. After the initial foray to explore the paddock your dog will always be engaged in training with you or stationed at a distance from the livestock where they can relax or at least remain relatively calm.

A good way to calm your dog when they are tied or crated away from livestock is to drop a handful of treats on the ground or in their crate. It is ideal to tie your dog and drop treats in the grass in front of them. The only behaviors your dog must perform to earn the treats are to be stationary and quiet. You can also use this technique anytime you are working around stock to calm your dog. Dropping a handful of treats in the grass while your dog is stationary encourages them to scent out the treats, which has a calming effect on your dog.

Your goal when taking your dog to livestock is to keep everyone safe and protect your dog's confidence. If your dog shows any fear do *not* let them approach too close to the penned stock until they show more confidence. Let your dog tell you how close they want to approach the livestock.

Although stock is safe in a small pen, they still may feel threatened by the approach of your dog and ram the pen. Be cautious and initially avoid getting your dog too close to the pen, especially if your dog lacks confidence.

Eventually you want your dog to be able to heel, sit, down, stand, recall, and perform all obedience behaviors near livestock. Heeling around livestock, on and then off-leash, is a great way to gauge both your dog's self-control and the level of distraction provided by the livestock.

Watch Sir heel with sheep across a fence at https://www.youtube.com/watch?v=b1aachoYY7I&feature=youtu.be

---

Initially keep your sessions around livestock short, only 3 to 5 minutes in length. Then take a break. Start with sit, down, stand, or tricks at a good distance from stock and when successful, move on to heeling and a few recalls off of stock. Working around livestock is stressful for most dogs, especially the first few times. If you do a lot of work around stock with your obedience behaviors, heeling, and recalls your dog is going to be much better prepared to move successfully into herding behaviors when you get to that point.

Here I am using a long line while working on obedience behaviors near cattle. On this recall I allow Sir to hook up to the cattle and then call him while keeping the tug hidden.
I have treats in the bowl on the crate for working stationary behaviors such as stand, sit, and down.

Even when your dog is doing well, be sure to take breaks and give them a chance to relax and decompress. Just watching stock is mentally taxing for herding dogs because they are constantly reading the stock by watching movement and their instincts are strongly telling them to react to that movement. Multiple short sessions are far more productive than one long training session.

Your demeanor in the paddock

There is a lot to keep in mind when you are working with your dog around stock. It is important to remember that your level of excitement will influence your dog's level of arousal. Stay as calm as possible; take a break if you get excited or frustrated. There is no way your dog will be relaxed if you are tense and breathing quickly and shallowly.

Don't yell, even if your dog charges the pen and tries to bite the stock through the panels. Yelling only increases your dog's arousal and sustains their attack. Instead, grab the long line, calmly tow your dog back away from the livestock, and give your dog a short time-out.

Also, remember to keep your cues calm and of course, do *not* repeat cues if your dog doesn't take them the first time cued.

Many people do not realize that they lean toward their dog when they cue behaviors. Leaning over your dog puts a lot of pressure on them and instead of helping them be successful, promotes failure. Stand up straight and give your dog space rather than crowding them. Have confidence in your dog!

In the pictures of the recall of Sir off of cattle, you can see that I leaned toward him as I gave my verbal cue. That picture shows the high value of video. I had no idea I was leaning when I recalled Sir. Because he was focused on the cattle he was not reading my body language, but my bending at the waist definitely could overshadow my verbal cue at other times.

Reading your dog

Some ways to read your dog are by how they take food or how willing they are to tug or play when they are around livestock. There are other body language cues that you can use to understand how confident your dog is around stock.

NOTE All breeds do *not* display the exact same body language, especially in regards to tail carriage.

Key body language indicators

- *Tail position* – If your dog's tail is held high, out straight, or over their back, they are indicating a lack of confidence and may act erratically.
- *Muscle tension* – A dog that moves stiffly, shivers, bounces or paddles feet, or shows other signs of muscle tension is overly aroused.
- *Hook up to stock* – If your dog does not look at the stock, it usually indicates avoidance due to fear or possibly no interest in the stock.
- *Zoomies* – If your dog stresses high, meaning they become very active when highly aroused, they may exhibit quick, jerky behaviors such as running in circles.
- *Freezing* – If your dog freezes they may be overly aroused yet their behavior may slow down or stop such that they move in slow motion or stand and stare.

In border collies their tail carriage is probably the best indicator of their mental state and one of the most important. Around livestock, the tail position you want to see is down but not tucked under the body. We call this a workmanlike tail position and it indicates your dog is able to think and process information. Your dog may start with their tail down but raise it as they begin to move fast or approach stock. When your dog's tail goes up it is a red flag telling you to stop and take a break. If your dog is showing any signs of over-arousal they need time and distance from stock to calm themselves. You want your dog to be confident and relaxed around stock.

While hooked up, 4-month-old Sir's tail carriage is down, his muscles are tense, and he is frozen. He is balanced on his feet, neither leaning forward nor backward, showing interest but not fear.
When a dog's tail goes up, they are usually going to behave erratically, often charging the livestock.

If you need to take breaks often to calm your dog, then consider sitting in a lawn chair and watching the penned stock while your dog chills out on a long line. You can mark and treat any relaxing of tense behavior, including standing still, sitting, lying down, lying down and rolling onto a hip, flicking an ear in your direction, turning their head toward you, coming over to you, or any other behavior that indicates they are calming down. By sitting down you will relax and encourage your dog to calm themselves.

If your dog starts bouncing, pacing, lunging, or displaying other inherently reinforcing high-arousal behaviors, interrupt them by bringing them back to you with the long line. Once they are close to you throw a big handful of treats in the grass next to you to encourage your dog to scent out the treats, which tends to lower arousal. Just having you close can calm your insecure dog and build their confidence. You may want to use a leash when you begin sitting down to keep your dog closer to you.

If your dog still cannot relax, move yourself and your dog farther away from the livestock. Once your dog can relax, move incrementally closer to the penned livestock to build relaxed confidence. Most likely, your dog will need several days or weeks to approach the penned stock.

Round robin recalls

A good way to transition from obedience to herding behaviors is by using your recall to call your dog around the paddock with stock in a small pen in the center. Both you and your dog will stay on the outside perimeter of the fenced area to start and your dog will be on a long line. Hold the long line until your dog demonstrates that they will readily come to you. At that point, you can allow your dog to drag the long line.

First, I call Sir from near the tree in the corner of the paddock. (I am no longer using a long line.)

Next, I move farther away from the tree and recall Sir. The recall has increased from 8 feet to about 15 feet. I can also move around the perimeter of the small paddock while keeping the recall distance the same and eventually I will recall Sir from the other side of the sheep.

Can your dog come to you if you move 3 feet away from them? How about 8 feet? Can your dog come to you when you are on the opposite side of the paddock such that they have to recall around the sheep to get to you?

Next, move closer to the sheep and call your dog in to you. Once they come in to you pick up the long line but keep slack in it, step to the fence, and call them back away from the livestock. This exercise's main purpose is to build *your* confidence in your dog. When you are confident your dog will come to you no matter where you or they are in relation to the stock and your dog can heel fluently and/or perform their obedience behaviors within 3 feet of the livestock in the pen, you are ready to start working on herding behaviors.

Building fluency of your obedience behaviors near livestock is critical foundation work for herding. Everyone is anxious to move on to the more sexy herding behaviors but your dog's success depends on a rock-solid obedience foundation.

As soon as you get your obedience behaviors trained, transition them to livestock. In the meantime, move on to teaching your dog their herding skills away from livestock. Once you have taken your obedience skills to stock and your dog is showing amazing self-control you will be ready to introduce their herding skills to livestock.

If you lay a strong foundation, by working your obedience behaviors around livestock until your dog has the ability to quickly and precisely perform these behaviors when cued, your dog will have leaped the first major hurdle that stands between them and becoming a capable herding dog!

Next, we will address putting herding skills on your dog in the comfort of your home. To start, let's look at the stop.

CHAPTER 14

Herding RAMs – Stop

Basic herding skills include stop, in/back, directionals, flanks, out/close, and easy/hurry. Each behavior, or set of behaviors, will have its own chapter in order to do it justice. To start, let's look at training *there* or stop.

Introduction to stop

I use *there* as my cue for stop. **Stop** means come to an immediate stop, don't move any paws, and stay stopped. The dog should remain stationary in a sit, down, or stand, until given another cue. Depending if you have a forward- or sideways-moving dog the struggle will be either for your dog to stop or to move into stock after stopping. Forward-moving dogs like to apply pressure to their stock and sideways-moving dogs like to flank around their stock. Both types of dogs want to control their stock but their instincts manifest in different ways.

A solid stop is one of the most important herding skills. You need your dog to stop and stay stopped when asked, no matter what the livestock is doing. This will be especially hard for your dog if you are allowing the stock to move away such that your dog perceives that they are losing control of the livestock. Allowing stock to escape is a real test of your dog's self-control!

*A **down** can be used as a stop and is usually easier to teach than a stop. The advantage of a stop behavior over a down is that your dog can remain in the position that is most comfortable for them. If your dog tends to clap and remain down when asked to move you may want to opt for teaching a standing stop.*

Sally says

I was quite tempted to teach a standing stop and in fact started teaching it along with a down stop, using different cues. But I found that I was much more inclined to let my criteria slip with a standing stop. On the first day I allowed the dog to take an extra step, by the third day it was half-a-dozen steps and pretty soon it had deteriorated to a slow down. So although I have a moderately useful "there" cue, in a trial I would only use the "lie down" stop which was more precise (not perfect, just less bad than the stand!).

To teach the stop I use a flirt pole. The stop can be taught using treats or other toys such as tugs and balls but I like a flirt pole because I can control my dog's access to the reinforcement of the "rat". The **rat** is the toy at the end of the flirt pole.

Flirt pole training
Before you start
Using a flirt pole is easy but it takes a bit of practice to place the rat where you want it. Practice without your dog around. Put a couple of targets on the ground, such as large bowls or hula-hoops, and practice until you can wing the rat onto the targets with confidence while using either hand on the flirt pole handle.

Practice with your flirt pole until you can hit a target with either hand. The goal is for the rat to hit the target, a metal bowl.

Your dog also needs to tug and release a tug or toy in order to use a flirt pole. If your dog will not tug or won't release the tug on cue, you need to get those behaviors in place before using a flirt pole. I use *mine* as the cue for my dog to drop or release the tug. The release cue will become important when you eventually teach the bite. If you don't know how to teach a release cue look ahead to teaching the bite in Chapter 21, Herding RAMs – Out and close.

PHASE 1 – Grip and release tug

You may use a toy or treats to teach the stop but the flirt pole gives you much more control over your dog's access to the reinforcer. It more closely simulates prey because you can move the rat and have it "come alive".

Placement of the rat, ball, or tug is important! You want the placement of your reinforcer to help you in your training, so precise placement is essential. Be sure to practice throwing any reinforcer that you plan to throw in training.

The small Tail Teasers flirt pole comes with two toys included. When you make your own larger and longer flirt pole with a lunge whip, from a farm store, you will need to come up with your own toy or rat. I like a toy that is long and narrow with a bit of weight to it so it is easy to whip around with accuracy. The rats I use look like a squirrel tail or a furry mouse.

The nearly worn out "rats". The rats take a lot of abuse so be sure to use toys that will stand up to frequent, intense tugging.

Flirt pole instructions

While learning to handle the flirt pole and the cues that go with it, practice *without* your dog. Hold the flirt pole with the handle in one hand and the rat in the other. As you move the handle with one hand, drop the rat. The rat should fly through the air and land where you want it to. Put out targets and practice until you can easily whip the rat to the target you choose. Then switch hands and hold the handle in your

Here I am whipping the rat off of the ground and into my free hand. Practice this with both hands as it is an essential skill for flirt pole work.

other hand. Again practice until you can easily whip the rat to the desired target. Also, practice whipping the rat from the ground into your free hand. Again switch hands and practice whipping the rat from the ground into your other hand.

While it is easy to handle a short flirt pole with precision, it is much more challenging to place the rat of a long flirt pole exactly where you want it. Use your long flirt pole outside unless you have a big room with a high ceiling. Be sure to practice with targets and your large flirt pole too. It is even more important to practice with both hands to gain control of the larger, more unwieldy flirt pole. Besides hitting a target on the floor it is essential that you also practice bringing the rat back into your free hand. If your dog tries to grab the rat before you want them to, you need to be able to remove it before they can get it. Practice this with both flirt poles using both hands.

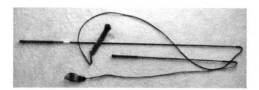

The larger flirt pole is a lunge whip, available at farm stores, with a toy added to the end and the smaller one is a Tail Teaser, available on Amazon.

I like using a flirt pole because I can have complete control of my dog's access to reinforcement. If I ask my dog to stop and they continue moving toward the prey, I can whip the rat away before they can get there, thus preventing them from gaining reinforcement. I only wish I could do the same thing with sheep!

Another key part of using a flirt pole is moving the rat to increase arousal. Prey moves so once your dog can perform cued behaviors while the rat lies still you need to ramp up the arousal by making the rat dance or run. Can your dog listen and respond now?

If your dog is not interested in the flirt pole, try whipping the rat along the ground in front of your dog. Most dogs cannot resist chasing escaping prey so have the rat run away from your dog, moving it quickly and erratically. Fast, sweeping rat movement can usually be used to get your dog into the game.

The tricky part of using a flirt pole, to train the stop, is not the physical manipulation of it but the timing of the verbals you use in the training. I use a verbal marker, such as *yes*, but the marker does *not* release my dog to get the rat. You also need to have or train a release cue. I use *free* as my release cue for most training but when using a flirt pole I use *get it*. The release cue tells your dog they have permission to grab the rat. Don't end a flirt pole training session with the release cue *get it*. Instead, use *that'll do* or some other cue to tell your dog they are done working. You want your dog to learn that they will not get the prey/stock when done working.

Practice using your flirt pole verbal cues *without* your dog. It takes time to get used to handling the flirt pole and giving the correct cues. The more consistent you are with your cues the easier it will be for your dog to learn them.

Using *get it* as a release for your dog to grab the rat also puts the foundation in place for your dog to "get a bite". All dogs should have a bite on cue and be reinforced for biting to protect themselves. Biting is your dog's only self-defense. A confident dog usually does not need to bite but having a bite bolsters confidence. Never punish your dog for biting, if aggressively challenged by stock, and instead reinforce the bite with tons of verbal praise.

I use yes *as my marker when training so that I can mark wanted behavior without releasing my dog to bite or lunge at the stock. If your marker releases your dog to the reinforcer, train a new marker that is not a release to use while herding, a keep going signal. Some people use* **yes** *as a marker and a releaser and* **good** *as a keep going signal, a marker that is not also a releaser.*

Flirt pole verbals
- A *cue* (*there*) tells the dog what behavior to perform to earn reinforcement.
- A *marker* (*yes*) tells the dog they performed the correct behavior and reinforcement is coming.
- A *releaser* (*get it*) tells the dog they may grab the rat, the reinforcer.
- An end of session *marker* (*that'll do*) tells the dog the session is over and the rat is not available.

Thus, yes *becomes a keep going signal in herding. It tells the dog they are correct and heading toward reinforcement but they have not been given permission to seize reinforcement. Often in herding, reinforcement is in the form of allowing the dog to continue interacting with the livestock.*

The reason it is important to *not* use your marker as the release to get the rat is that the rat is the prey. When you go to livestock the sheep or cattle are the prey. Since your dog will grab, bite, and tug on the rat you do not want your dog to bite the stock when you mark a correctly performed behavior.

An example would be when your dog is walking in to sheep. Maybe you have had some difficulty getting your dog to not rush and instead come in with a nice steady pace. Your dog gives you some nice walking in without rushing so you want to mark that behavior. If your dog is used to being released by your *yes* to bite the rat they may rush forward and bite the sheep! By keeping the two cues separate you have a way to mark your dog without releasing them to grab the reinforcer.

Your use of verbal releasers and markers are of the utmost importance when using a flirt pole. If you are consistent you can have your dog walking in toward the rat, mark that behavior (yes), and your dog will wait until you give your release cue (get it) before they grab the rat. Watch Sir wait for "get it" at https://www.youtube.com/watch?v=4R6_KgaOOj0&feature=youtu.be

If your dog is not very aggressive this might seem like nitpicking but if your dog is somewhat aggressive or a bit fearful, they may well go after the stock when marked, if you have not trained them to wait for a release cue. Using these two different verbal cues makes your training crystal clear to you and your dog. Although you may see the rat and livestock as completely different, your dog sees them both as prey.

After you become familiar with handling the flirt pole, be sure and practice using your marker and releaser. Consistency makes all the difference. If you give the cues consistently your dog will respond to them likewise. Once you are confident handling the flirt pole and giving your marker and release cues, bring your dog into the picture. To introduce your dog to the flirt pole, use the smaller flirt pole, put your cones away, and get out a timer.

Flirt pole use – Step by step
1. Set the timer for 5 minutes.
2. Flip the rat onto the floor.
3. Immediately give your release cue (*get it*).
4. If your dog does not go and grab the rat, use the flirt pole handle to move it, and make it seem to come alive. Get excited: verbally encourage your dog to grab it!

5. Once your dog grabs the rat let them tug for a moment while you hold the flirt pole handle.
6. Ask your dog to release the rat just as you would a tug.
7. Repeat this 5 times.
8. Take a break!

This should be a fun, fast-paced game! Most dogs behave as if the rat is a live squirrel and this level of intensity is the closest you can get to having a sheep on the end of your flirt pole!

The first step in flirt pole training is getting your dog to engage with the rat. To get Sir interested initially I made the rat "run" along the ground away from him and the movement of the prey kicked in his instinct to chase and grab. To keep your dog engaged, be sure to allow plenty of tugging time as reinforcement.

Troubleshooting

- ***Dog is afraid of the rat*** – If your dog is fearful of the rat, take it off of the flirt pole and use it as a tug. Then put it on a string, pull it quickly *away* from your dog, and get your dog to tug again. Finally, you should be able to put the rat back on the flirt pole and start training the exercise.

- ***Dog is reluctant to get the rat after it has been whipped back into your hand*** – If your dog becomes concerned when the rat flies off the floor into your hand, then you will need to encourage your dog to get the rat once it is on the floor again. Excite your dog by moving the rat quickly along the floor a bit to build some arousal in your dog. Arousal is the best antidote for fear.

- ***Dog isn't into flirt poles*** – If after a valiant attempt over several days, you decide your dog just won't interact with the flirt pole rat, you can move forward using a thrown tug, ball, or treat. The disadvantage of using these reinforcers is that you cannot physically control your dog's access to them.

Renn always seemed afraid of a flirt pole and I can't say I ever got the hang of it either, so in the end I used a toy on a string (paracord is light and strong) which suited us both a lot better.

After your dog is familiar with the rules of when they can get the rat, you can move outdoors to teach the stop. It is best to teach the stop outside with the long flirt pole because you have more room to flip the rat into the air at a height that will discourage your dog from leaping at it as it flies overhead.

Keep the rat near or on the ground unless you are quickly flipping it back into your free hand. When the rat is off of the ground you may find your dog jumping to grab it, which can lead to injury. Be careful!

The position of the stop is at the dog's discretion, however they are most comfortable. If you stop your dog and they have to wait in place they may change position as long as they remain stationary. If you decide to use a stand or down for your stop, follow the directions below substituting the down or stand criteria and cue.

Stop
THE RULES

1. *Goal* – The goal is for your dog to stop immediately when cued and hold position until given another cue. They may choose to stand, sit, or lie down while stopped.
2. *When to begin teaching* – Start teaching the stop as soon as you are familiar with handling, and your dog is into playing with, the flirt pole.
3. *When to move on* – You will teach the stop with the flirt pole outside and then use other exercises such as throwing a tug and having your dog stop before they get to it or on the way back with it to generalize the stop.
4. *Appropriate environment* – An outside fenced area is a good place to start with the longer flirt pole.
5. *Setting up the environment* – If your dog is into playing with the flirt pole you will not need to worry too much about distractions. Most dogs find the flirt pole rat as fixating as live prey.
6. *What props are needed* – Use your long flirt pole.
7. *Criteria in one sentence* – When cued the dog stops immediately and remains stopped, no paw movement, until given another cue.

8. ***Reinforcement to use*** – Use the flirt pole rat.
9. ***Cue to use*** – I use *there*.
10. ***When to add the cue*** – The cue will be added as soon as your dog stops and holds the stop until cued to get the rat.

THE MECHANICS

1. ***Your position*** – Start facing your dog with the flirt pole handle in one hand and the rat in the other.
2. ***Your dog's position*** – Your dog will be facing you.
3. ***What is marked*** – The stop, all four feet stationary, is marked with *yes*.
4. ***How and where the reinforcement will be delivered*** – Your dog will go and grab the rat, the reinforcer, when you release them with *get it*.
5. ***How to grow the behavior*** – Besides moving to different locations you will want to ask your dog to stop when going to get or bring back a thrown tug or ball, when they are heeling beside you while you continue walking or running, occasionally during recalls, and eventually while flanking and walking in to stock.
6. ***When to practice without your dog*** – Because of the use of both a marker and a release cue, you need to practice until you are confident and comfortable with all of the mechanics.

Watch the video (on page 186) of Sir working stop with the flirt pole. Pay particular attention to the use of the marker and release words. (Note in this video that I omitted the yes cue.) If you are consistent your dog will quickly learn the game. Watching the video will give you a better feel for what the final behavior looks like.

A correct stop is a weight shift from your dog's front end onto their rear end. You want your dog to lean backward as they stop not coast or glide into the stop.

Stop – Step by step
PHASE 1 – Getting the stop

1. Stand outside facing your dog while holding the longer flirt pole with one hand holding the handle and one the rat.
2. Flip the rat onto the ground about 6 feet in front of your dog.
3. As your dog moves toward the rat, and they may move very quickly so be ready, flip the rat off of the ground and back over your dog's head and onto the ground behind them before they can grab the rat. You don't want to say anything to your dog at this stage of training. You want to flip the rat high above your dog's head

so that they do not attempt to leap up and grab the rat as it passes over them. If they jump and twist they can hurt themselves.

4. Your dog should immediately turn around 180° and attempt to grab the rat again.

5. Keep flying the rat high over your dog's head and landing it behind them until they stop trying to get it and stand still.

6. The moment your dog stops, release them to the rat with *get it*. Tug with your dog and reset them for the next trial.

7. Repeat this several more times and grow the time your dog waits for the release until your dog is waiting 5 seconds for you to release them to get the rat.

---

8. When your dog stops on the next trial, mark the stop with *yes*, but do **not** say *get it* this time.

9. If your dog holds the stop, give your release cue *get it* and allow them to grab the rat, tug, and reset.

10. If your dog releases on *yes*, whip the rat high over their head and repeat step 8 until your dog holds the stop when marked and then release them to the rat with *get it*.

11. When your dog is consistently waiting for the release cue *get it*, after the mark *yes*, celebrate and take a long break.

The rat does not have to touch the ground in order to be flipped away from your dog. In fact you want to re-loft the rat as soon as you see your dog starting forward to grab it. The rat may only get within a yard of the ground before you need to flip it back up and away from your dog.

At first, Sir charges the rat as soon as it lands. As he approaches the rat I whip it high into the air and bring it down behind him. Note in the middle picture the rat is almost at the top of the picture.

You can start this training with a young dog, but you want to have very short sessions and avoid twisting and jumping to get the rat.

ABOVE: Again I whip the rat over Sir's head as he charges toward it.

RIGHT ABOVE: Finally, Sir stops so I immediately give the release cue (get it) and he is allowed to run and grab the rat. Once he was stopping I added the marker (yes) and continued using my release cue. I was not using my stop cue (there) at this point.

Initially, you will release your dog if they stand still while the rat hits the ground. Work up to having your dog stand still 5 seconds before you release them to get the rat, with *get it*, and then introduce your *yes* marker to the exercise. By the end of this session, your dog should be waiting up to 5 seconds after being marked until you give them the release cue to get the rat. No cheating!

Your dog must be able to stand for 5 seconds after the mark and wait for your release cue before you add the stop cue.

Troubleshooting

- **Dog gives up** – If your dog gives up trying to get the rat, go back to playing with the flirt pole as you would a tug and build more value for the rat.
- **Dog gives up** – Sometimes a dog will get discouraged if you are not consistent with your use of the marker and release word. If this happens, go back to practicing without your dog until you get your mechanics perfected.
- **Dog leaps into the air** – Be sure and use your longer flirt pole and practice flipping the rat high into the air. The rat does not have to land very far behind your dog, so work on height, rather than the length, of the rat's flight.
- **Dog gets the rat before released** – If your dog beats you a time or two, they will work a lot longer to get the rat. Be ready to re-loft the rat the moment it comes down as most dogs will not wait for the rat to land before going after it.

Safety first! Pull the rat quickly skyward to keep your dog from leaping after the rat to avoid injury.

Phase 2 – Adding the cue

1. Once you have a solid stop, start to say your cue, *there*, as you flip the rat onto the ground.
2. If your dog stops, mark with *yes* and then release with *get it*.
3. If your dog takes the word *there* as a release cue, loft the rat and land it behind them.
4. Repeat until your dog is not releasing on *there*.

---

5. Now flip the rat as far in front of your dog as possible while saying *there* as you do it. You want to extend the distance between your dog and the rat in front of them. Your dog should stop and wait, if not re-loft the rat until they stop and wait when you say *there*.
6. When your dog stops when cued *there*, mark with *yes,* and tell your dog to *get it*.
7. As soon as your dog starts toward the rat, because you gave your release word *get it*, say *there*. The sooner you catch your dog in motion the better.
8. If your dog stops a second time, mark with *yes* and immediately tell them to *get it*, tug, and reset.
9. If your dog ignores the stop cue, loft the rat and start again.
10. Repeat until your dog will stop and hold the stop on their way to get the rat *after* being released to the rat.

---

11. An **alternative** to releasing your dog to the rat is for you to flip the rat back to your dog while they are stopped. Give the release cue just as the rat flies back to them. Doing this reinforces the stop in place and builds mass for remaining stationary. Then tug and reset.
12. Randomly release your dog to grab the rat and to fly it back to them. Remember to always use your release cue *get it* in both situations. Always tug and reset after your dog earns the rat!
13. Take a break and celebrate!

You now have a cued stop on your dog! Play this game with your dog until your dog will stop when they are just about to grab the rat. Then play it until your dog will run right up to the rat, wait only inches from it for the release cue, before they will grab the rat. If you are consistent you will be amazed how quickly they will get to this point!

Go back to Phase 1 for a while if you notice your dog slowing down as they move forward to grab the rat. Once your dog is back up to squirrel chasing speed, start working Phase 2 again.

As a challenge, in a different environment, attach a leash to your dog's flat collar or harness. While they are standing facing you, give your stop cue and then put light pressure on the leash. Does your dog shift their weight back against your pull to hold the stop or do they move forward into the pull? No moving forward!

This is a fun, fun game! Most dogs love chasing squirrels and this is as close as you can get to that in training.

Troubleshooting
- ***Dog gives up trying to get the rat*** – If your dog pauses when released or quits trying to get the rat, go back to Phase 1 until they get back into the game. Until your dog learns that they will eventually get the rat, they may become frustrated and not want to play. Don't wait until your dog quits playing to go back to Phase 1!
- ***Dog won't wait for the release cue when close to the rat*** – If your dog usually does well waiting for the release cue but not when they are close to the rat, you need to be really quick flipping the rat out of their grasp so they cannot self-reinforce by grabbing it when no release cue is given.

Generalizing the stop
Eventually, you will introduce the stop into cone square or cone circle training, which will be introduced in Chapter 19, Flanks 1. For now, generalize the stop in every way you can think of to build mass on it in highly distracting situations. Especially work the stop when your dog is aroused, such as when they are rocketing toward a thrown toy, coming on a recall, or running with other dogs. You can further generalize the stop during fast heeling by asking your dog to stop while you continue forward and during any other game you can imagine.

You definitely want to work the stop around livestock but be sure to start with your dog on a long line to restrict their access to the livestock. Also have the stock in a small pen to limit their movement since moving stock is much more arousing than standing stock.

As you generalize the stop be sure to maintain your criteria. Most dogs will start to cheat at some point by moving one paw slightly, so initially deliver the reinforcer to them. Can you tempt your dog to take a step forward by slowing down your treat delivery? Your dog *must* keep all four paws stationary until you release them to move with either *get it*, a general release cue such as *free*, *okay*, or *break*, or another cue

As Sir recalls to me I ask for a stop.

such as *in*. Be on the lookout for your dog gliding into the stop, stopping slowly, or adding steps after they have stopped. Criteria, criteria, criteria!

 *Eventually, you will be using* in *or a flank cue as a reinforcer for the stop, depending on which behavior your dog finds most inherently reinforcing. Don't start reinforcing the stop with an* in *until your stops are super solid or you may find your dog starting to "coast" through the stop in anticipation of the* in *cue.*

Once your dog knows stop, you can switch to your small flirt pole and work stops inside, if you want. *Don't* start inside because you will not be able to flip the rat high enough to discourage your dog jumping up to get it. By the time you go back to using the smaller flirt pole your dog will already have learned how to gain reinforcement and will not be nearly as tempted to leap.

Usually, you cannot do too much practice stopping your dog. If you keep things fast and fun your dog should be able to stop around higher and higher levels of distraction until they finally have a solid stop around livestock.

Now that your dog has a stop, you can begin to work on the *walk in*. You will again be using your flirt pole and your stop will come in handy. Working on *in* with the flirt pole gives you a chance to further generalize the stop and have great fun doing it.

Now that your dog can stop on cue it is time to get them moving!

CHAPTER 15

Herding RAMs – In

In is the cued behavior that brings your dog directly toward the stock and makes it possible for you to cue your dog to drive livestock. Many variations are used to cue the in such as *walk in, get in, get up, in,* and *walk up.* **In** means your dog should walk directly into the stock and move the entire group of animals in a straight line. The line is determined by where you ask your dog in and where the stock is. The stock should move off in the direction from which your dog approached them and your dog should hold that line, flanking as needed to maintain the line, until given another cue.

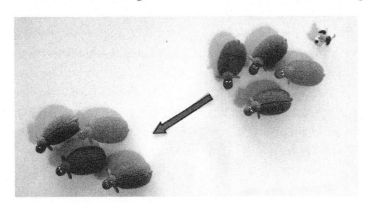

This is correct driving. The dog is holding the sheep on line. With practice, most dogs learn to hold the line and will automatically flank or lean, to keep the stock on line. Some dogs are particularly adept at holding a line and are called "line dogs".

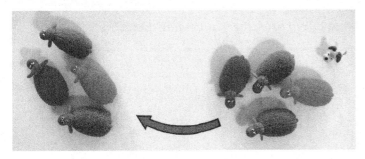

This dog is not holding the line and is allowing the sheep to get off line to the right. Since the dog is not correcting the line, the handler would step in and cue away to me *to flank the dog and put the sheep back on line.*

When driving a few head of livestock, your dog should not need to weave or flank back and forth behind them. If you are driving a large herd or flock, your dog will have to flank from side to side to tuck the corners and keep the group together and moving forward. In is a very handy behavior for your dog to know. You can use in to fetch, drive, move stock into a pen, barn, corral, or chute, or to hold livestock to you so that you can catch one, if need be. We will re-visit in when we get to advanced herding skills and go into much more detail about driving. For now, we will concentrate on teaching your dog to apply pressure by moving directly toward the stock.

If you have a forward-moving dog, *walk in* is usually easy to teach. If you have a sideways-moving dog, your dog may struggle with this behavior. It all depends on how comfortable your dog is moving toward livestock and applying pressure. Just because a dog is more comfortable flanking than walking in does not necessarily mean that one type of dog has less presence or power than the other.

If your dog happens to be afraid of livestock, try herding groups of 5 to 10 ducks, lambs, or kids (baby goats) to grow their confidence. You want livestock that moves freely and will not challenge your dog.

Presence is the ability of the dog to project self-assurance to the livestock and be readily noticed by them. **Power** is the confidence a dog projects such that the stock will be reluctant to challenge your dog. Presence and power are closely related. The main difference is that a dog may have presence and seem confident and at ease around livestock but may not stand up to stock that offers resistance by not moving away from or coming toward the dog. A dog with power usually also has presence but will readily stand up to and maintain eye contact with resistant stock. A powerful dog will bite if need be but usually doesn't have to, as the livestock read that the dog will not back down *and* the dog allows the stock time and space to retreat.

I believe that power is the most important trait a herding dog can possess!

To train the *in* we will go back to using our flirt pole. Since your dog is an old hand at flirt pole training, because of teaching the stop, you can start with either the small or large flirt pole.

In

Before you start – Flirt pole training

If you did *not* use the flirt pole to teach the stop, you will need to go back and learn how to use it before you begin teaching the *walk in*. If you are familiar with handling the flirt pole and have a solid stop or down on cue you are good to go!

If you are new to flirt pole training or haven't done it in a while, review the use of your marker and release cue protocol before starting to train the in. See flirt pole instructions and flirt pole use – step by step in Chapter 14.

You have to mark moving feet when training the in or you will end up with a standing dog!

The Rules

1. *Goal* – The goal is for your dog to walk directly in toward stock and apply pressure.
2. *When to begin teaching* – Start working on the in as soon as you have a solid stop (down or stand) on cue.
3. *When to move on* – I teach the in using a flirt pole and transition straight to stock.
4. *Appropriate environment* – Start training in a room or a fenced outside area.
5. *Setting up the environment* – Make sure the environment is safe and your dog has room to move around freely.
6. *What props are needed* – Use either the small or large flirt pole.
7. *Criteria in one sentence* – When cued the dog starts walking forward toward the stock and continues moving until given another cue.
8. *Reinforcement to use* – Use the flirt pole rat.
9. *Cue to use* – I use *walk in*, sometimes shortened to just *in*.
10. *When to add the cue* – You will start with a verbal prompt such as *let's go* and change it to *walk in* when your dog is reliably walking in after being prompted.

The Mechanics

1. *Your position* – Start parallel to your dog with the flirt pole handle in one hand and the rat in the other. You and your dog face the same direction.
2. *Your dog's position* – Your dog is standing parallel to you, slightly off to one side, and about 3 feet behind you.
3. *What is marked* – Initially, mark your dog taking a step forward. Then shape your dog to take more steps by withholding the mark. Ping-pong how many steps you ask for before marking to avoid constantly making it more difficult for your dog.

4. ***How and where the reinforcement will be delivered*** – Your dog will go forward and grab the rat, the reinforcer, when you release them with *get it*.
5. ***How to grow the behavior*** – You will grow this behavior by reinforcing your dog for starting forward when cued and then for walking farther and farther, until another cue is given.
6. ***When to practice without your dog*** – If you are comfortable using your marker and release cue you should not need to practice without your dog.

Study the video example (see link below) to get an idea of what you want your dog to do before you try a training session. Make sure your dog is engaged with, hooked up to, and willing to grab, the flirt pole rat before you begin training the in behavior.

Watch puppy Sir's introduction to a flirt pole in https://youtu.be/kA90NgsVSmc

In – Step by step
PHASE 1 – Getting movement
1. Stand facing the same direction as your dog while holding the flirt pole.
2. Your dog should be facing the same direction that you are but off to one side and 3 feet behind you.
3. Flip the rat out 6 feet in front of your dog.
4. Encourage your dog forward with the prompt *let's go* or other release cue.
5. When your dog takes a step forward toward the rat mark with *yes* and release them to the rat with *get it*.
6. Tug with your dog and reset.
7. Repeat marking one step forward 3 times. Then withhold your mark for two steps.

---

8. Start ping-ponging the number of steps you ask for before marking until you get up to 10 steps. You may have to drag the rat forward on the ground to make room for your dog to walk 10 steps forward. If your dog tries to grab the rat when it starts to move, flip it back into your hand and start again.

---

9. Start walking forward dragging the rat off to the side and in front of your dog as your dog walks forward.
10. Now work the same exercise with you on the other side of your dog.
11. Take a break!

At this point, your dog should be freely walking forward, not pausing or stuttering. When you start to move the rat forward away from your dog they may freeze, lunge forward, keep walking, or slow down. All of these are normal reactions to the prey coming alive or moving. Be ready to fly the rat back into your free hand if your dog reacts in any manner other than continuing to walk forward.

It shouldn't take long until you are able to start walking forward as your dog walks in.

In his first outside training session, I was able to start walking forward with Sir. Be sure to work the in with your dog on both sides of you.

Watch out for your dog getting sticky, slowing down significantly, when the rat starts moving. Mark moving feet! Mark while your dog is moving freely. Don't be afraid to withhold a mark or use your no reward marker and 10-second pause if your dog gets sticky. In the long run, it is easier to slow a dog down than speed them up.

Troubleshooting

- ***Dog gets stuck when rat moves*** – If your dog freezes or slows down significantly when the rat moves, give your no reward marker, flip the rat back into your hand, and pause 10 seconds. Then reset and try again. After a few tries your dog should be able to take a confident step or two forward, so be ready to mark, release, and have a rat tug party!

- ***Dog lunges at stationary rat*** – If your dog dives for the rat while it is stationary, whip it back into your hand, pause for 10 seconds, and reset. After a few reps your dog may walk forward, in which case continue with the exercise. If your dog instead becomes stuck standing, then encourage them by softly prompting *let's go*. Once your dog takes a step or two forward be ready to mark, release, and have a rat tug party!

- **Dog lunges when rat moves** – If your dog dives for the rat when it starts moving, be ready to whip it back into your hand before your dog can get to it. You have to be focused and on your toes especially during training with a moving rat!
- **Dog is sticky** – Dogs get slower and more cautious as they get closer to prey or as prey moves. If you have trouble with your dog being sticky when walking in, try to allow more distance between them and the rat: start with more distance between your dog and the rat. It is normal for your dog to slow down as they approach prey.

PHASE 2 – Getting distance

1. Stand facing the same direction as your dog while holding the flirt pole.
2. Your dog should be facing the same direction as you but off to one side and 3 feet behind you.
3. Flip the rat out 15 feet in front of your dog. (Use your long flirt pole.)
4. Encourage your dog forward with the prompt *let's go*.
5. If your dog starts forward as soon as you say *let's go* and keeps walking steadily along toward the rat for about 10 feet, or two thirds of the distance to the rat, then mark and release to the rat. Tug and reset.

---

6. If your dog starts forward as soon as you say *let's go* but stops before they get two thirds of the way to the rat, give your no reward marker, flip the rat back into your hand, and pause 10 seconds. Reset your dog to try again.
7. If your dog gets stuck partway to the rat, note where that is and mark, release, and tug a step or two before that spot on the next trial.
8. Shape your dog to walk all 10 feet by withholding your mark and ping-ponging how many steps or how far you ask your dog to walk without stopping or pausing.
9. Once your dog will walk two thirds of the way to the rat, starting when prompted, without stopping you are ready to start walking along with your dog.

---

10. Now work up to walking 10 steps forward while you drag the rat on the ground in front of your dog. Your 10 steps should increase the distance your dog walks in on the rat by 10 steps from step 9 above.
11. You will handle your dog's success or failure exactly as you did previously. The only difference is that now you and the rat are moving as your dog walks in.
12. Be sure to work this with your dog on both sides of you and at different distances from you.
13. Start inserting your *walk in* cue before *let's go* and when your dog begins to walk forward on the *walk in* cue then drop the *let's go* prompt.
14. Take a break!

The key to this exercise is aborting the trial if your dog stops walking before you mark and release them to grab the rat. It should be easy to change over to a new cue once you have the behavior established. Say your new cue before your old one, then start pausing between the two cues to give your dog a chance to respond to the new cue. Once they start walking in on the new cue just drop the old one.

The goal behavior is for your dog to start walking in when cued and to continue walking in toward the rat or stock until you cue them to do something else. Most traditional trainers will repeat walk in multiple times, whenever their dog stops or slows down. If you repeat the cue when your dog is not walking in you are reinforcing the behavior you don't want, stopping or pausing.

Once your dog can walk in while you also walk 10 steps, start mixing things up to generalize this as much as possible. Have your dog walk into the rat from a 90° angle or from straight in front of you. Run with the flirt pole instead of walk. Move much farther away, add a stop, and then ask them to walk in again. Have your dog walk in to a tug or ball you have thrown. Take the exercise to new locations and eventually work around livestock.

Old habits die hard and I admit I have been known to repeat a walk in or flank cue when my dog hesitates instead of using a no reward marker and pause. The more consistent you are in your training the more consistent your dog's behavior will be. If you think your dog is going to slow down or stop, repeat your cue while they are still walking in or flanking with speed. In this way you are using your repeated cue to reinforce the behavior you want.

Adding distance to the walk in, stops, and eventually flanks using a flirt pole all work to generalize the in behavior and build mass on it. Work on as many types of generalization off of stock as you can think of to prepare your dog for the massive distraction of livestock.

Troubleshooting

- ***Dog does not want to go beyond handler*** – If your dog will only come up even with you and seems unwilling to go beyond you to get the rat:

  1. Start with your dog next to you and place the rat about 3 feet in front of you.

  2. Release your dog with *get it* and encourage them to grab the rat.

  3. If your dog still will not go, set up again and take one giant step to the side and away from your dog.

  4. If your dog again doesn't want to go beyond you, have your dog stand next to you and dangle the rat from your hand, held out ahead of you and release your dog to the rat.

  5. As a final breakdown of this setup, stand perpendicular to your dog with your dog on your left and dangle the rat from your right hand.

  6. Release your dog and encourage them to pass in front of you and get the rat.

  7. Once your dog will cross in front of you, slowly start to pivot your body farther around each time you set up until your dog is going from behind you to get the rat in front of you.

  8. Now slightly increase the difficulty by asking your dog to walk in to the rat placed a few feet in front of you.

  9. Continue to shape the walk in past you until your dog is confident walking right by you.

This should be a fun exercise. If you are not laughing and really enjoying yourself you are doing something wrong. If your dog tends to be a sideways-moving dog they may struggle with walking in. The more you can relax and enjoy small victories the more your dog will free up and learn that they can be pushy.

When you take the walk in to livestock, it is important that you initially allow your dog to walk into the stock until you see a reaction from the stock. The reaction can be a head turn away from your dog, a step away, or any other sign that the livestock is giving in to the pressure your dog is applying.

You want your dog to elicit a reaction from the livestock so that your dog associates walking in not only with moving toward stock but putting pressure on them. This is especially important for sideways-moving dogs that may be reticent to apply pressure to livestock. It also helps dogs to learn how close they need to be to affect the livestock's movement.

The in behavior is the beginning of driving. Your dog is learning to apply pressure while maintaining self-control. We usually think of self-control as inhibiting excess movement but it takes even more self-control to move when your dog feels more comfortable stopping and standing still. Have patience now and you will be handily rewarded when you go to livestock later.

Releasing pressure

Nervous livestock will mill and behave erratically just before they panic. Don't get so focused on your dog that you miss the behavior of your livestock. If you sense that the stock is feeling overly pushed, stop or back your dog off and allow them to settle before you attempt to re-apply pressure. Most dogs will slow down as they feel the pressure building on the stock but some pushy dogs are apt to apply too much pressure. Sometimes we need our dogs to apply excessive pressure, including biting, but at this point, you should be working livestock that offers little resistance to and moves freely away from your dog.

Dogs can apply too much pressure and force livestock to blindly flee or fight. If the stock can escape, the easiest way to reduce the pressure on them is to stop your dog and let the stock move away. If the stock cannot escape you will need to back your dog off to diffuse the situation. Panicked stock may jump into or over you or your dog.

Once your dog is familiar with applying pressure, they need to learn how to release pressure. Dogs that like to push can end up being too close to their stock, especially in close quarters such as at a gateway, pen, or chute. If your dog gets too close you need them to back off but not lose contact with the stock. In these cases, you need your dog to move back while continuing to face the stock. To back away from livestock your dog needs to learn the next basic herding skill of backing directly away from livestock.

CHAPTER 16

Herding RAMs – Back

Moving back from livestock, without breaking eye contact, is a great way for your dog to reduce pressure on livestock without releasing the stock to get away. This behavior comes in handy when pushing the stock into any tight place they are reluctant to go. **Back** means that your dog walks directly backward away from the stock while remaining hooked up to and facing them.

The key to persuading stock to go where they don't want to go is to block every route, except the one you want them to take, and then allowing them to settle after each block, instead of continuously applying pressure.

Once livestock learns they cannot escape, they should be allowed to settle and discover the path you want them to take. Your dog's job is to block escape routes and then hold enough pressure on the stock so that they will follow the last available path, the route you want them to take. If you try to force livestock to take a path without allowing them to choose that path, you will most likely have a train wreck with stock running in every direction. Too much pressure on livestock can be just as much a problem as too little, such that the stock will not move at all.

When your dog gets in too close to stock there are usually a few moments when the livestock will **mill**, go around in a tight circle, or freeze. From experience, you will sense that either you and/or your dog needs to step back and release some of the pressure. If you don't release the pressure or add more, the livestock may go where you want them to but more likely they will explode and run in every direction.

Most dogs do not naturally back up but once taught will often find many situations where backing up is very handy!

Back

Before you start – New hand target

You will be using a hand touch in teaching the back so practice 10 hand touches while you are sitting on the floor. Your hand position will be different from when you used the hand target in Chapter 12, Obedient RAMs, for teaching the stand so you want to generalize the hand target with you in a sitting position.

Your position for targeting changes from standing with your dog beside you, to standing with your dog in front of you, to sitting with your dog in front of you. Your hand will look different to your dog as you change from standing to sitting so be sure to shape the new sitting hand target touch before you try to use it in teaching the back behavior.

This is the hand target position you will be using to teach the back behavior. Start teaching the hand target while standing in front of your dog, then kneel or sit in a chair, and finally sit on the floor or on a low stool or thick cushion.

The Rules

1. ***Goal*** – The goal is to have your dog walk directly back away from stock.
2. ***When to begin teaching*** – You can start teaching the back at any time.
3. ***When to move on*** – I teach the back with treats, move on to using a toy, eventually a flirt pole, and finally transition to livestock.
4. ***Appropriate environment*** – You want a room with few distractions to work in.
5. ***Setting up the environment*** – You need a clear, flat area 4 by 12 feet, a long hall is ideal. If you find your dog backs off to one side you may want to work next to a wall or set up a temporary barrier on that side using an X-pen.
6. ***What props are needed*** – Treats and possibly an X-pen, low stool, and/or thick cushion.

7. ***Criteria in one sentence*** – When cued, the dog starts walking backward away from the stock while continuing to face the stock and continues back for 6 front paw steps, unless cued to stop sooner.

8. ***Reinforcement to use*** – Use large treats that will roll and are easy for your dog to see on the floor.

9. ***Cue to use*** – I use *back* as a verbal cue. Initially, your hand movement will be the hand signal or cue.

10. ***When to add the cue*** – You will add the verbal cue when your dog is consistently backing straight away from you for 6 steps.

THE MECHANICS

1. ***Your position*** – Sit on the floor facing your dog with a bowl of treats between your legs, which are spread out to each side of the bowl. Alternatively, you can kneel with your treat bowl in front of you.

2. ***Your dog's position*** – Your dog will be standing facing you 4 feet in front of you.

3. ***What is marked*** – Initially you will mark any backward foot movement with *yes*. Eventually, you will mark 5 to 7 steps backward.

4. ***How and where the reinforcement will be delivered*** – Start by throwing treats between your dog's front paws, under their body.

5. ***How to grow the behavior*** – You will start marking any backward paw movement, front or rear paw, and shape more backward steps in a straight line away from you.

6. ***When to practice without your dog*** – No need to practice without your dog.

You want a steady foot by foot back, not a jumping backward with two feet in the air at a time. If your dog learns to jump backward they will most likely startle the stock you are trying to calm down. A calm, slow backing motion is preferable for herding.

Back – Step by step

1. Put 20 large treats that will roll into a bowl.

2. Settle yourself on the floor, either kneeling with the treat bowl in front of you or sitting with your legs spread out to each side, with the bowl between your legs. You may sit on a low stool or a thick cushion if you prefer.

3. Get your dog to stand facing you and get a treat in one hand.

4. Extend your other hand toward your dog as a hand target. Keep your hand as close to your body and the floor as you can and still have your dog willingly touch it.

5. When your dog touches your hand, drop your hand to your side. Your dog may step back to look at your face. Be ready!

6. If your dog moves any paw backward, mark with *yes* and throw the treat you have in your hand slightly under your dog and between their front feet. Reload your hands as they become empty. You should use alternate hands, right then left then right, to throw treats.
7. If your dog just lifts their head and stares at you without stepping backward, roll a treat between their legs to get the game started.
8. If the treat went behind your dog's front feet they will have to step backward to get the treat. As they step back to get the treat, mark, and throw another treat.
9. Repeat marking backward paw movement and throwing treats until your dog takes 3 steps backward, then reset by having your dog come to you to touch your hand target.

---

10. Start moving your hands, with treats in them, like you are throwing treats, as a cue for your dog to start backing and keep moving your hands while your dog is backing. When they get to the step number you have determined you will reinforce, then mark with *yes*, and throw a treat with one hand.
11. Call your dog forward to you for a hand touch and repeat marking and throwing treats for backward paw movement three times.

---

12. The next time you call your dog forward have them touch your hand, drop your hand, and wait.
13. If your dog moves any paw backward mark, throw a treat between their front legs, and keep marking and throwing treats for any more backward movement.
14. If your dog just stands or starts to lie down or sit, throw a treat over their head so it lands behind them.
15. When you have gone through your 20 treats, take a break!

Any time your dog starts to lie down or sit, pitch a treat over their head to keep them in the game and learning that reinforcement ultimately is delivered behind them.

If after one session your dog has not started offering any backward paw movement don't worry! Most dogs have not done much walking backward so this may be a new concept for them. Allow time for your dog to process the session and try again later in the day or the next day.

If your dog is offering a few steps, all the better. You will then grow this behavior to 6 front footsteps backward. Your hand movement, when throwing treats, becomes the hand signal or cue for now. Be sure to ping-pong the number of steps you mark and reinforce, 1, 1, 2, 1, 2, 2, 1, 3, and so forth.

Sir touches my hand, backs up as I move my hands back and forth as a physical cue, gets a mark while he is moving backward, receives a treat, and comes forward for another hand touch.

Troubleshooting

- **Dog curls off to one side when backing** – If your dog consistently curls to one side, move against a wall, erect a temporary barrier on that side, or if your dog is backing 4 to 6 steps, throw the treat to the opposite side. If they are curling to their left then throw the treat to their right. Behavioral economics should help you encourage your dog to back closer to where the treat will be delivered.

- **Dog will not take a step back** – If you do three sessions of Phase 1 and you don't see any backward paw movement you can try moving to a chair and placing a treat under the seat while you sit on the chair. Your dog will have to duck under the seat to get the treat and you should be ready to mark and toss a treat between their front feet as they back out. Keep marking and treating as you did in Phase 1.

- **Dog gets stuck after the same number of steps** – If your dog consistently takes the same number of steps backward but will take no more the tendency is to help your dog, usually be prompting verbally or through body language. Instead of prompting your dog when they don't take the number of steps you have determined they need to take before you will mark and reinforce, pause and wait for a few seconds to see if they will offer more steps. If they continue to stand still then offer your hand for a touch and start again. Repeat this step 5 times or until your dog offers another step.

- ***Dog just doesn't get it*** – If Phase 1 does not work for you and your dog an alternative approach is using a foot target to teach the back.

  1. First, you will need to find a mat or rug that has a different texture from the surface you are working on so your dog will be able to feel when they have reached the target.

  2. Put the target down and shape your dog to stand with their rear feet on it. Reinforce heavily.

  3. Then offer a treat a few inches ahead of your dog. You want them to move one rear foot off of the target. When they eat the treat, wait and look at the target.

  4. When your dog places their rear foot back onto the target, mark and treat. You may need to prompt your dog by leaning into them slightly a time or two.

  5. Then offer your treat so your dog moves both back feet off the target and wait.

  6. Once your dog starts moving both back feet onto the target you can begin pulling them farther forward off of the target, ping-ponging the distance, until they have to back 6 steps to reach the target.

  7. At this point, you would add your cue.

  8. Finally, fade the target by making it smaller until it disappears. This method works best if your dog has done some rear foot awareness or proprioception training. **Proprioception** is the ability to sense the position, location, orientation, and movement of the body and its parts. Most dogs do not know how to move their rear legs independently of their front ones unless they have been trained to have rear-end awareness. See training rear-end awareness in Chapter 8.

Once your dog is consistently taking 6 steps backward you want to work on different criteria, one at a time.

Backing criteria

1. ***Topography of the back*** – This simply means your dog should walk backward and not hop.
2. ***Number of steps*** – Work up to at least 6 front paw steps.
3. ***Speed of backing*** – Your dog does not need to back quickly but instead focus on slow, steady steps backward.
4. ***Straight backing*** – Since your dog will be using the back to release pressure on livestock, you need them to back straight and not curve to either side.
5. ***Handler standing*** – The final criterion, before you add the verbal cue *back*, is to *move* yourself from a sitting to standing position.

Once you have your dog consistently walking straight backward 6 steps at an even pace while you stand in front of them, you can install the back cue. Give your verbal cue and then start moving your hands as you did to cue the back while training it. Once your dog starts backing on the verbal cue, drop the hand motion.

Generalizing the back

To generalize backing you need it to be on a verbal cue. So far your dog has only been backing away from you. In essence, you are the target your dog focuses on during backing. Now we need to have your dog start backing away from new targets.

Start by standing in front of your dog; place a toy at your feet, between you and your dog. Ask your dog to back, mark and reinforce. You can either throw your dog an identical toy or throw them a treat. As your dog is successful, start stepping off to the side of where the toy is placed. The toy placement stays consistent, only you move.

When your dog can back away from the toy on cue, switch to using a tug instead of the toy. Again either throw an identical tug or a treat to your dog. Once your dog is backing away from the tug, place the flirt pole rat on the spot the tug had been. When your dog backs away you can reinforce by flipping the rat to your dog. Just remember to use your release cue, *get it*, before the rat gets to your dog.

Challenge your dog by eventually asking them to back away from a twitching or moving rat.

The important part of generalizing the back is the change of your position relative to your dog so that your dog learns to back independent of your position. Using a clock face as the basis for an exercise is a good way to strengthen and generalize the back.

Generalizing the back – Step by step

1. Set up a cone circle about 12 feet in diameter.
2. Stand on the perimeter of the circle, where you stand becomes 12 o'clock, and drop the rat into the center of the circle.
3. Your dog will be stationed a foot or two away from the rat and directly opposite but facing you.
4. Cue your dog back.
5. If your dog takes 3 steps straight back from the rat then cue stop, mark, release, and tug.

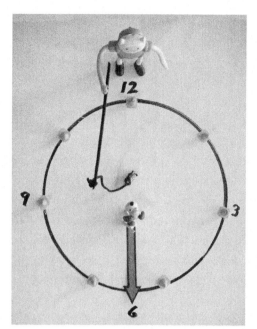 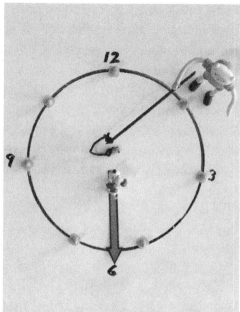

To generalize the back start at 12 o'clock and have your dog back directly away from you while facing the rat. Then move to 1 o'clock and have your dog back the same path they did when you were at 12 o'clock. Eventually you will be able to ask your dog to back away from the rat no matter where you are standing on the circle.

6. If your dog stands and stares at the rat, give your no reward marker, pause 10 seconds, and reset. Repeat the trial twice more. If your dog steps back one or two steps then cue stop, mark, release, and tug. If your dog still stands and stares, go back and work Back – Step by step above.

7. Shape your dog to back 6 steps, which should take them almost to the cone circle. Do not allow your dog to back into a cone! Make the circle larger if your dog needs more room. Vary the number of steps backward you mark, between 3 and 7.

8. Once your dog can back straight away 6 steps, with you at 12 o'clock, start moving to 1 and then 11 o'clock. Your dog should keep backing straight away from the rat on the same line they took when you were at 12 o'clock. They should not adjust their path so they are backing directly away from you.

9. When your dog is proficient with you at 1 and 11 o'clock then start moving to 2 and 10 o'clock.

10. Eventually, move all around the circle while your dog continues to back along the line they were on when you were at 12 o'clock.

11. Change your dog's position so they are now backing away from the rat toward 3 or 9 o'clock. Work this until your dog can back straight away from the rat, no matter where they or you are positioned.
12. Remove the cones and practice asking your dog to back away from the rat with you and them in random positions and for random steps, from 5 to 10 steps.

13. Now work the same exercise with penned stock replacing the rat.
14. Eventually, work the back on loose but stopped livestock.

Once you switch to livestock in a pen your dog may struggle. Be prepared to go back to kindergarten in challenging situations and re-teach the back. Your dog will usually get up to speed quickly. Try moving your dog farther away from the stock to make backing away easier. If they struggle, you may have to go back to an easier environment and build more mass on the back behavior.

Perfect dogs

Now you have a stop, in, and back on your dog. Congratulations! You and your dog have come a long way!

The next herding skill to build is flanking. Because flanks are based on directionals, right and left, you will start training directionals in the next chapter and then grow your directionals into flanks in the following chapters.

Directionals are usually challenging for dogs. Take your time, work short sessions often, and most importantly practice diligently without your dog. Don't be afraid to use wrist bands to make sure you keep the directional cues straight. It is very easy to mix up the cues and even the most experienced top handlers give the wrong flank cue once in a while. There are no perfect handlers, handlers that never make mistakes, and there are no perfect dogs. Be kind to yourself and your dog when mistakes happen. We are all doing the best we can.

CHAPTER 17

Herding RAMs – Directionals

As you start directionals, right and left, it is important to remember that we are always referring to your dog's right and left, not yours.

Right and left are simple for you to teach but often difficult for your dog to learn. Most dogs struggle learning directionals, so be patient. The problem is that most behaviors that we teach our dogs are a simple discrimination of a discrete behavior. In this case, you will be teaching two very similar behaviors with different cues. Your dog will quickly pick up that you are reinforcing a head turn but it will take them much longer to learn that head turns to one side are cued differently from head turns to the other side.

We start out teaching right, *away to me*, or left, *come bye*, but soon start mixing them up. Because we are teaching two behaviors at the same time, both discriminations, it takes most dogs quite a while to learn the cues to fluency. If you have used different cues for heeling on each side of you, your dog may pick up directionals more quickly since it is a similar type of discrimination, the same basic behavior but different cues for different sides.

The good news is that you can train directionals sitting in your house. It doesn't take much physical effort to teach directionals but it does take a lot of mental effort. Although your dog will initially be sitting and only turning their heads from side to side they will still be working very hard. Be sure to start teaching directionals early and practice often, using short sessions. Keep it fun but if you start to get frustrated, stop and take a break.

Stationary directionals
Before you start – Sit

You need a solid sit with substantial duration before you begin teaching directionals. The sit position is used to anchor your dog in place and allow you to isolate the head turn. Your dog will be sitting directly in front of you, about a foot or so away from you, facing you. Since most people initially train sit facing their dog, this should be a comfortable position for your dog.

THE RULES

1. **Goal** – The goal is to teach your dog their directionals, right and left.
2. **When to begin teaching** – Start early, train often, and keep sessions super short.
3. **When to move on** – Stay at this stage until your dog has reached a 95% to 100% rate of success. Don't be in a hurry to move on until you are confident your dog knows their right from their left.
4. **Appropriate environment** – Any quiet room in your house will work.
5. **Setting up the environment** – You will want to make the environment as distraction-free as possible. Your dog is really going to have to concentrate, so eliminate as much background noise as you can.
6. **What props are needed**
   1. You will need a low chair or a step stool to sit on. It should be low enough that when you are sitting on it and place your elbows on your thighs with your arms parallel to the floor that your hands are the same height as your dog's head. If you have a small dog you may have to sit on a cushion or the floor to get low enough.
   2. You will use a physical *and* verbal marker since your hands are required to train the behaviors.
   3. You need a small bowl to hold treats.
   4. You may want to use a wrist band or other marker to remind you which way is *come bye* and which is *away to me*. I sometimes use two wristbands, one with C on it and one with A. (It is very easy to get confused and realize at the end of a session that you were reinforcing right head turns for come bye and vice versa. Been there, done that!)
7. **Criteria in one sentence** – The dog should turn their head right when cued *away to me* and left when cued *come bye*. Remember you are training two behaviors.
8. **Reinforcement to use** – Treats are superior for getting a lot of reps in quickly. Start out using high-value treats since this is a tough behavior to learn.
9. **Cue to use** – Traditionally handlers have used *away to me* for right and *come bye* for left. You may want to use *go bye* if you use *come* as your recall cue.
10. **When to add the cue** – The cues are added quite soon, contrary to the usual procedure of getting the behavior and then adding the cue.

THE MECHANICS

1. ***Your position*** – Sit directly in front of your dog with both hands fisted, holding a treat, and resting on your collarbone while your elbows rest on your thighs. You will then lower one, eventually both, fisted hand to the level of your dog's head. You will have to lean your upper body forward to assume this position.

2. ***Your dog's position*** – Your dog will be sitting directly in front of you looking at your face with their head directly between your outstretched fists.

3. ***What is marked*** – Initially you will mark eye movement or slight head movement but eventually you will mark 90° head turns in the correct direction.

4. ***How and where the reinforcement will be delivered*** – You will hold a treat in your closed hand. After you give a directional cue you will open your hand, if your dog has turned toward the correct hand.

5. ***How to grow the behavior*** – See the next RAM – Moving directionals.

6. ***When to practice without your dog*** – It is absolutely critical that you practice without your dog! There is a lot to think about and observe. You also need to immediately reinforce by opening your hand when your dog is correct.

The RAMs give you an overview of the training that you can quickly refer back to without having to read through the entire directions, if you just need to check a detail or refresh your memory after a pause in training. Although the RAMs are useful they are not sufficient to explain exactly how to train a behavior. For that level of detail, you will need to read through and become familiar with the step-by-step directions.

Video of Phase 1 Directionals (Re-creation): https://youtu.be/5z1AKOBnGRY

Stationary directionals – Step by step
PHASE 1 – Setup and intro of cues (one hand at a time)

1. Gather your props which include: stool, treats, bowl, and optional wrist band(s).

2. Set up your video camera and turn it on. (Highly recommended!)

3. Count out 11 treats and place them in the bowl.

4. Sit on the stool and find a place, on the lower step of the stool is ideal, between your legs to place the bowl containing the treats.

5. Bend your knees and separate your legs to make room for your dog directly in front of you.

6. Call your dog, have them sit facing you. Reinforce the sit with one of your treats.

---

7. Put a treat in your *right* hand and close your hand around it.

8. Lower both elbows to your thighs but place your fisted hands on your collarbone under your chin. You will have to lean forward with your upper body.

9. Now drop the forearm of the hand holding the treat until it is at the height of your dog's head. Your other elbow will remain on your thigh but that hand will not drop down to your dog's head but instead will remain resting on your collarbone.

10. If your dog gets out of the sit, reposition them in the sit by touching their collar before continuing. Your dog must remain sitting during this phase of the training.

11. As you lower your hand your dog will look at it. You will immediately mark with *yes* and open your hand so your dog may eat the treat out of your hand, while remaining sitting. Repeat 5 times.

---

12. On trial 6 through 10 you will say *come bye* before you lower your hand. As your dog looks toward your hand you will mark with *yes* and open your hand so your dog may eat the treat.

When your treats are gone the trial is over. (Each set of 10 reps should take less than 1 minute.)

The initial trial will look like this: You will drop your right fisted hand down to your dog's head level. At this point, you will *not* give the *come bye* cue or say anything. As your dog notices your moving hand and looks toward it you will say *yes* and open your hand. Your dog will eat the treat and you will re-load your hand from the bowl between your legs and bring it back to your collarbone where your other hand has been resting. You will repeat this 5 times.

If possible you may want to separate your treats into two piles, one containing 6 treats and the other 5. Take the first treat from the pile with 6 treats. Now you do not need to count 5 treats for the first part of Phase 1, only mark. Once the first pile is gone you can move on to the second part of Phase 1, cue and mark. This is an easy way to keep track of 5 reps. A divided plastic container is perfect for organizing treats.

Now add the cue *come bye* as you drop your right hand. Again, say *yes* and open your hand when your dog looks toward your moving hand. Repeat this 5 times. That ends your first session! You should have used all 11 treats and be ready to re-load your bowl with 11 more treats. Release your dog from the sit before you fill your bowl again.

After a short break, you will do exactly the same 12-step procedure *except* you will switch and now load your left hand with a treat and keep your right fist resting on your collarbone. You also will be using the cue *away to me* instead of *come bye*.

With Sir sitting in front of me and a treat in my right hand I raise both hands to my shoulders. I then lower my right arm and open my hand. Once Sir has taken the treat I reload my hand from the bowl in front of me, raise it back to my collarbone and am ready to start the next trial. At first, I don't use a flank cue but after 5 reps I start to say come bye *before I lower my hand to the level of Sir's head.*

This should be a very easy exercise for your dog. The cues you are giving mean nothing to your dog at this point, as they are cueing off of your arm lowering and hand opening.

If your dog gets out of the sit, the base position, use a collar touch to reposition them back into the sit. If you re-cue the sit you will be reinforcing their movement out of the sit, exactly what you don't want!

Once you have finished working both sides, take a break. Congratulate yourself on getting through all of the mechanics, even though they felt awkward, and play with your dog as added reinforcement for playing this new game with you.

Troubleshooting

- **Dog stands** – Be sure that you are placing your hands close enough to your dog's head so that they do not need to get up to eat the treat once you open your hand. Your dog should only have to turn their head to reach the treat in your palm.
- **Dog lies down** – Because this is a new exercise, some dogs have trouble remaining sitting. If your dog goes down or stands up several times, work on the sit behavior and get it solid before you move forward with training directionals.
- **You get confused** – Although it seems simple, it is easy to forget what you need to do. If you make a lot of mistakes, stop and practice more without your dog. Consider using wrist bands.
- **Your mechanics suck** – If you find you fumble and stutter raising and lowering the correct arm or opening your hand as soon as your dog turns toward it, you will want to practice without your dog until you can perform the mechanics smoothly.

Phase 2 – Further intro of cues (both hands)

1. Place 11 more treats into the bowl.
2. Sit down and get your dog sitting facing you. Reinforce the sit with one treat.
3. Pick up a treat in your right hand and place both closed fists on your collarbone.
4. Lower both fists to your dog's head level with your elbows on your thighs.
5. As you lower both hands your dog should watch your face and not turn toward either hand. If they look at one hand, raise both hands back up as soon as you notice them focusing on either hand.
6. Say *come bye* as soon as both of your hands are down in the lowered position and still.
7. Your dog will look at one of your hands. If they look at your right hand say *yes* and open that hand so your dog can eat the treat. If they look at your left hand do nothing and wait for them to look at your right hand. Once they look at your right hand say *yes* and open your hand.
8. Repeat 4 more times.

---

9. Now you will switch to having the treat in your left hand and repeat steps 6 through 10 using *away to me* as the cue. Of course, your dog must now look at your left hand to get a mark and treat.

When your treats are gone the trial is over. (Each of these trials should also take only about a minute to complete.)

These 10 trials will look similar to your initial trials except both hands will be lowered to your dog's head level. Although you will be saying the directional cues, they still have no meaning for your dog. Your primary goal in this phase is to get you and your dog familiar and comfortable with the mechanics of the exercise.

For the Phase 2 exercise, you will be lowering both hands, giving a directional cue, and asking your dog to make a discrimination. At first, it will be 5 come bye cues followed by 5 away to me cues.

You will be lowering both hands in this phase and your dog may get anxious and stand or lie down, since you will now have a hand on each side of their head, which is new to them. They may change position as they try to figure out what earns reinforcement. If you have taught a down by prompting with your hand moving toward the floor, your dog may interpret your lowering hands as a cue to lie down.

In this phase, you will again be sitting slightly forward so that you can place your elbows on your spread thighs. You will take a treat in one hand but lower both hands to head level. Now you will give a verbal directional cue and your dog will have to make a choice. If they choose correctly you mark with *yes* and open that hand. If they choose incorrectly you do nothing and say nothing but wait for them to choose the other hand. Once they turn toward or look at the correct hand you mark, open that fist, and allow them to eat the treat.

Troubleshooting

- ***Dog looks at one hand while both hands are lowered*** – If your dog looks at one of your hands while you are lowering them, raise both of them to your collarbone under your face. This will help to encourage your dog to look at your face while you lower both arms, rather than stare at one hand. Repeat this as many times as needed to get your dog looking forward at you while you lower both hands.
- ***Dog looks at one hand while both hands are lowered*** – You may need to do a session reinforcing your dog for looking at your face, rather than at your moving hands. Remember, it is natural for your dog to be attracted to hand movement.
- ***Dog looks at one hand before a cue is given*** – If you get both hands lowered but your dog focuses on one before you give the directional cue, again raise both hands to your collarbone under your face. You need your dog to look at you until you give a cue. Once the cue is given they are free to choose either your right or left hand.
- ***Dog doesn't want to participate*** – Some dogs are very sensitive and may get frustrated or lose confidence due to uncertainty about how to successfully gain reinforcement. This frustration may cause them to shut down. Make sure you are keeping this training fun! Instead of frowning or sighing at mistakes, yours or your dog's, laugh instead. We all make mistakes and our dogs will too.
- ***Dog is not progressing*** – Be sure to take breaks and allow you and your dog some time for latent learning. **Latent learning** is learning that is not immediately expressed and occurs without any obvious reinforcement of the behavior. Latent learning may take place between training sessions when an animal processes the training.

Phase 3 – Mixing directional cues

1. Place 20 slips of paper in a bag, 10 will have the cue *come bye* and 10 *away to me*. Pull out one slip at a time and thus generate a random list of directional cues or use a random list generator on your computer or smart phone.
2. Place the list where you can see it while training.
3. Place 11 more treats into your bowl. You no longer need to divide treats into two piles in your bowl.
4. Sit down and get your dog sitting facing you. Reinforce the sit with one treat.

---

5. Pick up a treat in the hand that corresponds to the cue on your list and place both closed fists on your collarbone.
6. Lower both fists to your dog's head level with your elbows on your thighs.
7. As you lower both hands your dog should watch your face and not turn toward either hand. If they look at one hand, raise both hands back up as soon as you notice them focusing on either hand.
8. Say the cue corresponding to the hand holding the treat, *away to me* for your left hand and *come bye* for your right.
9. If they look at the correct hand, say *yes* and open that hand so your dog can eat the treat.
10. If your dog looks at the other hand, raise both hands, a physical no reward marker, and pause 10 seconds.

---

11. Look back at your random list of cues and go on to the next one for the next rep, even if your dog has chosen incorrectly.
12. Continue in this way until your dog has earned and eaten all 10 treats or you reach the bottom of the list.
13. Take a break!

In Phase 3 you are asking your dog to make flank cue discriminations that are given in random order. Now is when your dog really has to begin thinking to earn reinforcement!

The reason you move on to the next random cue is that if you re-cue and put your hands back down, your dog will quickly figure out that if their first choice was wrong all they have to do is choose the other hand. Since they have a 50% chance of being correct initially, they will, by chance, get reinforced 50% of the time for their first guess. Then the chance of being correct on their second guess, the other hand, becomes 100%. In other words, they will learn that they can guess once and if they are wrong just default to the other hand.

This phase will be a challenge for you and your dog! Your dog will have to use a lot of mental energy to figure out how to win this game consistently. For this training, it is best to do short sessions of 10 reps with long breaks and repeat often. In other words, you will want to train this often but not for long periods at one time. Always generate a new list of 20 random directional cues for each trial.

Be sure and use a different random list of cues every training session or your dog will learn the sequence rather than the discrimination of cues. You can use the same list twice if you follow it from the bottom up instead of the top down. If you get confused going back up the list, just rewrite the list in reverse order before you start training.

If you notice at any time when teaching directionals that your dog favors one side, such as always choosing away to me, then weight your random list to the other side, come bye. Do this by using 15 slips of paper indicating come bye and only 5 slips indicating away to me when you draw to set up your list of 20 cues.

Troubleshooting

- ***Dog is not progressing*** – If you do 10 sessions of 10 treats, with substantial breaks in between, and your dog doesn't seem to be making progress, try dropping back to Phase 2 for a session or two.
- ***Dog doesn't want to participate*** – If your dog struggles, your rate of reinforcement is going to plummet and your dog may not want to train directionals. Try to keep your training fun, take long breaks, and train other behaviors that allow your dog to earn a high rate of reinforcement. If necessary, change to higher value treats.
- ***You are unsure if your dog is progressing*** – The easiest way to keep track of how well your dog is doing is to note how far down the 20 cue list you get in each session. If you get to the bottom of the list three times in a row, after long breaks in between sessions, and you still have treats left you should go back to Phase 2 for a session or two.

Once your dog is correct 95 to 100% of the time, you are ready to move on to changing your and your dog's positions. Don't be in a hurry to move on to moving directionals. Build a lot of mass on stationary directionals. This will help you as you transition from you and your dog sitting to both of you standing. These changes of position may be highly distracting for your dog.

Start transitioning from both you and your dog sitting to standing by asking your dog to stand while you remain sitting. Your dog will quickly figure out this is the same game. If your dog struggles to remain standing, pull out the stand position and work it separately from directionals until you have a solid stand.

Then you too will need to transition to standing in front of your dog. You will probably want to change from a bowl to a treat pouch for this step. Once your dog has generalized the game with both of you standing you are ready to get your dog moving, which will transition your directionals into flanks.

CHAPTER 18

Herding RAMs – Moving directionals

Moving directionals are used to transition from directionals to flanks. Until now, your dog only had to turn their head to earn reinforcement. Now you will be asking your dog to move their feet as well as their head.

Moving directionals
Before you start – Stand and foot target

For this exercise, you will use the *stand* as your starting position. If your dog does not have a solid stand behavior, you need to shape and strengthen your stand to 10 seconds of duration. You may also want to use a very low platform or rug as a station for your dog to stand on. The platform/rug makes it easier to position your dog to start a trial and gives them a fixed place to return to after you finish a trial. The advantage of using a **platform**, a portable slightly raised area just large enough for your dog to stand on, is that it provides a specific place for your dog to be stationed during the exercise, a home base.

You also need to train a front foot target before you can do this exercise. A **foot target** is a target on the floor that your dog touches with their foot or feet. A foot target needs to be fairly large, to start, and have a texture different from the surface you will be using it on, so your dog can feel the difference in surfaces as well as see it. If you are working on carpet, then you want a smooth, firm target such as a Frisbee. If working on a wooden or concrete floor, you want a piece of carpet as the target. Make sure the target does not slide around on the surface it is placed on.

To teach a foot target, put out your target but be ready to mark and reinforce as soon as you put the target down. Stand near the target and look down at it. Most dogs will go over to investigate the target. Mark, verbally or with a clicker, and deliver your treat while your dog is on or near the target. Step away from the target and prompt your dog to come with you. You may toss a lower value treat to reset your dog if desired. Move back to the target and look at it again. Shape your dog to get closer to and stand on the target with one front foot. (If you have taught a foot target such that your dog must put both front feet on the target you can use that criterion for these foot targets too.)

The first time your dog actually touches the target with their paw, mark and feed several treats while they stand on the target. After your dog has touched the target a few times, up your criteria to having them stand on the target with one foot. Do this until your dog has placed one foot on the target 5 times. Again move farther away and get your dog to come with you. This time look back at the target but do not move toward it. Give your dog some time to think about where they have been getting reinforced. Most dogs, after a few reps of getting reinforced for standing on a target, will quickly learn that standing on the target pays and will happily offer a paw on the target.

Keep building this behavior until your dog will readily go 10 feet to get onto the target, no matter where you are standing or sitting. Also, move the target around the room so your dog has to go to different places to touch it. The foot target is the physical cue for this behavior. Do not add a verbal cue. When you are done working on the foot target, be sure to pick it up so your dog does not continue to offer the behavior and not earn reinforcement.

The main difference in this exercise, other than your dog is now standing and moving to a target, is that you want your dog to **flank squarely**, shift their weight back onto their rear end as they turn to go to the target. This means that they do not step forward to turn but shift their weight backward and start off perpendicular or square, 90°. A dog that squares their flanks does not move toward the livestock and thus does not put any added pressure on the stock as they turn but maintains a consistent distance from the stock. We will use cones or other barriers to encourage our dogs to shift their weight back while turning.

To encourage your dog to notice and avoid cones or uprights, they must be as tall as your standing dog's head.

The Rules

1. **Goal** – The goal is to get your dog moving right and left on cue by shifting their weight backward as they initially turn.

2. **When to begin teaching** – Start this exercise after your dog knows right and left, as taught in the Stationary Directionals exercise.

3. **When to move on** – You will move on to the flanking exercises after your dog can go to cued foot targets with a success rate of 95 to 100%.

4. **Appropriate environment** – Use the room where you taught Stationary Directionals. Eventually you will need an area 10 by 15 feet for the final exercise.

5. **Setting up the environment** – Continue to use a distraction-free environment.

6. **What props are needed** – For this exercise you will need 11 treats, a treat pouch or other means to hold treats, two tall cones or similar barriers, two identical foot targets (I often use two orange Frisbees), and a platform or rug is optional. You will again use a verbal marker.

7. **Criteria in one sentence** – The dog should shift their weight backward and then move right to touch the foot target when cued *away to me* and left to touch the foot target when cued *come bye*. (Your dog should *not* step forward as they turn!)

8. **Reinforcement to use** – High-value treats are again the best reinforcers to use.

9. **Cue to use** – Use *away to me* for right and *come bye* for left.

10. **When to add the cue** – Continue using the cues from the previous exercise.

The Mechanics

1. **Your position** – You will stand 1 to 2 feet in front of and facing your dog.

2. **Your dog's position** – Your dog will stand facing you, optionally on a platform or rug, directly between two tall uprights (tall cones or upright pool noodles) with two foot targets that are 3 feet on either side of your dog. The uprights should be in line with your dog's front legs and 3 to 6 inches to each side of your dog. The foot targets should be in line with your dog, about 3 feet away and slightly behind the uprights. (See illustration below.)

3. **What is marked** – You mark, with a verbal *yes*, your dog touching the foot target that corresponds to the directional cue given.

4. **How and where the reinforcement will be delivered** – After marking their paw touching the correct target, reach over and deliver a treat to your dog while they are touching or standing on the foot target.

5. **How to grow the behavior** – Once your dog is performing the exercise using random directional cues 95 to 100% of the time correctly, you will incrementally step back from your dog and then move the foot targets farther out to the side of your dog. If you have used a platform or rug, over time fade it out of the picture by making it smaller until it is gone. You may be able to remove it all at once since

your dog will still be standing between the tall uprights. The final behavior will have you standing 6 feet in front of your dog with your foot targets 6 feet out on either side of your dog.

6. **When to practice without your dog** – A short practice without your dog is advisable.

Again you may want to mark each target with an A or C so you don't get mixed up. You may mark the side of the target so you can see the letter but your dog cannot or use some other type of indicator so that you do not get mixed up. You may even mark your side of the uprights so that you know as soon as your dog moves if they are heading toward the cued foot target.

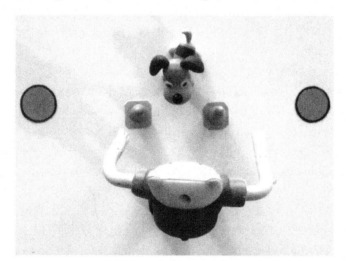

Sample initial setup for moving directionals:
2 cones
1 or 2 targets
Dog stands with front feet between cones (Dawg should be standing farther forward with front legs between the cones.)
Handler and dog face each other
Mat or platform for dog is optional

Moving directionals – Step by step
Before you start – Stand at home base

Before you start moving directionals you need a solid stand in place. Take 20 to 30 treats, set out your uprights and targets, and as soon as you get your dog standing at home base, quickly feed 5 treats, one at a time. Then feed 5 treats at a slower pace with more time in between each treat. You may verbally mark before each treat or just feed the treats without any marks. Continue stretching out the time between the treats, increasing duration, until your dog will stand still for 10 seconds, between reinforcers, without attempting to move.

The following exercises can be broken into several different sessions over a day or several days. Take the time you and your dog need to be comfortable and confident at each step before moving on.

Phase 1 – One side at a time

1. Place 30 treats in your treat pouch.

2. Place two cones or uprights about a foot apart such that there is just enough room for your dog to stand between the cones.

3. Place *one* foot target about 2 feet to one side and slightly behind where your dog will be standing.

4. Stand about 1 foot in front of your dog and get your dog standing and facing you with their paws directly between the uprights.

5. Reinforce the stand with 3 treats.

6. When your dog is looking at you, cue a directional, either come bye or away to me, depending on which side you placed the foot target. (Do not look at the cued target, instead keep looking straight ahead at your dog.)

7. If your dog turns their head in the correct direction, mark and reinforce by luring your dog onto the appropriate foot target. Your dog should shift their weight backward and go behind the uprights. Feed the treat with your dog standing on the target.

8. When your dog is done eating, prompt them to go back to home base and reinforce their return to starting position with a verbal marker such as good or feed a treat.

9. If your dog turns their head or steps in the wrong direction, prompt them to go back to starting position and pause for 10 seconds.

10. Repeat 5 times.

11. Take a short break.

---

12. Move your foot target to the opposite side of your setup, about 2 feet beyond the cone.

13. Repeat steps 6 through 9, cueing the opposite directional. If you started with come bye, switch to away to me, etc.

14. Repeat 5 times.

15. Take another short break. (Keep your setup in place.)

---

16. Now cue the same directional you have just been working on but *wait* for your dog to turn and move to the foot target. If your dog does not begin to move toward the cued foot target, instead they just turn their head in the correct direction, withhold your mark for a few seconds and allow your dog to figure out what they need to do to earn reinforcement. (If necessary, look down at the cued target while you wait for your dog to make the connection between the cue and the foot target. As soon as your dog starts moving toward the target, go back to looking straight ahead and not at the cued target.)

17. Mark and feed the treat while your dog stands on the target.
18. Repeat 5 times.
19. Take another short break.

---

20. Move the foot target to the other side of your setup.
21. Cue the opposite directional and wait for your dog to turn and go to the foot target.
22. Mark and feed the treat while your dog stands on the target.
23. Repeat 5 times.
24. Take a long break!

Troubleshooting

- **_Dog is afraid of cones_** – If your dog seems overly worried about the cones, you may need to set them around the house and let your dog desensitize themselves as the cones fade into just another object present in their life. Don't call attention to the cones, just set them out of the way, and over a few days move them around and then closer to where your dog eats, sleeps, and trains.

- **_Dog goes to foot targets when no cue is given_** – If your dog continues to offer foot targeting without waiting for a directional cue, you need to build more mass on the stand at home base. See the _Before you start_ instructions above.

Now you are ready to work with both foot targets. You will also need a list of 20 random directional cues, placed where you can see them.

PHASE 2 – Putting it all together

1. Generate a random list of 20 directional cues.
2. Place the list where you can see it while training.
3. Place 13 treats into your treat pouch.
4. Place two uprights as you did for the previous exercise.
5. Now place _two_ foot targets, one to each side of your dog and about 2 feet away.
6. Stand and get your dog standing facing you with their paws directly between the uprights and centered between them. You should be about 1 foot in front of your dog.
7. Reinforce the stand with 3 treats.
8. When your dog is looking at you, cue the first directional on your list, either _come bye_ or _away to me_. (Do not look at the cued target, instead keep looking straight ahead.)
9. If your dog turns their head in the correct direction but does not move, mark and reinforce by luring your dog onto the appropriate foot target. Your dog should

shift their weight backward and go behind the uprights. Feed the treat with your dog standing on the correct target.

10. When your dog is done eating, prompt them to go back to home base and reinforce their return to starting position with a verbal marker or feed a treat.

11. If your dog turns their head in the wrong direction or goes to the wrong foot target, prompt them to go back to start position and pause for 10 seconds. Then go on to the next directional cue on your list. (Do *not* repeat the same cue unless it happens to be next cue on your list!)

12. Continue in this manner for 5 reps, following your random list of cues.

---

13. Once your dog begins to move to and *stand on* the cued foot target, mark and feed on the target before prompting them back to starting position. Continue in this manner until you have fed all of your treats. (Once your dog learns they must stand on the cued foot target with one foot to earn reinforcement they will quickly begin to offer standing on the target.)

14. Continue in this manner until you feed all 10 treats.

15. Take a long break!

16. Repeat this exercise, taking breaks along the way, until your dog is performing with 95% accuracy.

These exercises are very similar to Stationary Directionals. The main difference is that now you are asking your dog to move their feet instead of just their head. Directionals are the start of flanks and we want *square flanks*.

As mentioned, squaring a flank means that when your dog flanks you want them to make a 90°, right angle, turn and not move closer to the stock or in this case you. If your dog starts their flank by turning less than 90° they are said to slice their flank. A **sliced flank** is a flank that your dog begins by moving forward toward the stock. A **square flank** is started by your dog shifting their weight backward. With a sliced flank your dog shifts their weight forward and usually moves toward the livestock putting unwanted pressure on them. (See diagram on next page.)

To encourage your dog to turn, without stepping forward, have your dog stand with their front legs between the uprights. The targets are then set farther out to each side of your dog. Thus a foot target, an upright, your dog, another upright, and then another foot target are all on the same line:

Target --- Upright --- **Dog** --- Upright --- Target

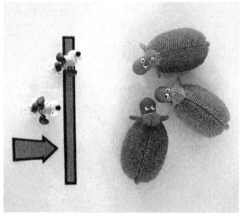

Square flank *Sliced flank*

When performing a square flank your dog does not move closer to the stock but instead maintains the same or greater distance as they flank. When slicing a flank your dog moves closer to the stock as they flank. The dog's black nose in the diagrams above really shows the difference in their distance from the sheep as they flank. The arrows indicate the direction of the dog's weight shift before turning.

Start with the targets close enough that your dog has only to take a step or two to get to them. Also, stay close so you can lean over or just take one step to deliver a treat to your dog when they touch the cued target. If you are using a platform or rug as a station, place it midway between the uprights and get your dog standing on it facing you.

At first, your dog may go and touch one of the foot targets before being cued. Don't say anything. Allow your dog to stand on the target for a few seconds and then encourage them back to their starting position between the two uprights. They may then go to the other target. Repeat the same procedure of waiting a few seconds, then have them go back to home base.

Now that you are attaching the cues, *come bye* to one target and *away to me* to the other, you may want to label your foot targets to prevent confusion. Once your dog is standing still in front of you, looking at you, cue a directional. If your dog turns their head in the correct direction, mark and reinforce by feeding far enough to the side that they have to shift their weight back and then step onto the foot target to get their treat. Your dog should already know their directionals so they should quickly figure out that not only do they need to turn their head but they also need to step onto the foot target on that side to earn reinforcement.

I find it easier to hold 11 dry treats in my hands rather than try to get them out of a treat pouch quickly. See what works best for you.

Again you will need to generate a random list of 20 directional/flank cues to use. As before, if your dog makes a mistake and goes to the wrong foot target, do not repeat that cue unless it is next on your list. If your dog makes a mistake do *not* use a no reward marker! Instead say nothing and the lack of reinforcement will tell your dog all they need to know. A 10-second pause, when back in home base, after an incorrect choice will help to communicate to your dog that they did not choose correctly.

Sir is waiting to start Moving Directionals (L). We are both in position (R). I am standing about a foot in front of Sir and he is standing with his front feet even with the two cones.

After an away to me cue Sir moves to the target to his right, my left. To reset Sir I prompt him with a hand target but no verbal cue is given for the reset.

A no reward marker is not used in this situation because you are actually asking for two behaviors, a compound behavior: a discrimination (which direction to go) and a foot target behavior. If your dog goes in the correct direction but doesn't hit the foot target and you give your no reward marker, your dog may think they have gone in the wrong direction instead of realizing they did not meet criteria for the foot target. On the other hand, if they go in the wrong direction but hit the foot target they may become confused about the criteria for foot targeting.

Troubleshooting

- **Dog is afraid of cones** – If your dog seems overly worried about the cones you may need to set them around the house and let your dog desensitize themselves as the cones fade into just another object present in their life. Don't call attention to the cones, just set them out of the way, and over a few days move them around and then closer to where your dog eats, sleeps, and trains.
- **Dog goes to foot targets when no cue is given** – If your dog continues to offer foot targeting without waiting for a cue you need to build more mass on the stand at home base.

From directionals to flanks

Once your dog is confidently going to the cued foot target on each side, your work on directionals is pretty much finished. If you find your dog is dropping below a 95% success rate you may want to go back and work directionals sitting in front of your sitting dog for a while to get them back up to speed.

The next step is to go from directionals using foot targets in a line to flanks around a cone square. Before you move to flanking, you need to replace the tall cones or other uprights with regular-sized cones (about 12 inches). Continue to set your dog up with their front paws directly between the cones to encourage your dog to shift their weight back and not step forward as they begin flanking.

Most dogs transition to flanks easily because they already know which direction to go when cued and they enjoy the movement of circling. In Chapters 19 and 20 you will teach your dog to flank around cone squares, cone circles, an empty pen, and eventually to flank around livestock in a pen. Finally, you will generalize flanking around stock in a pen to loose livestock.

There is still a lot of work to do before you can take your dog to stock, since flanks are just one of the skills your dog needs. Fortunately, almost all of the herding behaviors can be taught using cone circles and a flirt pole without a ewe in sight!

CHAPTER 19

Herding RAMs – Flanks 1

For our directionals, *come bye* and *away to me*, to become true flanks we need to change our straight line setup into a circular one. The advantage of using a line of uprights and foot targets as props is that you have encouraged your dog to square their flanks, turn right and left at a 90° angle, instead of stepping forward before turning. Now you will be teaching your dog that the directional cues tell them which way you want them to flank or circle while maintaining the square start of the flank.

Flanks are the curved or circular paths that your dog takes to move around livestock, either clockwise or counterclockwise. The goal of a flank is to move your dog around stock to a new position *without* affecting the livestock. This means that the sheep, if stationary, remain stationary for the most part while your dog is moving. To prevent applying pressure to the livestock as your dog flanks, your dog needs to maintain the same (or more) distance from the stock as they flank. There are times your dog's flanking will cause the sheep to move, such as when your dog is very close to the sheep or when your dog flanks away from the pull and the sheep move toward the pull, such as toward a gateway.

If asked to flank, and not stopped, a dog should circle completely around the livestock while keeping the same distance away from the stock. Flanks are divided into two categories; flanks and off-balance flanks. A **flank** is the part of the circle where your dog is going to balance. **Balance** is the point where your dog needs to be to control the livestock *or* apply pressure to bring the stock directly to you. If you send your dog from your side to flank around the sheep, they are on a flank until they reach the point of balance. Once your dog reaches the point of balance and continues flanking back toward you, they are on an off-balance flank.

An **off-balance flank** is the part of the circle where your dog has gone past balance and is heading back toward you.

In these diagrams, the "B" teardrop or arrow is pointing to the circle that marks the point of balance, the place your dog has control of the stock. When your dog flanks toward balance the movement is just called a flank (R) but when they are flanking away from balance the movement is labeled an off-balance flank (L).

Dogs with a lot of herding instinct love to go to balance naturally and find it difficult to flank past balance. Thus for most dogs flanking is easy and off-balance flanking is difficult. The reason your dog finds it natural to go to balance is that balance is the point at which your dog is in control of the livestock.

Herding dogs are control freaks! They do not want their livestock to get away from them. Your dog needs to gain confidence in you to allow the stock to "get away" by going off-balance when you cue an off-balance flank.

As you work flanks you will want to be careful to vary what flanking behavior you ask of your dog. Sometimes you will ask for flanks and sometimes for off-balance flanks. You will *not* permit your dog to circle round and round or orbit the stock. A dog that is **orbiting** is running around the stock obsessively without thinking about where balance is. You want to maintain your dog's sense of balance at all costs! If you allow your dog to orbit excessively they will no longer seek balance and you will have to tell them where to be to control their stock. If your dog does not have strong herding instinct, you too will be in charge of cueing your dog's every move by telling them where to be to control and move their livestock.

The easiest place to get your dog to stop is at the point of balance because your dog is in control of the stock's movement at that point.

Flanks are an essential skill for your dog to have to be successful herding. Don't skip steps or move forward until you are confident your dog has completely mastered the directional exercises. Flanks are grown from directionals, so if your dog doesn't know their directionals they will flounder when you try to build on a shaky base. Your goal should be to grow flanking fluency from the moment you begin training directionals with your dog sitting in front of you in your house. Once you get out around stock you will be glad that you took the time necessary to give your dog a strong foundation that will set them up for herding success.

The most important thing to do before you jump into training flanks is to focus on giving your dog a solid foundation of stationary and moving directionals. A strong foundation is the way your dog learns what behavior they will need to perform to earn reinforcement.

Flanks

Before you start – Cone square setup

To teach flanks you need to set up a cone square. I use 8 plastic orange traffic cones. The cones I use are 12 inches tall and flexible, not rigid. I also recommend having about three dozen 18 inches stiff traffic cones that do not bend.

I use the smaller, heavier cones primarily inside but also outside when it is windy. The taller cones are less expensive and I use them primarily outside. The downside of the taller, cheaper cones is that they will not bend if you or your dog runs into them and they tend to fall over if it is windy.

Initially, as you did previously, you will set up two cones about a foot apart and have your dog stand with their paws between them to encourage square flanks as they go to their foot targets which are positioned off to each side. As soon as possible set your dog up *behind,* rather than between, these cones and watch to make sure they are shifting their weight back and not stepping forward to flank. Once they are flanking squarely, when set up behind the cones, you are ready to move on to using cone squares.

The reason you start with a cone square instead of a cone circle is that you want to encourage your dog to maintain square flanks. Although your dog starts out moving along the front of the square in a straight line, to their right or left, the momentum of their flanking movement will swing them out into a circular flank as they continue flanking around the square. In no time we will change the cone square to a cone circle.

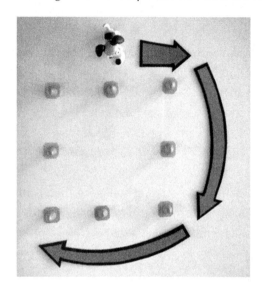

As your dog starts to flank along the flat side of the square they will tend to turn 90° and start the flank squarely. As they continue flanking, their momentum will carry them out away from the sides of the square and the flank will become circular.

Use 8 cones to set up a cone square that is 48 inches (4 feet) along each side. Make sure that the square is set up away from walls and other obstacles. Your dog will be going around the outside of the square so make sure they have at least 24 inches (2 feet) of clearance between the cones and any obstructions.

Before you start training, allow your dog to investigate the cones and get comfortable around them. Do not mark or reinforce their approach of the cones unless they are concerned about them. You want your dog to realize that the cones are just part of the stimulus picture but you do not want your dog to target the cones. The cones are a portable barrier to guide your dog along a path. You will be on the inside and your dog is to stay on the outside of the cone square.

The Rules

1. ***Goal*** – The goal is to teach your dog flanks and off-balance flanks.
2. ***When to begin teaching*** – Start this exercise after you have completed the Directionals and Moving Directionals exercises and have your dog positioned *behind* normal-sized cones rather than between two of them.
3. ***When to move on*** – Start by teaching very short flanks and once your dog is proficient move on to longer flanks.

4. ***Appropriate environment*** – Start in a fairly large room, move outside, go to livestock in a pen, and finally work with loose stock.

5. ***Setting up the environment*** – Work initially in the room where you taught Moving Directionals, if it is large enough. Otherwise, you will need to start outside in a fenced yard.

6. ***What props are needed*** – You will need 8 traffic cones or other 6 to 12 inch identical markers and your two foot targets from the Moving Directionals exercise. You may also use a barrier that your dog can see through such as an X-pen or short gate or panel. The barrier is placed against and to the inside of the cone square. Barrier use is optional but suggested.

7. ***Criteria in one sentence*** – The dog circles clockwise when cued *come bye* and counterclockwise when cued *away to me*.

8. ***Reinforcement to use*** – Use treats to start and then transition to a flirt pole, ball, or tug.

9. ***Cues to use*** – Use *come bye* and *away to me*.

10. ***When to add the cues*** – The cues should already be installed. If your dog does not know that *come bye* means move left and *away to me* means move right, they are not ready to start this exercise.

The Mechanics

1. ***Your position*** –Stand in the middle of your cone square to start.

2. ***Your dog's position*** – Your dog will stand in the center of a side of the cone square and on the outside of it facing you.

3. ***What is marked*** – You will mark your dog flanking *come bye* or *away to me*.

4. ***How and where the reinforcement will be delivered*** – Initially you will be handing your dog treats but eventually, you will reinforce using a flirt pole, tug, or ball.

5. ***How to grow the behavior*** – This behavior grows in several ways. The cone square becomes a cone circle, gets larger, and moves outside. You also transition from using treats to toys. Finally, you start off training only flanks and then add off-balance flanks later.

6. ***When to practice without your dog*** – Since this is new to you and your dog, you will definitely want to practice each new phase of this exercise without your dog. There are more new skills for you to learn than there are for your dog to master.

Feel free to use a wrist band to remind yourself of which direction is which. It is easy to get confused on directionals, especially if you are new to herding.

This is the setup you will be using for Phase 1 of Moving Directionals. A home base or station mat is optional. The RZ triangle indicates the Reinforcement Zone, the area in which you will reinforce your dog. Initially, you will reinforce your dog turning their head toward or moving toward a target but you will quickly withhold your mark and reinforcement until your dog gets to the target.

Flanks – Step by step

PHASE 1 – Cone square using foot targets

1. Generate a random list of 20 directional cues.
2. Place the list where you can see it while training.
3. Set up a square 4 feet in diameter using 8 cones.
4. Place each foot target about 3 feet on either side of where your dog will be standing, just *around* the corners of the cone square. The targets should be in the circular path your dog will be taking as they go around the cone circle and *not* in a line directly to each side of your dog. The targets should be placed about 12 inches away from the cone square and on opposite sides of your dog.
5. Place 11 treats into your treat pouch or hold them in your hands.
6. Stand in the center of the cone square and get your dog standing facing you. Reinforce the stand with one treat. You may use a piece of carpet or platform as a home base initially but it should be faded quickly.

---

7. When your dog is looking at you, cue the first directional on your list, either *come bye* or *away to me*. Look straight at your dog and don't look or turn toward the correct target.
8. If your dog turns their head in the correct direction but does not move, mark and reinforce by luring your dog onto the appropriate foot target. Lean over to feed the treat with your dog standing on the correct target. Your dog will be standing perpendicular to you on the target, not facing you.
9. When your dog is done eating prompt them to go back to their starting point with your hand and reinforce their return with a verbal marker such as *good*.
10. If your dog turns their head in the wrong direction or goes to the wrong foot target, prompt them to go back to where they started and pause for 5 to 10 seconds. Then go on to the next directional cue on your list.

11. Continue in this manner for 5 reps, following your random list of cues.

---

12. If your dog begins to go and *stand on* the cued foot target, mark and feed on the target before prompting them back to the start position. Continue in this manner until you have fed all 10 treats.

13. If after 5 reps your dog does not begin to move onto the cued foot target, instead they just turn their head in the correct direction, withhold your mark for a few seconds. Help your dog to figure out what they need to do to earn reinforcement by looking down at the appropriate target. Looking at the target should help your dog to make the connection between the cue and the foot target.

14. Once your dog learns they must touch the cued target with a foot to earn reinforcement, they will quickly shift to offering movement to the target.

15. Continue in this manner until you have fed all 10 treats and then take a break!

Sir goes from his station to touching the foot target on his right when given the away to me cue. I have marked and am feeding him while he stands on the target.

Next, I prompt Sir back to home base. I then cue come bye, mark and feed him a treat as he stands on the foot target to his left.

Your dog will likely take the addition of the cones in stride and not be concerned about their addition to the setup. Place the foot targets fairly close to your dog so that they can see them from their starting position. The foot targets should have a good amount of mass on them at this point and most dogs will immediately go to the cued foot target. Do not look at the cued foot target unless your dog needs a prompt to go to it, instead look straight ahead as you cue the flanks.

Troubleshooting

- ***Dog comes inside square to handler*** – If your dog consistently comes inside the square to you, rather than going to the cued foot target, you need to temporarily add a barrier to make the correct behavior easier for your dog. Set up an X-pen or other see-through barrier along the front of the square, or completely around yourself, and place the traffic cones on the outside with your dog. Once your dog learns to go to the foot targets, instead of coming inside the square, you can remove the X-pen.

- ***Dog does not hit foot target*** – If your dog moves in the correct direction but misses hitting the foot target consistently, try removing the foot targets. Your dog may have already figured out that the game is flanking and not foot targeting. Since you will soon need to transition from foot targeting to flanking, the sooner your dog makes that transition the better. Most herding breeds will find flanking more reinforcing than foot targeting.

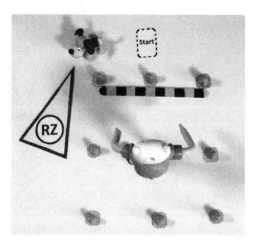

In Phase 2 you will fade or remove the foot targets and start having your dog flank farther around the cone square in order to earn reinforcement.

Note that the Reinforcement Zone has moved to the side of the cone square.

Phase 2 – Cone square without foot targets

1. Generate a random list of 20 directional cues.
2. Place the list where you can see it while training.
3. Place 11 treats into your treat pouch or hands.
4. Remove the foot targets from the cone square setup.

5. Stand in the center of the cone square and get your dog standing facing you. Reinforce the stand with one treat.

6. When your dog is looking at you, cue the first directional on your list, either *come bye* or *away to me*.

7. If your dog turns their head in the correct direction but does not move, mark and reinforce by holding the treat over the spot where the appropriate foot target was.

8. When your dog is done eating, prompt them to go back to their starting point and reinforce their return with a verbal marker such as *good*.

9. If your dog turns their head or goes in the wrong direction, prompt them to go back to start and pause for 5 to 10 seconds. Then go on to the next directional cue on your list.

10. Continue in this manner for 5 reps, following your random list of cues.

---

11. If your dog begins to move in the cued direction, mark and feed after they have gone around the circle and are at 2 or 10 o'clock. Then prompt them back to home position.

12. Continue in this manner until you have fed all 10 treats.

13. Take a break!

Use the foot targets *only* until your dog goes to them each time they are cued during *one* training session. You want to eliminate the foot targets as soon as possible. If necessary you can fade the targets by reducing their size and then removing them. Once the foot targets are gone your dog may get confused. To help your dog figure out what earns reinforcement mark anything your dog gives you in the correct direction; an eye flick, head turn, or step. Be sure to present the treat such that your dog has to take a few steps around the cone square to get it.

In Phase 2 you do the same training as previously but no longer have foot targets as a cue for your dog. Be sure to bring your dog farther around the square to mark and reinforce them.

After I prompt Sir back to home base I then cue away to me, mark, and feed him a treat for flanking to his right.

After you have done a few reps on each side, on the next trial wait and let your dog think, if they don't start to move immediately. Stay still and don't move your hand, turn your shoulders, or look where you want your dog to go. Your dog only has to take one step to get marked and you will then place the treat so that your dog takes another step or two to get it.

Soon your dog should start moving around the square when cued. You will then want to shape more steps by withholding your mark. The easiest way to keep track of how far your dog is going is to pick a cone to the side you are going to flank your dog. When your dog gets to the selected cone, you mark and feed a treat out ahead of them. Work this exercise until your dog will circle halfway around the square and end up almost behind you. Then begin to change your dog's starting point. Move their start point around the square to different positions but always turn to face your dog before you cue them.

Once your dog can flank in both directions halfway around the square, fade or remove the barrier between you and your dog. Do a session or two using the cone square *without* the barrier.

Cone square to cone circle
Next, reconfigure the square into a circle. Repeat Phase 2 using a cone circle. It will not take your dog long to adapt to a circle in place of the square.

Once you remove any barriers and are using only cones, you will want to pay close attention to your placement of reinforcement. To encourage your dog to stay on the outside of the cone circle be sure to feed as far outside of the circle as possible. It is easy to feed between cones and pull your dog into the center of the circle with you. Instead, place the reinforcer (treat) well outside the cone circle, as far outside of the

At the end of Phase 2, I removed the barrier and make the cone square into a circle. This should be done in two steps rather than both changes at the same time.

Place your reinforcer (treat) well to the outside of the circle to encourage your dog to stay out of the circle.

circle as you can comfortably reach. Other exercises will have your dog entering the circle but for this exercise, you don't want your dog to **slice** their flank, move closer to the center of the circle as they flank by entering the circle.

The next step will be to introduce your no reward marker. Since flanking is inherently reinforcing for most herding breeds, allowing your dog to continue to flank the wrong direction reinforces that incorrect behavior. In the next chapter, you will continue to shape your dog's circling into usable flanks by adding speed, distance, transitions, and new locations to your training. Flanks are a critical herding skill for your dog so don't rush through the phases of flank training.

Herding RAMs – Flanks 2

For my dogs, the fun really begins once I start using a flirt pole in training. Having prey as the reinforcer increases my dogs' arousal, focus, and speed. You may begin to throw your treats in Phase 3 of flank training but changing to a reinforcer such as a flirt pole or a thrown tug adds more arousal and energy to the training. I prefer a flirt pole but you can also use a thrown tug, as long as your dog will readily bring it back to you.

If you use a flirt pole you will want to use a small one inside. The following Phase 3 instructions can be followed substituting a tug or treat for the flirt pole but as the circle gets bigger it is quicker to use a flirt pole for reinforcement because your dog is always attached to you so you don't have to wait for them to bring a toy or tug back to you. If your dog is not interested in the flirt pole you may use a thrown tug or treat but the real advantage of using a flirt pole is that the rat truly imitates prey and brings out your dog's herding instinct. The sooner you can elicit and control your dog's herding instincts, the sooner your dog will be ready to herd livestock.

Phase 3 – Introduce flirt pole and no reward marker to cone circle

1. Generate a random list of 20 directional cues.
2. Place the list where you can see it while training.
3. Set up your cone circle using 6 to 8 cones but enlarge it to 6 feet in diameter.
4. To limit the length of your training session set a timer, estimate a 3 to 5-minute session, or stop when you get to the end of your list of directional cues.

5. Stand in the center of the cone circle holding your small flirt pole in one hand and the rat in the other. Get your dog standing facing you and reinforce with the verbal cue *good*.

6. When your dog is looking at you cue the first directional on your list, either *come bye* or *away to me*.

7. If your dog takes a step in the correct direction, mark with *yes* and immediately follow the *yes* with your releaser, *get it*, as you drop the flirt pole rat a foot or two in front of your dog on the circular path around the outside of the cones.

8. When you are done tugging with your dog, have them release the rat, and prompt them to go back to their starting point. Reinforce their return to start with *good*.

9. If your dog steps in the wrong direction use your *no reward marker*, prompt them to go back to start, and pause for 5 to 10 seconds. Then go on to the next directional cue on your list.

10. Continue in this manner following your random list of cues.

---

11. As your dog begins to move readily in the cued direction, withhold your mark and shape them to go farther before they get a mark and release cue. When you are done tugging with your dog, have them release the rat, and prompt them to go back to home base.

12. Continue this routine until you have done 10 to 20 reps, set a timer for 2 minutes, or estimate the number of reps or minutes. Don't go too long but if you and your dog are having fun don't worry too much about stopping exactly at 2 minutes.

13. Take a break!

You will add two new elements, the flirt pole and the no reward marker, to the exercise as well as using a slightly larger cone circle. To sort out all these new mechanics, practice without your dog. You need to start using a no reward marker because most dogs find flanking inherently reinforcing. If you don't say anything when they start heading in the wrong direction, they will most likely just keep right on flanking!

Sir is waiting for a cue and then flanking come bye.

I give my mark (yes) and say "get it" as I drop the rat to the floor in Sir's path. Then we tug to reinforce the correct flank.

I like to allow my dog to continue in the direction they were flanking while carrying the rat in their mouth. I usually allow them to continue flanking carrying the rat for about half a circle or so.

Troubleshooting

- ***Your mechanics are not precise*** – If you find yourself floundering as you try to use your flirt pole, directional cues, marker, releaser, and no reward marker while navigating a larger circle, you need to do more practice without your dog. Practice what you will do if your dog goes in the incorrect direction as well as in the correct direction. Make your cone circle smaller if you need to and then grow it later.

- ***You are confused*** – If possible, video your training and watch it either in slow motion or stop it often. Watch not only what your dog is doing but what you are doing during the training session.

- ***Dog gets stuck at the same spot around the circle*** – If your dog seems to get stuck at the same point around the circle, try moving your dog's starting point back a few cones. For example, if your dog is only comfortable going a quarter of the way around, by the time they get to the place they usually get stuck they will be closer to halfway around the circle.

*It is at this point, when my dog and I are fluent working with the flirt pole, the no reward marker, and the larger cone circle, that I start adding cues to begin and end our training sessions. I use **ready**, when we start training, and **that'll do** when we finish. These are optional so use them or not, as you see fit.*

PHASE 4 – Move your position outside the cone circle and off-balance flanks

In the last major shift before completing this exercise, you will move from the center of the cone circle to outside facing in, the same position as your dog. Before moving outside the circle, shape the rat's position from in your hand to the floor in front of you.

Start by standing in the center of the cone circle. Slowly lower the rat to your thigh and let it dangle there. Can your dog still flank? Once your dog can do this, lower the rat to your knee, then your ankle, and finally to the floor. Many dogs need a lot of practice to be able to work flanks with you standing in the circle with the rat at your feet.

After your dog can flank with the rat at your feet you will back up, step by step, to the outside of the circle. Now drop the rat into the center of the circle like the rat is a fish in the middle of a cone pond hanging from your flirt pole/fishing pole.

You and your dog will always be facing the center of the circle where the prey (rat) is located. Start with your dog standing beside you and send them away from you around the circle. Once you are sending them past balance, directly opposite you, you have begun to work on **off-balance flanks**. By definition, once your dog goes past the

These pictures show Sir hooked up to the rat on the floor and flanking away to me when cued. He will then be marked, released to get the rat, and have a tug session.

Sir really gets into this training, once the rat enters the picture. His level of arousal is very similar to what it would be with livestock present. Using a flirt pole brings prey into the training while you remain completely in control of your dog's access to it.

halfway point of the circle they are doing an off-balance flank because they are then moving past balance and toward you. Most dogs won't have much trouble going all the way around the circle if you shape this in small steps. Plus, although your dog will react to the rat as prey, this rat cannot look at your dog or turn its head so your dog will not react exactly to the rat as they will to livestock. It is much more difficult for your dog to know where balance is when there are no eyes or heads to get control of. Balance is the point of control.

As soon as your dog goes all the way around the circle from your side and returns to your other side in both directions (one complete revolution), start working on your dog flanking behind and, finally, in front of you. For this exercise have your dog sporadically flank in front of you, between you and the cone circle and, mostly, behind you.

Also remember not to do a lot of full-circle flanking, especially refrain from allowing multiple circles, as you want to preserve your dog's sense of balance. Do much more flanking half or three-quarters of the way around the circle rather than in complete multiple circles. To stop your dog, mark, release, and whip the rat either ahead of them or directly to them.

Remember not to repeat cues when your dog makes a mistake, instead continue to the next cue on your list. Sometimes it will be the same cue but often it will not. You don't want your dog to learn that if they make a mistake they just have to go in the other direction to be correct.

To shape your dog to do **off-balance flanks *behind*** you will use placement of your flirt pole rat. With your dog positioned at your side, step forward until you are between

When reinforcing your dog with the flirt pole an important goal is to keep your dog on the outside of the cone circle. Once in a while, your dog will inadvertently end up inside the circle. When this happens just maneuver your dog back outside the cone circle as they tug.

the cones in front of you. Be ready to flip the rat over your shoulder, the one farthest away from your dog, if your dog looks at you or turns their nose in your direction. Now cue the off-balance flank that will bring your dog behind you, mark, release, and flip the rat onto the floor behind and to the side of you. Your dog will go behind you to get the rat. If your dog heads in the other direction use your no reward marker, pause 5 to 10 seconds, and call them back. Shape your dog to go farther around behind you by withholding your mark, release, and toss of the rat. Work one side until your dog is confidently going behind you and then work the other side.

Use super high-value treats or the rat to shape **off-balance flanks *in front*** of you. Stand against a wall about 2 feet away from the cone circle and set your dog up on either side of you but slightly in front of you. Cue the flank that would bring your dog in front of you. If your dog heads in the other direction use your no reward marker, pause 5 to 10 seconds, and call them back. If your dog looks or turns their nose in your direction, mark and offer the treat or rat hidden in your hand that is opposite from where your dog started such that your dog has to come across in front of your body to get the treat or rat. Your dog will always stay to the outside of the cone circle.

Reset your dog to their original starting position and work this exercise until your dog is freely flanking in front of you. I like to toss the treat or rat in front of my dog as they are flanking to encourage movement. When your dog will flank one way in front of you, change your setup to the other side and get your dog to flank in front of you in the opposite direction. Make sure to take breaks and do lots of short happy sessions.

Eventually your dog will be able to change flank directions on the fly without stopping to change directions: https://youtu.be/24XARV7xyX0

You can work on your dog going behind or in front of you in either order. See which is easiest for your dog and work on that one first. Your dog will then have the idea that they can flank around the cone circle past you so going past you on the other side of you should be easier. It is usually more natural for your dog to flank behind you. Have your dog flank between you and the cone circle only occasionally at this point. You don't want your dog crossing over between you and the livestock to become a habit as it is only acceptable in limited herding situations.

Troubleshooting
- ***Dog struggles to go all the way around the circle*** – If your dog has trouble going around the circle and back to you, go back to standing inside the circle and shape your dog to flank behind you by slowly taking backward steps until you are outside of the circle.
- ***Dog struggles to go behind you*** – Take a step forward toward the center of the circle so that you are in line with the cones of the circle to make it easier for your dog.
- ***Dog struggles to go in front of you*** – Break it down so that your dog only has to do minimal movement to earn reinforcement such as look, lean, or tilt their head in the correct direction and raise the value of the reinforcer you are using.

Remember occasionally to practice having your dog flank between you and the cone circle only as you don't want crossing over, going between you and the livestock, to become their default choice for flanking past you. It is just good stockmanship for your dog to normally flank behind you and not between you and the livestock. Plus, if your dog crosses over between you and the stock at a trial when you send them to fetch livestock, you will lose all or the majority of your outrun points.

Phase 5 – Enlarge cone circle, move outdoors, and fade cones
Your dog has now mastered the basics of cone circle flanking! From here on out you will use the exact same mechanics but continue shaping flanks by:
1. Moving your circle outside.
2. Transitioning to your large flirt pole.
3. Growing the cone circle larger.
4. Fading cones out of your cone circle by removing every other cone.

5. Working flanks with no cones.
6. Finally moving the cone circle around a pen in a paddock.

Fading all of the cones is important for your dog's understanding that flanks are not dependent on cone props. To fade the cones you can start by laying them on their sides. Then over several training sessions remove every other cone until none remain. You may want to initially use a tree or trash cans to generalize and separate flanks from cones, if your dog struggles to flank without any props.

Flanks, with no circle markers, do not need to be perfect. The important thing is that your dog understands that they need to square off and flank the direction cued even when no cones are present.

This is the cone circle that Sally set up outside for Renn. Sally was able to use a very large circle because she threw a toy for Renn rather than using a flirt pole.

One big problem I have had to overcome over the years, concerning my training mechanics, is failing to pause for 10 seconds after giving a no reward marker. The pause is the most important part of the no reward marker sequence as it is a mild negative punisher. It is also the pause that separates cues so that the second cue does not reinforce the incorrect response to the first cue. Without the pause, the next quickly given cue reinforces the unwanted behavior.

Eventually, you will want to work on fading out the use of cones for flanking. You can always go back to using cone circles, and you will, but you want your dog to realize that flanking is not dependent on cones being present. Don't wait until you take your dog to stock to practice flanking without cone circles. You can use trees or trash cans as props to help your dog learn that they can flank without cones in the stimulus picture.

Sir is flanking away to me around the flirt pole rat with no cones.

The next phase of flank exercises will give you an idea of where you and your dog are heading as you generalize flanking around livestock. Your dog is *not* currently ready for Phase 6 but by understanding the final flanking exercises you will have a better grasp of why you need to work flanks away from livestock until they are fluent and have wrecking ball strength.

Here I am introducing Sir to flanking around an empty pen in my training area using my large flirt pole.

Phase 6 – Introduce flanks around stock with cones (for future reference!)

1. Move to a paddock *without* livestock and set up a large cone circle. Practice flanking.
2. Now add a small pen *without* stock that is inside of your larger cone circle (the cones should be at least 20 feet from the pen). Again practice flanking.
3. Put stock in the small pen with your dog on a long line and work your flanks.
4. Next have stock in the pen with your dog loose flanking around the pen and cones.
5. Start fading cones out of your cone circle by removing every other cone.
6. Continue fading cones by removing every other remaining cone.

7. Finally, work flanks around stock in the pen with no cones.
8. Have stock loose and your dog on a long line.
9. Have both stock and dog loose.

Generalizing flanks in Phase 5 gives you an idea of how you will transition your herding and obedience behaviors to livestock. Currently, you are not ready for Phase 6, taking flanks (or any herding skills) to stock, but when you are you will make the transition step by step. Taking a herding skill to livestock is no different than shaping any other behavior. Herding behaviors are just behaviors that include livestock.

The more you work your dog on cone circles, the longer it may take to fade the cones out of the picture. Move on as quickly as possible to flanking without cones, but plan to return to using cone circles in your more advanced training.

Combining flanks with in

Although you are not ready to take your flanks to stock, there is one more exercise that is vital to generalizing square flanking. After your dog can flank without cone circles (Phase 5 above) try having your dog alternate between walking in and flanking.

1. Start with your dog flanking around the rat, using your large flirt pole. Stop your dog and ask them to *walk in* to the rat. If they walk directly in to the rat, mark with yes, and release with *get it*.
2. Reset your dog and this time ask them to *walk in*. If they walk in, stop them and flank them, starting with a regular (not off-balance) flank. If they flank correctly, mark with yes, and release with *get it*. Be sure to loft the rat out into the path your dog is flanking.
3. Reset and alternate walking in with flanking. Eventually, ask for off-balance flanks too.

After your dog can alternate walking in with flanking, with a stop in between, move on to ask for a flank while your dog is walking in without stopping them. In the video I use cones so feel free to do this exercise *with* cones. The cones give your dog extra help in squaring their flanks, if you ask them to flank just as they are about to move into the center of the cone circle. If you use cone circles, later practice without them.

Watch Sir transitioning from walk in to flanking at https://youtu.be/gNapx917EGg

The important thing to keep in mind, once your dog can take random ins and flanks, is square flanking. No cheating!

Most dogs don't have trouble transitioning from flanks to walk in or from walk in to flanks but Sir did. I had to go back and work on these transitions away from livestock. I should have gone back sooner in our training but since I never have had a dog that struggled with transitions, I kept hoping he would improve. He didn't and we eventually went back and trained the transitions he struggled with.

When your dog can take their flanks **on the fly**, transitioning from walking in to flanking, flanking to walking in, or from one flank to the other without stopping, they have taken a huge step toward successfully herding. Most dogs take this exercise in stride but some struggle. If your dog struggles you want to train these transitions now and give your dog a head start on being successful when they are asked for the same behaviors around livestock.

We will revisit this exercise with livestock in a small pen before we ask your dog to take flanks on the fly around loose livestock, to set them up for success.

The next step
Before you can take your flanks to stock you will need to have obedience behaviors as well as a stop, walk in, and other basic herding skills trained. If you are anxious to work around livestock, work on sit, down, stand, heel, and recalls around penned stock. The more self-control your dog is able to demonstrate with obedience behaviors, the more likely they are going to be successful when you eventually take your herding behaviors to livestock.

Teaching directionals and flanks are a giant step toward herding proficiency. Spend the time your dog needs to gain proficiency at flanking. At the end of this section, Basic Herding Skills, I will talk more about transitioning to livestock. In the meantime, the next herding skills we will tackle are out and close.

CHAPTER 21

Herding RAMs – Out and close

There are several cues that are vital for precise herding:

- *there* or down to stop movement
- *walk in* and *back* to add or release pressure
- *come bye* and *away to me* to indicate direction to flank
- *out* and *close* as flank distance modifiers
- *easy* and *hurry* as flank and *in* speed modifiers

These cues give you a way to fine-tune your dog's movements as they interact with livestock. Herding is all about distance, angles, and speed of the interaction between your dog and the livestock. These three elements combine to create a moving picture that can look like a dance or turn into a train wreck.

An out or close allows you to move your flanking dog away from or toward stock to increase or decrease pressure they are applying to the livestock as they flank. Inexperienced dogs can get caught up reacting instead of thinking. By adjusting your dog's distance from stock, using *out* or *close*, or their speed while flanking or driving, using *easy* and *hurry*, may help them to relax and use their minds as well as their instincts to calmly control livestock.

---

*Changing your dog's flanking trajectory or speed necessitates a modifier cue. A **modifier** is a cue that labels a concept such as hurry up or move closer. The behavior is flank and the modifiers tell your dog to change their speed or distance from the livestock while continuing to flank.*

The difference between modifiers and other cues is that other cues name a **behavior** *and modifier cues label* **concepts.**

In this chapter, you will learn how to train out and close since they are trained similarly. **Out** means your dog widens out as they flank, moves farther away from the stock as they circle. **Close** means your dog comes in as they flank, moves closer to the stock as they circle. Being able to ask your dog to move farther away from or closer to stock as they flank is an important skill because many young or dogs new to herding tend to work too close to their stock.

Your dog will move a set distance for the *out* and *close* cues and then hold that distance as they continue to flank. These modifiers should *not* mean move farther and farther from or move closer and closer to the stock. Thus you do *not* want your dog to spiral farther and farther away from or closer and closer to the stock. Rather, these cues mean your dog should move from the circular flank path they are traveling to another circular path either farther or closer to the livestock.

It is easier for a dog to control stock if they are away from or off of the stock at a good distance. When a dog is in close, they have to flank much farther to affect movement of the entire group or flock as compared to when they are off at a greater distance. Having an *out* on your dog is almost as important and useful as having a stop!

Controlling a set of livestock more easily from a distance, rather than being in close, seems counterintuitive but if you go out and try moving a small flock of sheep you will quickly realize it is true.

The out cue modifies the flank and tells your dog to widen out or increase the distance between themselves and the stock while continuing to flank. Once your dog has moved out farther from the stock they should begin to flank on a new circular path that is beyond the circular path that they were on. Unless your dog tends to naturally flank too wide you will be using out more often than close.

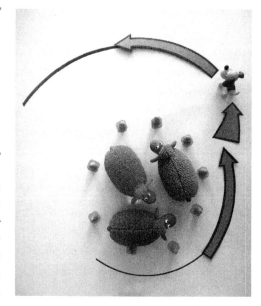

Sideways-moving dogs tend to flank out too far away from and forward-moving dogs tend to flank too close to their stock. Thus teaching *close* may be more important for a sideways-moving dog while teaching *out* may be more important for a forward-moving dog. The main problem with working too far away from the livestock is that your dog may lose contact with their stock.

Losing contact means that the dog is no longer controlling the movement of the livestock except in a very minor way. The stock is not affected by the dog even though the dog may be hooked up to the livestock from a great distance. The dog may flank along the farthest perimeter of a paddock, run fences, or purposely go out of sight of the stock. Some dogs run wide because they want to avoid interaction with the stock while some are very sensitive to pressure from the stock and are more comfortable at a greater distance from them. Note that if you push a young dog off too far, too soon they may learn to run too wide.

Dogs tend to widen out as they mature and gain experience herding. Don't be in a hurry to push your dog out if they are not causing the sheep to move as they flank around them.

*Some dogs like to **wind** in as they flank. They start flanking at the appropriate distance but as they flank they move closer and closer to the stock.*

Double cone circle setup
Training *out* and *close* requires *two* concentric cone circles. The inner circle has a diameter of 6 feet and consists of 5 or 6 short cones and the outer circle has a diameter of 16 feet and is composed of 15 or 16 tall or short cones spaced approximately 4 feet apart. Vary the number and spacing of cones in each circle as necessary for your situation.

I have two different sized sets of cones, the smaller I use for the inner circle and the taller for the outer circle. If you only have one size cones, place them quite close together for the inner circle and farther apart for the outer.

Out

THE RULES

1. **Goal** – The goal is for your dog to move away from the stock while continuing to flank in the original direction.

2. **When to begin teaching** – You can start training the out once your dog can proficiently flank both directions around a cone circle 16 feet in diameter.

3. **When to move on** – I teach the out using the large flirt pole and transition straight to penned stock.

4. **Appropriate environment** – Any flat area that has good footing, and is large enough for your dog to flank around the outside of the 16-foot cone circle.

5. **Setting up the environment** – Make sure the area you work in is free of obstacles or holes.

6. **What props are needed** – Use the large flirt pole and as many cones as necessary. (Sets of 2 different sized or colored cones are ideal but not mandatory.)

7. **Criteria in one sentence** – When cued *out* the dog immediately moves from the inner to the outer cone circle while continuing to flank in the same direction.

8. **Reinforcement to use** – Use the flirt pole rat.

9. **Cue to use** – I use *out*.

10. **When to add the cue** – The cue is used at the onset of training.

THE MECHANICS

1. **Your position** – Stand between the 2 circles and next to an outer circle cone. You will be about 3 feet from the cone and facing your dog.

2. **Your dog's position** – Your dog stands facing you at the next cone in the large circle, about 4 feet in front of you with their shoulder 1 to 2 feet from the cone.

3. **What is marked** – You will mark your dog as they cross through the large circle, moving from the small circle.

4. **How and where the reinforcement will be delivered** – Your dog will go and grab the rat, the reinforcer, when you release them with *get it*. The rat will be flipped into your dog's path along the outer circle.

5. **How to grow the behavior** – At first you will lure your dog by flipping the rat out to where you want your dog to go. After 3 reps you will no longer lure your dog but instead will wait for them to turn their head or start moving outward when cued *out*. Once your dog is moving, after the cue, you will release and reinforce your dog for moving through the correct cone circle. In time you will shape your dog to flank around the small circle, cue an *out*, mark, and reinforce them for immediately moving to the large circle and continuing to flank in the same direction. You will work the *out* in both directions, *come bye* and *away to me*.

6. ***When to practice without your dog*** – There are a lot of mechanics that happen quickly so you need to practice without your dog. You may want to use a bucket or other prop to stand in for your dog during this practice.

 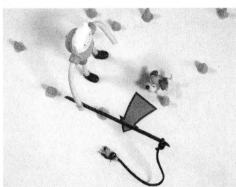

Start facing your dog while standing between two cones (one from each circle) and holding the rat in your hand. Your dog starts facing you, standing between the two cone circles, and next to a cone on the outer circle. You will drop the rat to the outside of the large cone circle, just beside and beyond the cone next to you as a lure, 3 times, cueing out *and then get it (release cue) each time. Once your dog starts moving on the out cue you can begin to mark your dog moving outward, with* yes, *before giving your release cue.*

This exercise is not as difficult to do as it is to explain. Once you have the mechanics sorted out in your mind, practice without your dog.

Before you start – Flirt pole training

You need to be comfortable with the mechanics of handling the flirt pole to teach *out* and *close*. If you need to refresh your flirt pole skills, go back to Chapter 14, Herding RAMs – Stop, and follow the introduction to the flirt pole instructions. Remember to use your marker and release cue every time you use the flirt pole, unless instructed to temporarily omit the mark. Practicing without your dog is highly recommended!

You also need to set up the two cone circles and do a few sessions with your dog flanking around both the inner and outer circles separately so that they learn to flank both directions on both circles. Your dog should stay on the circle they start on at this point. If your dog starts flanking come bye around the inner circle they should not switch by moving to the outer circle while continuing to flank come bye.

Start this exercise with both you and your dog facing each other in the 5-foot area between the two circles (ie not standing in the middle of a cone circle).

NOTE

You will work one flank direction at a time, *come bye* or *away to me*, for 5 to 10 reps, as noted in each exercise. Maintaining the same flank direction for several reps in a row eliminates the need for your dog to discriminate which direction to go; instead they can focus on learning only the new behavior, the out. You want your dog to develop a pattern for going out as they circle in each direction. In the final phase, you will ask your dog to listen for random flanks and then perform the out behavior when cued.

This series of pictures show me luring the out. I set Sir up, flip down the rat, and release him to get it (Phase 1 steps 1–7). Note that his position is not correct, he should be squarely facing me in his start position.

Out – Step by step
PHASE 1 – Getting movement

1. Stand next to and 3 feet away from a cone on the large circle, facing your dog, while holding your flirt pole in one hand and the rat in the other. You will be standing between the cone circles.
2. Your dog should be standing about 4 feet in front of you with their shoulder next to and 2 feet away from the next cone in the large circle.
3. Flip the rat 2 to 3 feet beyond the cone you are standing next to, and outside of the large cone circle. You are standing a yard away from a cone: flip the rat 3 feet to the opposite side of the same cone. The rat will land 5 to 6 feet away from you, on the opposite side of the large circle, in line with your shoulder.
4. Your dog should stay standing still, watch the rat fly over to the outside of the large circle, and land on the ground. The rat is now a lure for your dog.

5. Say *out* to prompt your dog to move toward the rat and then immediately say *get it*. Your dog will go between cones to get to the rat and will end up on the outside of the large circle.
6. Tug with your dog and then reset them to their start position.
7. Repeat luring your dog with the rat 2 more times to give your dog the idea of what they need to do to gain reinforcement.

8. Reset your dog to their starting position but instead of flipping the rat over to the other side of the large circle just say *out*. If your dog moves forward, outward, or looks in the correct direction flip the rat over the large circle and say *get it*. Then tug with your dog.

9. Repeat this step 4 more times, always going in the same flank direction.

10. Reset your dog and release and reinforce as your dog moves outward by taking at least one step. Repeat this step 4 more times, still in the same flank direction.

11. Take a short break!

---

12. Now change your setup by turning 180°. You will be facing the opposite direction and your dog will again be in front of you such that to move outward they will now turn in the opposite direction from your previous reps. If your dog was turning to the left they now will turn to the right to move outward.

13. Repeat steps 1 through 10 in this new flank direction and take a break!

When cued, your dog should take a step toward the outer, large circle in order to earn reinforcement. The cue *out* is just a release word at this point. Once you have shaped a step or two the next phase is to get more movement, more steps. Because you are using a flirt pole rat as the reinforcer your dog should think this is a really fun and exciting game.

After luring Sir 3 times I am now giving the out cue while still holding the rat. Once he starts to move out I release him to get the rat that I flip onto the floor in front of him (Phase 1 steps 8–10).

Troubleshooting

- ***Dog is confused*** – If your dog acts confused by heading the wrong direction or not moving at all, you are probably confused too. This is a simple exercise for your dog with a somewhat complicated setup. Look again at the diagrams to get a better understanding of the setup and your mechanics. If you are videoing, watch your video to see where things fall apart.

- ***Dog doesn't move on out*** – If your dog doesn't move when the rat is not on the ground to lure them, you can add a general release word after the *out* such as *okay, free,* or *break*. Your verbals would then be: *out, free,* and *get it* in quick succession.

PHASE 2 – Getting more movement

1. Set up your dog as in Phase 1. You move one cone back, away from your dog.
2. Give your *out* cue and wait for your dog to start moving outward. Then mark, release, and reinforce by dropping the rat 3 feet in front of your dog. (You are now adding a click or verbal marker between the cue and the release to the rat.)
3. If your dog does not move, reset twice more. If still no movement, go back to Phase 1.
4. At this point, you will shape your dog to take more steps by withholding your mark until they are flanking a few steps around the large circle before marking, releasing, and reinforcing.
5. Repeat, in the same flanking direction, until your dog trots or runs while flanking a few steps around the large circle.

---

6. Do the same exercise in the opposite direction.
7. Take a break!

---

8. Now start moving your set-up point around the cone circle for generalization.
9. Take another break after 10 reps on each side, 20 total trials.

Your dog should be getting into the game by this point. Phase 2 is very similar to Phase 1 but you want your dog to go all the way to the outside of the large circle immediately when cued and to move at a trot or faster.

In Phase 2 you are adding a mark and asking your dog to move a bit farther around the larger cone circle before reinforcing them. You are looking for your dog to go a bit farther and faster after moving out.

Troubleshooting

- ***Dog walks or hesitates*** – If your dog moves outward slowly, change how you present the rat. Instead of dropping it a few feet in front of them and letting it lie there, land the rat and *immediately* draw it away from your dog along the ground in the direction you want your dog to go around the outside of the large circle. The movement of the rat away from your dog should trigger their chase instinct and increase their level of arousal.

PHASE 3 – Flanking farther

1. Change your set-up point by moving a cone farther away from your dog. Turn toward the outer cone circle and step back against the inner circle. Your dog will now be perpendicular to you instead of being face to face. (See diagram.)
2. You will now change your initial cue to a flank and then add the out. So you would say *come bye, out, yes* and *get it*. The *out* should quickly follow the flank cue, after your dog has taken just a few flanking steps. Your dog should then move to the outside of the large circle and continue flanking. As your dog flanks around the outer circle you will mark, release, and reinforce by tugging. You are just adding a bit of flanking before and after the *out*.
3. Repeat 5 times in the same direction or until your dog goes out and keeps trotting or running around the outside circle.

---

4. Switch and work the other flank by going the other direction.
5. Repeat 5 times or until your dog meets criteria going this direction.

It should not be difficult for your dog to master Phase 3. Your position will change slightly and you will shape your dog to flank farther before and after moving from the inner to the outer cone circle when cued to do so.

Your position has changed in Phase 3 from facing your dog to standing perpendicular to them while facing the large outer circle. Your dog is going to flank a few steps before being cued out. This diagram shows the placement of the rat for reinforcement.

In Phase 3 you will change your position to move farther away from your dog and just in front of or in line with the small cone circle. You are at the intermediate stage of shaping your position from directly in front of your dog to the center of the small cone circle, the final handler position for these exercises.

Troubleshooting

- ***Dog doesn't want to flank before the out cue is given*** – Move another cone away from your dog to give them more distance from you and more time to flank before you ask for the out. Your dog may not be comfortable flanking very close to you so this gives them more space.

PHASE 4 – Handler moves to center of small cone circle

1. Now change your setup so that you are standing in the middle of the small circle and your dog is standing between the two circles facing you. Use large flirt pole.
2. Your dog will be doing the same behavior as previously, except that your position has changed relative to the cone circles and your dog. Your dog's position remains the same, except they are now turned toward the middle of the circles, facing you.

3.   This phase is similar to the one before it. Your dog should begin flanking, move out, and then continuing to flank on the outside circle. The main differences between this phase and the previous are the positions of you and your dog.

4.   Repeat 10 times and change to the other flanking direction.

5.   Now ask your dog to flank around the inside circle until they can complete one complete circle *without* switching to the outside circle. Repeat in the other direction. (This may take a while so have patience!)

6.   After a complete circle on the inside cone circle, ask your dog to flank again on the inside circle but after 3 to 6 steps cue the *out*.

7.   If your dog immediately moves to the outside circle and continues to flank around it in the same direction you initially cued then mark, release, and reinforce. Then throw a party with tons of tugging and laughing required!!!

8.   If your dog does not immediately move to the outside circle, give your no reward marker, get your dog to stop flanking, wait 10 seconds, reset, and go again. If your dog does not succeed after 2 resets go back and work Phase 3 but move to the center of the small cone circle. If need be, go back even further and set your dog up, cue *out, yes* and *get it*. Then try adding the flank cue back into the exercise. Work both directions. Go back in your *out* training as far as necessary for your dog to achieve at least a 90% rate of success and then move forward again.

9.   Take a break!

One final position change for you and your dog in Phase 4. You are now in the center of the small cone circle and your dog is now facing you. At this point, you will need to switch to your larger flirt pole, if you have been using your shorter one, to flip the rat outside of the large cone circle.

Most dogs quickly learn the out behavior, while flanking before and after it. You are going to build this behavior to the point that your dog will flank on the inside circle, in both directions, until you cue out. Your dog will then immediately move to the outside circle and continue to flank in the direction they were cued until you ask them to stop or you mark, release, and reinforce.

In Phase 4 you will have moved to your final position in the center of the small cone circle. At this point, you will have to use your large flirt pole to flip the rat to the outside of the large cone circle.

Break the exercises down as much as you need to for your dog to be successful!

Troubleshooting

- ***Dog outs before cued or doesn't out when cued*** – Both of these situations call for a no reward marker, stopping the flanking movement, a 10-second pause, and a reset. If your dog isn't successful after 3 tries, stop and take a break to think and plan what you need to work on. Is your dog not taking the out cue or offering the out when no cue has been given? You will have to play with this a bit and work on whichever part your dog struggles with. If you or your dog get frustrated quit for a while. If you are not having fun something is wrong so stop, take a break, and come back to the exercise at a later time.

- ***Dog struggles to stay on the inner circle for one complete revolution*** – You will need to break this down and ask for a quarter circle, then a half, three-quarters of a circle, another half, an entire circle, and finally a half-circle. Keep working one direction until your dog makes one entire circle but do *not* have your dog go farther than once around. No orbiting! Then work the other direction in the same way and take a break.

You never go wrong taking a break!

PHASE 5 – The final exercise

1. The last change of your setup, before going to penned livestock, has you again standing in the middle of the small circle with your dog between the two circles facing you.
2. Randomly cue *come bye* or *away to me*. (Random flank.)
3. Once your dog is flanking in the correct direction, randomly ask for an out before they complete one full revolution, before they get back to their starting point. (Pick a random point on the circle to ask for the out, such as halfway around.) Now your dog has to flank in the cued direction and go out when cued.
4. Occasionally throw in a full circle *without* an *out*.
5. Mix it up so your dog really has to listen and don't get upset or frustrated when your dog makes a mistake. You are making your dog think hard and tune in to your cues!

When your dog can confidently complete this exercise, they will definitely have a new capability! Congratulations on working through a lot of shaping to end up with solid flanks and an awesome out!

Don't be surprised if your dog gets confused with their flank cues when you try adding them to the final exercise. If they head the wrong direction, give your no reward marker, get them to stop, pause 10 seconds, and start again.

Most dogs find flanking inherently reinforcing and being cued *out* at different times and places around the circle gets them thinking and listening. This becomes a fast-paced, extremely fun game!

*If you have a sideways-moving dog, don't dwell on the out. You don't want your dog to become a fence runner. A **fence runner** is a dog that falls out and attempts to find and then run along a nearby fence rather than doing an outrun just wide enough to get behind the stock without disturbing them.*

Repeating modifier cues

Once you take out to livestock, remember that the criteria are to *move out* immediately when asked and then *stay out* and hold the new distance. There is no set amount of distance a dog has to move outward to be correct. If your dog moves out 5 feet but you need them farther out, you are free to repeat the out cue. In this situation, your dog has performed the correct behavior and you need them to perform it again. This also applies to cueing close. Thus your appropriately repeated cue reinforces the first correct out response and cues the second out.

This is one of the few times in herding that it is necessary and correct to repeat a cue.

Since *easy* and *hurry* are also modifier cues, you are also free to repeat them. For instance, if your dog is running and you cue them to slow down they may drop down to a trot. If you really need them to walk, you are free to repeat *easy* again. More on these modifier cues in the next chapter.

Teaching close

Teaching close *is* very similar to teaching out. Once you have taught your dog out you simply change your and your dog's starting positions to begin teaching close. Your dog is on the outside circle and you are between the circles. You start by flipping the rat between the circles as a lure. All of your verbals will be the same except that you will be cueing *close* instead of *out*. Work through all five phases above just as you did before. The exception is that you will need to get your dog flanking on the outside circle in Phase 4 – step 5 and Phase 5 rather than the inside circle.

If your dog is a sideways-moving dog, I suggest you concentrate more on close; if your dog is a forward-moving dog, work more on out. Your job is to know your dog and move them toward balancing behaviors on opposite ends of a continuum by putting more time and effort into the ones your dog struggles with. For example, if your dog prefers to flank come bye then spend a bit more time on away to me flanks and so on.

For training close, you will start between the circles and your dog will be on the outside of the larger cone circle. This diagram shows luring the close behavior. Follow the training plans for out but substitute the close cue and work at having your dog move inward toward the smaller circle instead of outward beyond the larger circle. Again, you will eventually end up in the center of the small circle, as shown in the picture, but your dog will be flanking around the large circle and moving to the smaller circle when cued.

Work close separate from out. Even when my dogs know both out and close, I usually only work one of the behaviors per session when using cone circles. Eventually, you can work both out and close in the same session if you want to really challenge your dog!

All herding dogs need to know the cued behaviors for moving closer to or farther away from stock as they flank but all dogs also have their preference for the distance from stock that they find comfortable. Just because your dog is comfortable very close or very far from livestock does not mean that is where they need to be to effectively handle and control stock. You will have to give your dog guidance until they learn how best to approach and control livestock. The key to knowing if your dog is the correct distance from stock is the reaction of the livestock.

If your dog is flanking fairly close, while not disturbing their stock, they may not need to be farther away but, even if your dog is flanking quite far from the stock, they may need to be even farther off, if their movement is affecting or unsettling the livestock. No two dogs (or people) interact with livestock in the exact same way. One dog may need to be really far off of a set of sheep to handle them calmly while another dog may be able to work very close to the exact same sheep without upsetting them.

Transitioning to livestock

When you are ready to transition the out and close to livestock, work in a small paddock and have your livestock in a small pen in the center. If you have a sideways-moving dog don't spend much time on out, to prevent them from becoming a fence runner, rather concentrate on close.

If your dog struggles with close around livestock, you may help them, if you are in the center of the pen near the livestock, by prompting them with your recall cue, here, *a few times to encourage your dog to flank closer to you and thus the livestock. Drop the prompt after three trials.*

There are only a few more Herding RAMs we need to cover before your dog is ready to start herding livestock. In the next chapter, we cover *easy* and *hurry*, which are the cues for slow down and speed up. These two cues are also walk in and flank modifiers and can be used to change your dog's speed while driving or flanking.

CHAPTER 22

Herding RAMs – Hurry and easy

Two more vital herding concepts are *easy* and *hurry*. If your dog tends to flank slowly or walk in quickly, the solution is to teach them cues that modify, speed up or slow down, their rate of movement. These modifiers are useful for changing the speed of flanks as well as walk ins. As you remember from the *out* and *close* training of the previous chapter, the difference between modifiers and other cues is that other cues designate a behavior and modifier cues label concepts.

Hurry and easy are also modifiers because they tell your dog how to change their speed, whether it is while flanking or walking in, but not to change the base behavior they are performing.

Often your dog will adjust their speed appropriately to the situation but sometimes you need your dog to get moving to catch escaping stock or slow down while driving or flanking. Using modifiers finetunes your handling and may not be essential for your dog and what you want or need them to do but training modifiers gives you more precise control on your dog. For example, by changing their speed, you can give your dog experience flanking at the speed that is appropriate for the situation.

Often if your dog is over-aroused and flanking too quickly, just by slowing their movement down their arousal level drops. Instead of trying to reduce their arousal so that they slow down, by slowing them down their arousal level naturally drops. This also works for under-arousal. By speeding your dog up their level of arousal naturally increases. You can also affect the reaction of the livestock by changing just the speed of your dog's movement. Stock will react more calmly if your dog slows down and more abruptly if your dog speeds up. Slower movement of your dog tends to be perceived as less threatening to livestock while faster movement is perceived as more of a threat.

Sir is trotting as he goes around the sheep in the small paddock. Note how the sheep have turned back in front of me as they head away from the camera.

Now Sir is cantering or running instead of trotting. Notice how far the sheep move off of the fence as Sir approaches at greater speed, the distance the sheep move away from the fence as Sir passes between them and the fence, and that the sheep turn back beyond me. Speed affects livestock movement!

Teaching the speed up modifier is usually easier because dogs seem to naturally respond to it. The hurry or speed up cue is a quick, excited *"chit-chit"*. Chit is a made-up word that generates a feeling of excitement and repetition of it naturally tends to speed dogs up, especially while flanking. When you give the cue you should notice a significant increase in the speed of your dog's flank. To make things easy for training, I have defined speeding up as moving up one gait and slowing down as dropping down one gait.

In dogs, the four main gaits are: walk, trot, canter, and gallop. Certainly, your dog may slow down or speed up while remaining at the same gait but, by initially looking for a change in gait to determine when your dog has met criteria, you have simplified things for both you and your dog. Eventually, you can accept your dog's change of speed while maintaining a gait but for these training exercises it is easiest to keep gait changes as the primary criterion since gait changes are easily seen.

The easiest way to teach hurry and easy is to use a 6 to 8 feet cone circle and a long target stick. A target stick at least 3 feet in length with a ball the size of a ping-pong ball or approximately 1½ inches in diameter is about right. Make sure the color of the ball is easily seen by your dog in the environment where you will train hurry and easy.

Before you start – Target stick

If you did not use a target stick to teach the stand in Chapter 12, Obedient RAMs, let's do a recap of target stick training.

A **target stick** is just a stick or dowel rod with a ball on the end. I like to use a clicker for training nose targeting because it is a precise behavior. So grab a clicker and have several good treats ready. Be sure to set a timer for 2 minutes or count out 20 treats to limit the length of your training session.

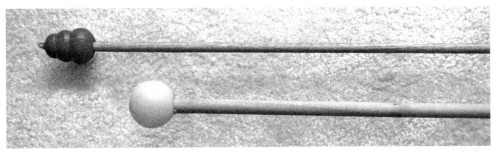

These are a couple of homemade target sticks that I use in my training. Target sticks are easily made with a dowel rod and a ping-pong ball or other rounded objects on the end as a target. Dowel rods are readily available in lengths up to 3 feet.

If you have a long target stick, start by holding the stick fairly close to the ball, within a foot. Hold out the ball on the target stick a foot or two in front of your dog and at nose level. Be ready to click! Usually, your dog will investigate the ball by coming up to it with their nose. As they approach the ball with their nose, click and then feed near the ball.

Now move the ball about a foot away and allow your dog to approach it again. Repeat this until your dog touches the ball with their nose. As they touch the ball, click, and feed a treat near the ball. Repeat several times with your dog touching the ball with their nose. Then move the ball about 2 feet away from your dog and repeat having your dog touch the ball with their nose.

If your dog does not readily touch the ball, then you will have to shape the ball touch. Move the ball away from your dog so that they will notice it. That movement may arouse your dog's interest enough to approach the ball. If not, mark and reinforce your dog looking toward the ball, then approaching the ball, and finally touching the ball.

Be sure and click just as your dog touches the ball. If you click too early you will get your dog putting their nose near the ball but not touching it and if you click too late you will reinforce your dog moving their nose back away from the ball. Also, you want to make sure your dog is not touching with their open mouth or biting at the ball. Sometimes it is better not to click than to mark the wrong behavior. Initially, the presentation of the ball will be the physical cue or signal for the nose touch. Once your dog is readily touching the ball you can add a verbal cue such as *touch*, *ball*, or *nose*.

Work this behavior several sessions, until your dog can touch the ball, held high or low, and even jumping off of the ground to touch it. Now start moving the hand holding the target stick back away from the ball. Incrementally shape the position of your hand holding the target stick until you are holding it at the end opposite the ball.

Work to get your dog following the ball on the target stick high or low, and walking, trotting, or cantering. You are ready to start training hurry and easy.

This is the basic setup for teaching both hurry and easy – a long target stick, a cone circle, and a dog that knows how to follow a ball target.

Notice I turn my body as a prompt for Sir. The speed I turn initially indicates for him to speed up or slow down his movement. Eventually, this prompt is faded.

Hurry

THE RULES

1. **Goal** – The goal is for your dog to speed up one gait while continuing to flank in the original direction or to speed up one gait while walking in. (For example, if your dog is moving at a walk they should begin trotting.)

2. **When to begin teaching** – You can start training the hurry once your dog can proficiently flank both directions around a cone circle 6 to 8 feet in diameter.

3. **When to move on** – I teach hurry using a target stick and transition straight to stock.

4. **Appropriate environment** – Any area that is flat and large enough for your dog to flank around the outside of the 6-foot cone circle.

5. **Setting up the environment** – Make sure the area you work in is free of obstacles or holes.

6. **What props are needed** – Use a target stick, treats, and as many cones as necessary.

7. **Criteria in one sentence** – When cued *chit-chit*, the dog immediately speeds up one gait while continuing to flank in the same direction.

8. **Reinforcement to use** – Use great treats.

9. **Cue to use** – I use *chit-chit*.

10. **When to add the cue** – The cue is used at the onset of training.

ABOVE: Be sure to work both directions, come bye and away to me. When I trained this, I held the target quite high, way above the level of Sir's nose. I should have either made the cone circle smaller or the target stick longer so that I could keep the target ball at a lower level that would promote a more natural head carriage.

ABOVE RIGHT: I switch my hands on the target stick, depending on which direction Sir is heading, so that I am leading with my hand rather than my body.

THE MECHANICS

1. *Your position* – Stand in the center of your cone circle.
2. *Your dog's position* – Your dog stands on the outside of your cone circle facing you.
3. *What is marked* – You will mark your dog as they drop down one gait when cued.
4. *How and where the reinforcement will be delivered* – You will hand your dog a treat slightly ahead of their circular path.
5. *How to grow the behavior* – At first you will verbally cue the behavior but the increase in speed of the target stick will prompt your dog to speed up.
6. *When to practice without your dog* – No need to practice without your dog.

Hurry – Step by step

1. Set up a cone circle 6 to 8 feet in diameter using 8 to 10 cones.
2. Use a target stick that is long enough to reach a foot beyond the cone circle.
3. Reinforce your dog for following the target stick around the outside of the cone circle in both directions at a walk. Keep the target at head level or a bit above.
4. Give your *chit-chit* cue and move the target stick faster, ahead of your dog.
5. If your dog starts trotting mark and reinforce with a treat.
6. If your dog continues walking after 3 trials, you need to increase your dog's arousal level. Now as you cue *chit-chit* you will start to trot in a very small circle in the center of the circle. Your increased movement will increase your dog's level of arousal and should prompt your dog to trot. Fade your quick movement once your dog starts to trot when cued.
7. Work this in both directions until your dog will speed up immediately when you cue *chit-chit*. Then work on your dog moving from a trot to a canter.

Most dogs figure *hurry* out quickly. High energy dogs, in particular, like to move quickly and respond instinctively to the sound of the *chit-chit* cue by speeding up.

Training hurry and easy: https://youtu.be/o9Rb7WRx_FE

Teaching easy

Easy is taught just as you taught hurry, using a cone circle, target stick, and treats. Just follow the steps you used for teaching hurry and substitute *easy* for *chit-chit* and slow down the target stick instead of speeding it up. Be sure to say easy in a calm, quiet voice.

Unfortunately it is not natural for a dog to slow down when they hear the easy cue but it is an essential behavior for your dog to master. Some dogs don't seem to realize they can move slowly and be relaxed around livestock. It is truly a game-changer to have a cue that can be used as a brake that slows your dog down without stopping them!

Your dog probably will not take an easy cue if they are tense when working stock. Work your dog in small areas taking breaks until both you and your dog relax. Slowing down is almost impossible for a dog in high arousal.

Easy is more difficult to teach because it too is a concept and although dogs naturally respond to an exciting-sounding word by speeding up they do not naturally slow down when they hear *easy*. Other cues that people use for slowing down include *time*, *take time*, and *steady*. The criteria for easy is to slow down one gait while continuing to flank or walk in.

Sadly, sticky dogs tend to learn easy as they are more comfortable slowing things down and pushy dogs tend to learn hurry since they like to move quickly.

Easy, then easy and hurry together – Step by step

1. Once your dog is speeding up reliably, start working on *easy* by repeating the 7 steps above for teaching hurry. Change to using the cue *easy* while slowing down the movement of the target in front of your dog at the same time.
2. Take a break.

---

3. Work hurry and easy several times separately until your dog is performing them fluently. You can now work at having your dog move from a trot to a canter and from a canter to a trot. (It may be difficult to keep your dog cantering for any length of time unless you also run around the center of the cone circle to keep your dog's level of arousal high.)
4. When your dog is fluent with both cues, start fading the target stick. At first, just extend your arm and later keep your arms at your side. You probably will have to continue to turn around the circle with your dog, especially at the trot and canter.
5. Finally, work both *easy* and *hurry*, including the canter if you can, until your dog is reliably speeding up and slowing down on cue in both directions.

---

6. Generalize these speed modifiers by using them when your dog is recalling to you, going out on a retrieve, or when loose leash walking.

7. Take your speed modifiers to penned stock. At this point, return to prompting your dog by holding out your arm as you walk around the pen. Eventually, you can stand still with your arms at your side and let your dog do all of the work.

Once your dog responds to the hurry and easy cues, while flanking around livestock, you can generalize the modifiers to walking in too.

You may have to prompt your dog to speed up or slow down their flanks when first taken to livestock. To prompt your dog, hold your arm out toward and in front of your dog, as if holding a target stick, and walk or trot around the penned livestock as you give your cue. Quickly fade the arm prompt and your movement.

Be sure to give the cues with the speed and volume that you want your dog to match in their response. *Easy* should be cued softly while being drawn out. *Chit-chit* should be cued more loudly and quickly.

Knowing how to speed up and slow down can help your dog learn to appropriately respond to different herding situations. Initially, most inexperienced dogs are only comfortable flanking or walking in at one speed. It is not uncommon to find, with a forward-moving dog that flank = gallop and walk in = trot while with a sideways-moving dog flank = trot and walk in = hesitate or clap. This is when modifier cues come to the rescue!

For example, Sir, a very forward-moving dog, became much more relaxed once he learned an *easy* cue and slowed down while flanking. He quickly generalized slowing while flanking to offering to drop down a gait on short outruns in a small paddock. He learned that if he slowed down as he approached the stock that they lifted more calmly and he could drive them off at a controlled pace. He no longer startled the stock and then frantically tried to regain control. Until Sir was taught to slow down on cue, I never saw him voluntarily offer to slow down while working livestock.

With basic herding skills in place, the last RAM to cover is the bite. All dogs should have a cued bite for self-protection and confidence while herding. Even if your dog won't bite stock, their confidence around stock will soar after bite training. As the bite cue is just an adaption of the *get it* cue you are well on the way to having a cued bite!

CHAPTER 23

Herding RAMS – The bite

Every dog needs a bite. Without a bite, your dog has no way to protect themselves from aggressive livestock. Having a bite and the self-protection it embodies gives your dog confidence when facing truculent stock. Often your dog will be moving livestock into a confined area where they do not want to go. Sometimes an animal will be ornery and will not move away from your dog unless your dog can enforce their eye with their teeth.

Often a confident dog will not need to bite. Their confident body language convinces the stock that they mean business and they will not be tested. Other times your dog may be working in close quarters where the stock cannot see them and your dog may need to bite a rear leg to encourage the stock to move forward.

The bite defined

A bite is using the teeth to grip something. In herding, a **bite** is a grip of an animal, usually on the nose or lower leg with a quick release. It can be dangerous for a dog to grab and hold on. You want your dog to bite to increase pressure on the livestock to move away from your dog. If the livestock is facing your dog, they should bite the nose and if the livestock is facing away from your dog, they should bite the lower rear legs.

When biting rear legs, it is safest if your dog bites as low as possible to avoid being kicked. Because of their anatomy, animals kick up and out. Where your dog bites is determined by instinct, to a large degree.

Some dogs like to grab onto tails and hang on. Tail hairs have sensory nerves around the hair follicle, but pulling hair is generally less painful than biting skin. Biting tails also puts the dog into a dangerous situation as they are directly in the kick zone when hanging near an animal's hocks. Besides tails, other unwanted bite targets include: ears, sides of the face and body, and hocks or upper rear legs.

Usually, the less confident a dog is, the less likely they are to bite directly on the nose. Some dogs may even lack the confidence to look directly at the livestock. If a dog is in front of stock but averts their eyes and looks away from the stock, even if they don't turn their head, the livestock will read the look away as a lack of confidence and act accordingly.

Often if a dog maintains eye contact with livestock, the stock will become insecure and give to the dog by turning away or backing up.

A cued bite

Having a bite on cue is particularly helpful for dogs working within sight of their handler. Especially in a trial situation, you usually do not want your dog to bite unless you cue the bite. Cattle in trials often require your dog to bite in order to move them, while at sheep trials your dog will usually be disqualified if they bite. Some judges will allow bites on sheep if the sheep are aggressive to the dog and the dog bites directly on the nose. A dog that grabs the side of a sheep is almost certain to be disqualified. A **cheap shot** is a bite to the side of an animal and may include the dog hanging on as they run alongside the animal.

A bite is also essential for practical livestock handling. Having the bite on cue gives you a lot more control of its use, although I encourage my dogs to use their bite anytime they deem it is necessary to protect themselves or move livestock. You will find that the more confident your dog becomes, the less they will need to bite.

Will all dogs bite?

Although a bite provides self-protection and boosts confidence, not all dogs will bite. Part of the difference is breeding and part is personality and experience. If a dog bites and is punished, by the handler or the stock, they may refrain from biting. If a dog is shy or lacks confidence they may be too inhibited to bite.

The first time or two a dog attempts to bite may well determine if they will develop a solid bite. A good first experience doesn't guarantee a good bite but a bad first experience often sets them up for being reluctant to bite. Bad experiences may include being injured by the livestock on the first few attempts or being severely punished for attempting to bite.

Some dogs have confidence without a bite and some don't. Not all dogs without a bite lack confidence but a bite definitely helps boost a dog's confidence!

Puppies and young dogs tend to have undeveloped confidence and are more prone to lose confidence if injured or punished. Protect your young dog's confidence at all costs by not putting them in harm's way too soon and helping them whenever the livestock refuses to give to them or becomes aggressive toward them.

Bite
THE RULES

1. **Goal** – The goal is for your dog to bite on cue and quickly release.
2. **When to begin teaching** – You can start training this when your dog fluently takes their cues while training with a flirt pole.
3. **When to move on** – I start teaching this with a flirt pole rat or tug and eventually transition to stock.
4. **Appropriate environment** – Start inside.
5. **Setting up the environment** – You don't need a lot of room for training because you are initially training a grab and release of a toy.
6. **What props are needed** – Use 2 identical tugs or rats. The best tugs to use are ones that have some stiffness or rigidity to them such as a firehose tug.
7. **Criteria in one sentence** – You are teaching two behaviors in this exercise, bite and release: When cued *get it*, your dog immediately grabs the part of the animal in front of them, nose or rear leg. When cued *mine* they immediately release the animal. (Although you will cue the release of the grip of the tug/rat, you most likely will not need to cue the release of the bite on an animal.)
8. **Reinforcement to use** – Use tugging to reinforce the grip and use gripping a second tug to reinforce the release of the first tug.
9. **Cues to use** – I use *get it* and *mine*, to release if necessary.
10. **When to add the cue** – The cues are used at the onset of training.

The Mechanics

1. ***Your position*** – Stand facing your dog.
2. ***Your dog's position*** – Your dog stands facing you.
3. ***What is marked*** – You will mark with *yes* when your dog grabs one tug and then mark again with *get it* (to cue grabbing the other tug) when they release the first tug.
4. ***How and where the reinforcement will be delivered*** – The reinforcement for grabbing the tug, when cued, is tugging with your dog and the reinforcement for dropping or releasing the tug, when cued, is cueing *get it* and having your dog grip the second tug. The cue *get it* is the reinforcer for letting go of the first tug.
5. ***How to grow the behavior*** – At first you will have your dog grab one tug on cue, tug, and then have your dog release that tug and grab the second tug. When your dog is readily grabbing and releasing on cue, eliminate the second tug and have your dog grab, release, then re-grab the same tug when cued.
6. ***When to practice without your dog*** – No need to practice without your dog.

I like to use two tugs that are quite thick and fuzzy or hairy to imitate the nose of a sheep. When you are teaching the first phase use softer, smaller tugs to start.

Before you start – Flirt pole and tug training

The groundwork for the bite has been laid in your precise use of cues when training with the flirt pole, specifically the *get it* cue. If you have not used the flirt pole to teach the stop, refer back to Chapter 14, Herding RAMs – Stop. In the flirt pole directions, the marker (*yes*) is separated from the release to grab the rat or toy (*get it*). The other foundational behavior your dog needs to have is releasing a tug on cue. I use *mine* as the cue for my dog to release the rat or tug but any reliable verbal release cue will work. If you have worked with a flirt pole and you have a release cue, then your dog is ready to transfer your *get it* cue from grab the rat to bite livestock.

Bite – Step by step

Phase 1 – Grip and release tug

1. Start facing your dog with a tug in your hand. Have the second, identical tug in your back pocket or tucked into the back of your waistband such that your dog cannot see the second tug.
2. Cue *get it* and offer the tug to your dog. If your dog does not grab the tug, move it around to increase your dog's arousal.

3. When your dog grabs the tug, mark with *yes* and tug with your dog.

4. After a short tug (a few seconds) make the tug go "dead" by holding it still. If your dog continues to tug, place your hand with the tug against your leg to hold the tug still.

5. When your dog stops pulling on the tug, even for just a moment, mark with *yes* and bring out the second tug.

6. Immediately cue *get it* as you offer the second tug to your dog.

---

7. Repeat steps 2 through 6 until your dog can begin, stop, and drop or disengage from the first tug when cued.

8. Take a break

9. Now repeat the exercise with only one tug. Your dog should grip and then release the tug when cued.

Troubleshooting

- ***Dog will not grab tug*** – You may have to whip the tug around to get your dog interested in it.

In this sequence, I am holding the tug parallel to the ground at head level. The tug imitates the nose of a sheep. Sir is moving at speed from 6 foot away to grab, tug, release, and then eat a treat.

- ***Dog will not grab tug*** – If moving the tug does not get your dog grabbing it, try putting it on a string and dragging it along the floor to increase its resemblance to prey.
- ***Dog will not release tug*** – If your dog will not release the tug even though you keep it very still, bring out the second tug before your dog stops pulling on the first tug. When your dog sees the second tug and releases the first tug mark the release with *yes*, cue *get it*, and tug for just a moment. Eventually, wait for your dog to release the first tug before bringing out a second one.

For the next phase, you start out holding the tug parallel to the ground in your hand at your dog's head level. When your dog is fluent with you holding the tug and driving from 4 or 5 feet away to bite, you are ready to move on to the next step. Now you will need to devise a way to secure your tug such that the end your dog will bite sticks out parallel to the ground at the level of your dog's head.

Now Sir is going to grab the tug as I stand next to it. I point to the target while giving my get it *cue. He comes in fast and grabs the tug without hesitation. After the grab, I mark with* yes *and feed a treat.*

I made a simple tug holder by sliding my tug through the handle of a milk crate and then tying the tug and the milk crate to a fence. This setup put the tug at a good height for Sir to bite. Make sure the tug holder is secured in place so that if your dog pulls on the tug neither the tug nor the tug holder pops forward and scares your dog.

Phase 2 – Grip and release stationary tug

1. If you have been offering the side of the tug to your dog, start offering the end of it for them to grip.
2. When your dog is grabbing and releasing the end of the tug on cue, start holding it parallel to ground at the head level of your dog. Repeat trials with the tug in this new position until your dog is biting and releasing it fluently.

---

3. Now attach the tug to some type of holder and have your dog grab it, when cued, as you stand next to it. Initially, point to the tug and then fade pointing.
4. Once your dog grabs the stationary tug, immediately cue your dog to release it, and offer another tug as the reinforcement for releasing the stationary tug. You may also reinforce with food if you prefer.
5. Move yourself away from the stationary tug over a few sessions until you can send your dog 4 to 6 feet to grab and release it.
6. Move to new locations to generalize the behavior.

This is basic shaping and generalization. Once your dog can grip and release a tug in your hand on cue, it should be fairly easy for them to do the same to a tug off of your body.

In this sequence, Sir goes in for the bite without me prompting him by standing near the tug or pointing to it. He is now grabbing the tug on a verbal cue alone.

Phase 3 – Get a bite

Once I go to livestock, I switch my verbal cue from *get it* to *get a bite*. The cues start with the same word and probably make more difference to me than to my dog. You may stay with the *get it* cue, if you prefer.

If your dog does not bite when cued you will be left with capturing the behavior, naming, and reinforcing it, when your dog bites spontaneously. Most dogs don't bite frequently because they are not challenged by livestock often. If your dog snaps near or nips a nose or leg, mark the bite attempt, then reinforce and encourage your dog with praise. If your dog takes a cheap shot, a bite on the side of an animal, use your no reward marker protocol to discourage this behavior.

Remember you should still be working unaggressive livestock. At this point, whenever your dog is working and the stock stands up to or comes after your dog, you should move to help your dog by coming up next to them to present a united front. Then cue and encourage them to bite. You want your dog to know that they can protect themselves and that you will back them up, if need be.

Never discourage your dog from standing up to and biting stock that is acting aggressively by repeatedly lowering their heads, pawing, stomping their feet, trying to butt, or come after your dog.

As this is not a setup, be on guard and ready to encourage your dog to bite as soon as you realize that the stock is resisting your dog. If your dog holds their ground and keeps eye contact, the stock may turn or back off or they may come after your dog.

If your dog bites or attempts to bite unruly stock, reinforce their behavior with lots of excited praise. You want your dog to learn that their bite is reinforced by the stock giving to them as well as your praise.

There are some setups you can use to allow your dog to practice their bite on livestock. One way to work on a heel bite is by walking with your dog behind a flock of sheep in an enclosed area such as an alley. Have your dog on a 6-foot leash and carry a stock stick or crook. Follow the sheep and when you get within a few feet of their rear ends encourage your dog to get a bite. After your dog is taking heel bites on cue you may be able to alter the setup so the sheep are facing your dog and you can walk in with your dog and encourage them to bite noses too. Just remember, safety first!

The best setup I have come up with to transfer the nose bite to livestock involves using a few dairy heifers or steers weighing 300 to 500 pounds or several dairy cows. In a small paddock, feed some grain over a few weeks to settle the stock and allow it to be comfortable in the paddock. Then put your dog on a 6-foot leash and carry a crook or stock stick. Walk into the paddock, close the gate, and stay near the gate. You are looking for the stock to remain settled and eating.

If the stock doesn't pay much attention to you and your dog, stop and wait for them to finish eating. Once finished they will soon become curious and walk over to investigate your dog. Watch your dog to make sure they are not trying to escape as the cattle approach. If your dog is afraid, step toward the cattle and encourage them to back off using your crook or stock stick. Gauge your dog's reaction and if they are still afraid, exit the paddock and try again another day. If your dog does not seem afraid as the cattle come within the range of your leash with their heads down to sniff your dog, encourage your dog with *get it* as you step forward with your dog. Your dog may not even need to bite to startle the cattle and turn them around. If your dog does get a bite, all the better! Reinforce a bite with enthusiastic praise!

A similar setup can be used with sheep, if you have a barn where they can stick their heads out through a gate or between boards into an alley. If a curious ewe puts her head into the alley encourage your dog to *get it*. You might entice some ewes to put their heads into the alley by feeding a bit of grain or hay, if the floor is suitable. If your dog grabs or snaps at an ewe, they will figure out quickly that they don't want to tangle with your dog and will refrain from sticking their heads out, no matter the enticement.

*Be sure you are not using ewes that are jugged with lambs. A **jug** is a small enclosure where a ewe and her newborn lambs are kept for a few days to ensure that they bond and that the lambs get off to a good start. Ewes with newborns may be quite aggressive as they protect their lambs and should not be used.*

Working to maintain and build your dog's confidence in all aspects of training is vital but nowhere is it more important than in bite training. A confident dog will project power to livestock and will have much less need to bite but, they will have the skill to do so if need be.

At this point, your dog has all of the basic herding skills in place that they need to control and move livestock. Your dog should now know stop, in, back, come bye, away to me, out, close, easy, hurry, and bite. Getting all of that training on your dog is a huge accomplishment and hopefully, your training has been a lot of fun!

Now that your dog has all the skills they need to herd, you may be surprised to learn that they may not instinctively know how to use these skills. In the next chapter, we will look at a few examples of teaching our dogs how to implement the instinctual and learned skills they have in order to move and control livestock.

The real fun and excitement come when your dog takes their new skills to livestock. If you have been working on your obedience behaviors around stock and your dog can sit, down, stand, heel, and recall next to penned livestock, you are ready to experience the awe and magic of "working dogs". I hope you find herding as fulfilling and addictive as I do. I know your dog will!

CHAPTER 24

Generalizing the herding RAMs

As amazing as your dog is, they may still struggle to work stock to the best of their ability. Although they instinctively know how to control stock, they may need guidance to apply both instinctive and learned behaviors. Skills your dog may struggle with include rating stock, distance to flank away from stock, speed of approach or flank, and negotiating tight spots.

Rating stock is adjusting the speed of approach to livestock such that they are controlled but not startled. Stock needs to be rated while fetching and driving, where a steady, calm pace is desirable.

Most herding breeds have the instinct to read and handle livestock that is far superior to our abilities. It is awe-inspiring to watch your dog move and control stock with ease. Seeing such awesome ability can lull us into thinking that our dogs have all of the knowledge necessary to handle livestock. The truth is, although your dog may have amazing ability, they probably don't know how to use those skills to optimally accomplish every herding maneuver.

When driving or fetching livestock, your dog needs to rate their livestock by reading the situation and applying just enough pressure to control the stock and move it calmly and smoothly. Too much pressure and the stock will bolt; too little pressure and the stock will drift or stop and may begin to graze.

Your dog will approach or handle stock at a certain speed or in a specific way. Their instincts and personality may dictate that they are too pushy or too sticky. They may not even realize that they can handle stock in a different way from what is natural for them, so they may need to learn a new way to interact with stock in certain situations. In some situations, their method of dealing with the situation is just plain wrong.

When your dog struggles to cope with a situation or maneuver, it becomes your job to help them learn how to be successful. You need to step in and help your dog generalize learned skills to new situations.

Go between fence and stock

An example of using generalization to grow your dog's skills is training your dog to go between stock against a fence or stock in a corner. If your dog can get stock off of a fence, they can then generalize that skill to getting stock out of a corner. Some dogs have this skill in their innate repertoire but many do not.

In this situation, I have asked Sir to go around four ewes, in a tight corner, who are all facing him. He needs to turn his head, or at least his eyes, away from the ewes and toward the fence to break his hook up with them and indicate that he intends to go along the fence and around them. Once a dog acquires this skill, pulling stock off a fence or out of a corner, it is theirs for a lifetime.

The problem is that the dog attempts to stay hooked up to the livestock, maintain their eye on the stock, while they slip between the stock and the fence. This is natural because herding dogs' modal action pattern has "eye" as a strong and integral component but the behaviors of flanking past the stock and staying hooked up to them are mutually exclusive, in this situation. To get between the fence and the stock, your dog *must* turn their head away from the stock, thus indicating to the stock that they intend to go between them and the fence. If they stay hooked up as they flank along the fence, they will push the stock along the fence rather than slightly away from it, so that they can get between the stock and the fence. So how do you teach a dog to get stock off of a fence, if they don't naturally have that skill?

Shaping to the rescue

I ran into this exact situation with my young dog, Hart of Gold. Hart had no fear of going between the stock and the fence but lacked the skill of turning her head away from the stock. She would stay focused on the sheep and push them along the fence a few feet until she would stall out and stop.

My traditional training had dealt with this problem. The solution I had learned was to take the dog by their collar and "help" them by pulling or dragging them between the sheep and the fence. My presence, between my dog and the sheep, encouraged the sheep to move away from the fence.

While doing traditional herding training I had often thought that there must be a better way to teach this exact skill to my dog. Here was a chance to come up with a better way. I needed to define the behaviors that comprised the skill, teach those behaviors, formulate a plan to implement those behaviors in this situation, and work my plan. Simple!

Developing this plan was dependent on me really knowing my dog. How was she reacting in this situation? How did she normally react when she was confused? Was she afraid or just confused about how to handle this situation? What skills did she have in place that I could use? It all came down to using Hart's learned skills to shape a new behavior.

Here are the steps I came up with for – **Go between sheep and fence**:
- *Define behaviors*
    1. *Flank*: Move forward between stock and fence
    2. *Head turn toward fence*: Turn head away from stock and toward fence.
- *Teach behaviors* – In this situation, I already had both of these behaviors in place. Hart knew how to flank and I had taught her a head turn as a puppy, as the first steps of teaching a spin.
- *Formulate plan* – The tricky part of teaching this was that Hart needed to do both behaviors at the same time, turn her head while moving forward. The plan I came up with was:
    1. Set up the original scenario with Hart standing along the fence facing the sheep on the fence while I held a box clicker.
    2. Cue the flank that would take her between the sheep and the fence.
    3. Click for a step forward, even if she was still looking directly at the sheep.

4. Let her push the sheep along the fence until she stopped and stood still.

5. Pause and wait for Hart to look at me for direction, which was her normal reaction when she was confused.

6. Remain stationary when she looked at me.

7. Click as she turned her head away from me to look back at the sheep.

8. Pause and wait for Hart to either look at me again and repeat step 7 or click if she turned her head farther away from me and toward the fence.

9. Re-cue flank, if necessary.

- **Work plan** – After Hart stopped and stood, it only took a few clicks to get her turning her head toward the fence and away from the sheep. She then offered a few more steps forward so I did not need to re-cue the flank to get forward motion. Once Hart had moved forward a few steps, with her head turned outward, the sheep moved away from the fence and Hart flanked cleanly through.

I immediately reset the trial and Hart needed only a few clicks, of either feet moving forward or head turning toward the fence, and then she flanked through again. By the third trial, Hart needed only the flank cue to flank immediately and cleanly between the sheep and the fence. I never had to work on this again because in just a short time Hart had gained a new herding skill to use for a lifetime.

In this situation, as in most when marking around livestock, I used the continuation of herding as the reinforcer for the click. I don't usually use a clicker when herding but I did in this situation because it was novel and stood out clearly as a salient marker.

In this case, my dog had the skills necessary but not the knowledge of how to use them. Don't assume your dog knows how to control and handle all situations with livestock, no matter how much herding instinct they possess.

Generalizing easy from flank to fetch

Another example of teaching a dog to implement a known behavior in a new situation, generalization, is one I faced with Sir Gold. Sir is very athletic and quick. He likes to flank fast and this often leads to reacting instead of thinking. I needed to teach Sir to flank easy, the slow down behavior explained in Chapter 22, to get him to relax and slow down when flanking. When I taught Sir to slow down while flanking I did not realize he would generalize this behavior to his outrun and thus vastly improve his lift.

The fetch situation with Sir was that he would do a nice outrun but come in too fast on top behind the sheep and startle them instead of starting or lifting them calmly toward me. When he did occasionally come in and lift the sheep calmly, the fetch that followed was picture-perfect but, when he flushed the sheep, the fetch was too fast with quick, frantic flanks as Sir overreacted to the sheep's erratic movements that he had caused.

Sir had no problem generalizing speed changes when I moved from my front yard to sheep. I worked in a small paddock with penned sheep to transition slowing down while flanking. I put a long line on Sir so that I could give a small tug to lightly punish his maintaining the current gait when cued to drop down one gait. Since Sir liked to flank quickly, continuing to flank at speed was inherently reinforcing for him. Waiting for him to tire and slow down voluntarily was my preferred option but I did not want him mindlessly orbiting the sheep. Because of his previous training of hurry and easy with a target stick away from livestock, Sir was soon slowing down and speeding up around sheep on cue.

When transitioning the easy cue to livestock (present in the paddock but not in this picture) I had Sir on a light long line and used my extended arm to prompt him to slow down when cued. At the beginning of this session, when Sir was highly distracted by the sheep's movement, I needed to give a light tug on the line when he did not drop down one gait when cued. After 2 or 3 tugs, he started taking my easy cue so I dropped the line and let him drag it. Later in the session, I also faded my arm prompt.

Once Sir had generalized speed up and slow down around loose sheep in a small paddock, I decided to try a very short fetch in that paddock. The length of the outrun was constrained by the size of the little paddock. Before teaching Sir to slow down, his fetch in the small paddock was virtually nonexistent. He would flank around the sheep so quickly that they would flush off of the far fence long before he could get behind them and they would be at my feet before he had any chance to fetch them.

I gave Sir his fetch cue as usual and expected him to blast around behind the sheep with the usual explosive result. I purposely did not ask him to slow down on his little outrun, to see how he would handle it. I expected a rocketing outrun, since we had not worked on generalizing the slow down while flanking to slow down while fetching. When flanking I was in the center of the paddock near the sheep but when fetching I sent Sir from my feet.

As soon as I sent Sir, everything was different! He trotted on his outrun, which was the appropriate pace given the space constraints, calmly lifted the sheep, and fetched them the short distance to me. I was amazed! Sir had generalized slowing down to a new behavior without any help from me. The behavior generalized because it helped Sir control and handle the sheep and thus was inherently reinforcing for him. I believe Sir just did not realize that he could slow down while fetching, it was not in his innate repertoire. Once it was introduced, he immediately adopted it because it worked for him.

Sometimes we assume that our dogs behave in a certain way because they find it inherently reinforcing, and they may, but they also may behave in that way because they don't know any other way to behave in that situation.

Jump sideways

Another behavior that spontaneously generalized to herding was rear foot awareness. **Proprioception**, awareness of body and limbs in space, is great for herding dogs since they will be working in difficult footing at times. I taught Sir to keep his front feet on a small platform and pivot his rear feet around in a circle in both directions. Great puppy training but not terribly useful for herding, or so I thought!

One day I was working Sir on several ewes along a fence. The ewes split and some ran along the fence, so I sent Sir to bring them back. Once they were all gathered together I asked Sir in to put pressure on the ewes. I wanted Sir to take responsibility for preventing them from getting away again. As he moved closer the ewes became more nervous and eventually started to split. Sir jumped sideways with all four feet and landed about a foot to his right, exactly on balance to prevent the ewes from splitting.

As much trouble as it is to video every session, I guarantee that if you don't you will miss something incredible! I regret that I don't have videos of the amazing sessions when Hart learned to go between the sheep and the fence and Sir jumped sideways.

I was amazed! I had seen many dogs jump sideways with their front feet but I had never seen a dog jump sideways with all four feet. I then realized, by jumping sideways, Sir was now perfectly positioned to flank in either direction. If he had only moved his front feet, he would have been at a disadvantage to move the direction he had come from. Too cool!

Unfortunately, I don't have a video of Sir jumping sideways with all 4 feet but I know for a fact that his training in proprioception was the foundation for that amazing sideways jump.

I called my friend, who owns Sir's mother, to ask if jumping sideways ran in the bitch's line, since I owned his sire and had never seen his sire do this behavior. She replied that she had *never* seen a dog jump completely sideways when working stock. Sir had generalized a behavior because it worked for him, it was inherently reinforcing.

You will find other behaviors that your dog spontaneously generalizes, as well as seemingly simple herding behaviors that your dog needs your help to accomplish. Don't assume your dog knows everything there is to know about herding. Dogs may come with a lot of instinctive behaviors that are far beyond your capabilities but new situations may require you to shape new behaviors that are beyond your dog's current capabilities. I guarantee your dog will amaze you with what they can do but will also amaze you with what they struggle to do.

Positive herding is a journey of learning for you, your dog, and your livestock. Have fun and enjoy the journey!

Positive Herding 102

If you have successfully completed the exercises in this book, you and your dog are now prepared to start herding livestock! *Positive Herding 102* is the companion book to *Positive Herding 101* and provides instruction on transitioning the herding skills your dog learned, apart from livestock, onto stock: from introduction of stock in a pen to advanced herding skills necessary for trial or farm work. Stockmanship is also covered in detail as it is the key to reading, controlling, and moving livestock with the least stress possible.

Be sure to visit my website at *positiveherdingdog.com*. I hope to join up with you again in *Positive Herding 102*. Happy trails, happy trials!

Acknowledgements

I am truly grateful for those who have believed in my ability to learn, transform, and then teach herding in a different way. The people who taught me invaluable lessons and believed in me when I doubted myself include: Kathie Arnold, Alesia Schauf, Debbie George, Ron Kilstrom, Kate Malatratt, Diane Spisak, Curtis Dukes, Tom Damewood, Scott Rupert, Parvene Farhoody, and Sally Adam. Your unwavering support and encouragement has meant the world to me.

I would be remiss if I did not mention Barb Bennett, although she is no longer with us. Barb was one of the earliest and staunchest believers in my ability to make a difference in the lives of herding dogs. And she was a heck of a lot of fun!

Sincere thanks also need to be extended to Nyle Sealine for the hundreds of hours he spent showing and explaining herding and stockmanship to me and fellow herding student and friend, Joel Hollatz. Those truly were the "good old days". You taught me to stand still and shut up, profound herding concepts.

This book never would have seen the light of day without the extensive time and effort invested reading and re-reading my attempts to put thoughts into words. Thanks so much Chris Bond and Jane Roznovsky. Also, many thanks to my great formatter and more, Jo-Anne Friedlander; proof readers Helen Zulch and Connie Krider; and photographer and friend Laurie Burbank.

Special thanks to Bob Bailey for generously penning the Foreword and allowing me to participate in Chicken Workshops and learn about behavior from a truly extraordinary teacher.

The person most deserving of my profound thanks and respect is my ever-patient husband, Kerry. He has cheerfully listened to more "dog talk" than any non-dog enthusiast should have to endure and then offered simply brilliant insights that I had missed. Thanks for always encouraging and supporting me through the years and the tears.

Through all of the years of questing for herding knowledge, my dogs have been an unwavering source of love and enthusiasm for any and all schemes I have put forth in the name of training. They have been my patient teachers and willing students, as they taught me invaluable lessons over the years. I've loved you one and all!

BB
Purdin
June 2021

References

Alexander, Melissa. 2003. "'NRMs' No Reward Markers." *clickertraining.com*. July 1. Accessed 2009.

Bailey, Robert E. & Parvene Farhoody. 2013–2015. 40 Hour Discrimination Operant Conditioning Workshop. Bailey–Farhoody Chicken Workshop. Columbia, MD.

Bertilsson, Eva & Emelie Johnson Vegh. 2010. *Agility Right from the Start*. Waltham: KPCT/Sunshine Books.

Burch, Mary R. & Jon S. Bailey. 1999. *How Dogs Learn*. New York: Wiley Publishing, Inc.

Chance, Paul. 2006. *Learning & Behavior*. Belmont: Thomson Wadsworth.

Coppinger, Raymond & Coppinger, Lorna. 2001. *Dogs: A New Understanding of Canine Origin, Behavior, and Evolution*. Chicago: University of Chicago Press.

Farhoody, Parvene. 2018. *Behavior Technology 101: Discrimination and Generalization*. St. Charles: Behavior Matters.

Fisher, Gail. 2009. *The Thinking Dog: Crossover to Clicker Training*. Wenatchee: Dogwise Publishing.

Garrett, Susan. 2005. *Shaping Success*. Chicopee: Clean Run Productions, LLC.

Laurence, Kay. 2008. Whippits – Teaching: self control & play skills. Waltham: Karen Pryor Clicker Training (video).

Luck, Laurie. 2015, July 24. My Dog Knows It, He Just Won't Do It! How to Achieve Fluency. Retrieved 2015, from *clickertraining.com*.

Pryor, Karen. 1985. *Don't Shoot the Dog!* New York: Bantam Books.

Pryor, Karen. 2005. Clicking With Cues: A Powerful Tool in Agility Handling. *clickertraining.com*. March 1. Accessed 2010.

Ramirez, Ken. 1999. *Animal Training: Successful Animal Management through Positive Reinforcement*. Chicago: Shedd Aquarium.

Reid, Pamela, J. 1996. *Excel-erated Learning*. Berkeley: James & Kenneth Publishers.

Glossary

Arousal: The state of being alert, awake and attentive. Performance will be affected if a dog is under- or over-aroused.

Aversive: Anything an animal will work to escape or avoid. Can be primary or conditioned.

Back chaining: Teaching the last behavior of a chain first, then the next to last, etc. until you have trained the first behavior of the chain.

Balance: The point where a dog controls the stock and if they turn into and apply pressure to the stock at this point, the livestock will move straight toward the handler.

Behavioral momentum: Consists of the mass and velocity of behavior, and is a theory developed by John A Nevin to explain why behaviors differ in strength.

Bite: A grip of an animal usually on the nose or lower rear leg. A desired bite is a grip with a quick release.

Bridge: A marker that "bridges" the time between the marking of the correct behavior and the reinforcement that is to follow.

Bump flank: A mini-flank that ranges from a dog taking a step or two sideways while continuing to face the stock, to just shifting their weight from one front foot to the other.

Chain: A series of behaviors that always occur in the same order. The chain starts with one cue and the following behaviors are cued by the behavior that came directly before them.

Clapper: A dog which often lies down quickly and is reluctant to get up and move when working stock.

Classical conditioning: Also known as Pavlovian conditioning. Determines involuntary responses – an animal responds automatically and has no control over the response, eg. the sound of a bell causes a dog to salivate.

Conditioned emotional response: A learned emotional reaction or response to a certain conditioned stimulus.

Contact (with stock): The mutual attention between the dog and stock or predator and prey. If a dog works too far away from their stock the livestock will no longer pay attention to them and the dog is said to have "lost contact" with their stock, which is highly undesirable.

Cover: The desire to control stock by instinctively flanking around them to prevent their escape.

Criteria/Criterion: The parameters that define a behavior. Almost every behavior is composed of many criteria. Criterion is singular, criteria is plural.

Cross driving: Driving stock perpendicular to the direction the handler is facing.

Crossing over: Any time on an outrun that the dog goes over an imaginary line between the handler and the stock, the dog has "crossed over". This is highly penalized at trials.

Crossover dog: A dog that was initially trained using primarily positive punishment but has been switched to being trained with primarily positive reinforcement.

Cue: A discriminative stimulus: a stimulus, an event, or thing that elicits a certain reaction, that when present the behavior will be reinforced.

Extinction: The gradual lessening of a behavior due to lack of reinforcement.

Extinction burst: The tendency of a dying behavior to return in full force for a short period, often right before it finally extinguishes.

Fading (a cue): Making a physical cue, such as a hand motion or a target, smaller and smaller until it is eliminated.

Fence runner: A dog that, instead of doing an outrun just wide enough to get behind the stock without disturbing them, falls out and attempts to find and then run along a nearby fence.

Fetch: The drive from the lift to the handler's feet.

Flank: The curved or circular path that the dog takes to move around livestock, either clockwise or counterclockwise. The flank can be split into two parts; flank, going to balance, and off-balance flank, flanking away from balance. (See "Off-balance flanks".)

Flight/fight zone: The stock's comfort or safety zone. The size of this zone varies depending on the dog or person involved and the livestock's perception of the threat they embody.

Flirt pole (FP): Light flexible pole or lunge whip with a toy on the end of an attached line.

Foot target:: A target on the floor that the dog touches with their foot or feet.

Forward chaining: Teaching the first behavior of a chain first, then the second, and so on until the end of the chain is reached.

Generalization: A process in which an animal takes a learned behavior and performs that behavior to criteria in new environments and situations.

Gripping: The dog biting the stock. (See also "bite".)

Hold: The dog freely flanks, without cues, to keep stock in front of them while not allowing the livestock to get away from or past them.

Hook up: The instinctive behavior of herding dogs to look at and immediately lock onto their prey with laser focus.

Instincts: Innate behaviors an animal is born with, which they have not had to learn. Instinctual behaviors generally override learned behavior. (See "Modal action patterns".)

Jackpot: Giving a large quantity of treats for exceptional performance, a form of differential reinforcement.

Jug: A small enclosure where a ewe and her newborn lambs are kept for a few days to ensure that the lambs and ewe bond and that the lambs get off to a good start.

Latent learning: Learning that is not immediately expressed and occurs without any obvious reinforcement of the behavior. Latent learning may take place between training sessions when an animal processes the training.

Lift: The point at which the stock begin to move under the influence of the dog

Line dog: A dog which naturally holds a line on the fetch or drive, once it is established.

Modal action patterns: A set of instinctive behavioral sequences that usually run to completion. For herding breeds this would be: orient > eye > stalk > chase > (grab bite).

Modifier cue: A cue that labels a concept rather than a behavior, eg. "hurry up".

No reward marker (NRM): A verbal cue that tells the dog they are no longer heading towards reinforcement, in other words they are incorrect. A form of negative punishment.

Off-balance flank: The part of the circle where the dog has moved off of balance and is heading away from the point where they have control of the livestock.

OIL behavior: Override Instinctual with Learned behavior

Operant conditioning: Also known as Skinnerian conditioning. Determines voluntary behaviors. The animal has a choice over its response, which will be influenced by the consequence to its past behavior. (See also "Reinforcement" and "Punishment".)

Outrun: Flanking from the handler's feet out and around stock before lifting and fetching them.

Power: The confidence a dog has in their ability to deal with truculent stock. The dog will stand up to and bite, if necessary, stock that challenges them.

Presence: The ability of a dog to project self-assurance to the livestock, be readily noticed by them, and thus be less likely to be challenged.

Pressure: Pressure is the opposite of pull – it is the desire of the stock to move away from perceived threats. (See "pull".)

Proprioception : The ability to sense the position, location, orientation, and movement of the body and its parts in space.

Pull (or "draw"): The desire of the stock to move towards perceived safety and comfort.

Punishment: Anything that weakens a behavior and decreases the probability of recurrence.

Ram: Intact (un-castrated) male sheep.

Rate of reinforcement: The number of reinforcers earned and delivered in a set amount of time.

Recall: The behavior of the dog coming back to the handler immediately when cued.

Reinforcement/Reinforcer: Anything that strengthens a behavior and increases the probability of a behavior occurring.

Release word: Word which tells the dog the behavior has ended.

Response cost: Removing the handler's attention from the dog for 10 seconds to decrease the behavior they just performed by withholding reinforcement. Response cost is by definition a negative punisher.

Reward: Something given in return for wanted behavior, but a reward is not necessarily reinforcing. A reward is not another word for a reinforcer. (See "reinforcer".)

Sequence: A series of behaviors that follow each other in no particular order. The most common example of sequences are found in agility. An agility run consists of many numbered obstacles but each run is unique in terms of the order of the obstacles.

Shaping: A training procedure that uses the reinforcement of successive approximations to build a desired behavior. Almost all training is shaping.

Shedding: Separating one or more animals from a group and maintaining control of those animals.

Sliced flank: A flank that the dog begins by shifting their weight forward and moving towards the stock.

Square flank: The desired movement of a dog when flanking, so as not to put added pressure on the stock. The dog shifts their weight backward and turns to start their flank at a 90° angle to the stock.

Stimulus: A thing or event that sets the stage to elicit or initiate a behavior.

Stimulus control: Four requirements for control of a behavior to be complete; animal responds to the cue each time, animal does not perform the behavior without the cue, animal responds with the correct behavior, animal doesn't offer this behavior for another cue.

Stockmanship: The knowledgeable and skillful handling of livestock.

Time-out: A form of negative punishment. Removing the dog from a situation the dog likes such as working sheep for several minutes, to reduce unwanted behavior such as lunging at sheep.

TRaC skills: Timing, Rate of reinforcement, and Criteria.

Tucking the corners: To keep a larger group of livestock bunched together while driving them a dog will flank out to a corner to push the animals fanning out back into the group.

Wearing: The lateral movement of the dog behind stock to move a large group or the dog holding stock to the handler.

Wether: Castrated male sheep.

Appendices

Chapter 8 (page 102)

Liver cookies recipe (for dogs)
- 2 ½ cups sifted whole wheat flour
- ½ cup dry milk powder
- 1 cup liver puree
- ½ teaspoon salt
- ½ cup farina cereal (Cream of Wheat)
- 1 cup grated carrot - optional
- 6 tablespoons bacon grease – optional
- 1 egg
- ½ cup cold water

Mix all ingredients together and add only enough water to form a thick dough. Use tablespoons to scoop up dough, drop into extra wheat flour, and form into balls. Press balls onto cookie sheet to flatten.

Bake 8 to 10 minutes at 350°F. Cookies will be soft.

Once cooled put into plastic bags and freeze until needed.

Chapter 10 (page 129)

The Traffic Light Record Form

Date: ....
....
....
....
....

Date: ....
....
....
....
....

Date: ....
....
....
....
....

Date: ....
....
....
....
....

Date: ....
....
....
....
....

Resources

Behavior and Learning

Burch, Mary & Jon Bailey. 1999. *How Dogs Learn*.

Chance, Paul. 2006. *Learning & Behavior*.

Clothier, Suzanne. 2002. *Bones Would Rain from the Sky: Deepening Our Relationships with Dogs*.

Coppinger, Raymond & Lorna. 2001. *Dogs: A New Understanding of Canine Origin, Behavior, and Evolution*.

Donaldson, Jean. 2005. *The Culture Clash*.

Garrett, Susan. 2005. *Shaping Success: The Education of an Unlikely Champion*.

Pryor, Karen. 1999. *Don't Shoot the Dog: The New Art of Teaching and Training*.

Pryor, Karen. 2009. *Reaching the Animal Mind: Clicker Training and What It Teaches Us about All Animals*.

Reid, Pamela. 1996. *Excel-erated Learning: Explaining How Dogs Learn and How Best to Teach Them*.

Marker training

Barney, Carolyn. 2007.*Clicker Basics for Dogs and Puppies*.

Bartlett, Katherine. 2018. *Teaching Horses with Positive Reinforcement: A Guide to Achieving Success with Clicker Training*.

Book, Mandy & Cheryl Smith. 2001. *Quick Clicks: 40 Fast and Fun Behaviors to Train with a Clicker*.

Book, Mandy & Cheryl Smith. 2006. *Right on Target: Taking Dog Training to a New Level*.

Fisher, Gail T. 2009. *The Thinking Dog: Crossover to Clicker Training*.

Laurence, Kay. 2009. *Teaching with Reinforcement: For Every Day and in Every Way*.

Laurence, Kay. 2008. *Clicker Training: The Perfect Foundation* combines *Clicker Foundation Training*, by Kay Laurence (2003) & *Clicker Novice Training*, by Kay Laurence (2003)

Laurence, Kay. 2008. "Whippits – Teaching: self-control & play skills" (DVD).

Laurence, Kay. 2004. *Clicker Intermediate Training*

Theby, Viviane. 2009. *Dog University*.

Zulch, Helen & Daniel Mills. 2012. *Life skills for puppies: Laying the foundation for a loving, lasting relationship*.

Herding

Hartnagle-Taylor, Jeanne Joy & Ty Taylor. 2010. *Stockdog Savvy*.

Holland, Virgit. 1994. *Herding Dogs: Progressive Training*.

Companion website: To purchase the second book in the Positive Herding Dog series, *Positive Herding 102*, visit *www.positiveherdingdog.com/book2*

Printed in Great Britain
by Amazon

53427858R00178